Work in America Institute's National Policy Studies

With the publication in 1989 of Work in America Institute's newest national policy study, *Allies in Educational Reform: How Teachers, Unions, and Administrators Can Join Forces for Better Schools,* the Institute will have completed its eighth major study since January 1978. Previous studies are:

> *Job Strategies for Urban Youth: Sixteen Pilot Programs for Action*
> *The Future of Older Workers in America*
> *New Work Schedules for a Changing Society*
> *Productivity Through Work Innovations*
> *Employment Security in a Free Economy*
> *Improving Health Care Management in the Workplace*
> *Training—The Competitive Edge*

About Work in America Institute

Work in America Institute, Inc., a nonprofit, nonpartisan organization, was founded in 1975 to advance productivity and quality of working life. It has a broad base of support from business, unions, government agencies, universities, and foundations, as reflected in its board of directors, academic advisory committee, and roster of sponsoring organizations.

In a series of policy studies, education and training programs, an extensive information resource, and a broad range of publications, the Institute has focused on improving the effectiveness of organizations through the use of human resources.

Allies in Educational Reform

Jerome M. Rosow
and
Robert Zager
with
Jill Casner-Lotto and Associates

Allies in Educational Reform

*How Teachers, Unions, and
Administrators Can Join
Forces for Better Schools*

A WORK IN AMERICA INSTITUTE PUBLICATION

 Jossey-Bass Publishers

San Francisco   •   London   •   1989

ALLIES IN EDUCATIONAL REFORM
How Teachers, Unions, and Administrators Can Join Forces for Better Schools
   by Jerome M. Rosow and Robert Zager with Jill Casner-Lotto and Associates

Copyright © 1989 by: Jossey-Bass Inc., Publishers
                      350 Sansome Street
                      San Francisco, California 94104
                                &
                      Jossey-Bass Limited
                      28 Banner Street
                      London EC1Y 8QE
                               &
                      Work in America Institute
                      700 White Plains Road
                      Scarsdale, New York 10583

Library of Congress Cataloging-in-Publication Data

Rosow, Jerome M.
    Allies in educational reform : how teachers, unions, and
administrators can join forces for better schools / Jerome M. Rosow
and Robert Zager with Jill Casner-Lotto and associates.
        p.   cm. — (The Jossey-Bass education series)
    "A Work in America Institute publication."
    Bibliography: p.
    Includes index.
    ISBN 1-55542-158-X
    1. School improvement programs—United States.   2. Teacher
participation in administration—United States.   3. Urban schools—
United States.   I. Zager, Robert.   II. Work in America Institute.
LB2822.82.R66   1989
371.2′0973—dc19   88-46095
                                                              CIP

Manufactured in the United States of America

JACKET DESIGN BY WILLI BAUM

FIRST EDITION

Code 8932

The Jossey-Bass Education Series

Published in association with
Work in America Institute

Contents

Tables

Preface

The state of public education in the great cities of the United States has been the subject of much handwringing but shockingly little action, a victim of malign neglect. The public and its representatives, unable to ignore the palpable horror of urban schools, sought catharsis through scapegoats. Teachers provided an easy target. Not until the business community voiced alarm did politicians feel the need to do something, and their first actions declared teachers the enemy.

In the early 1980s, Work in America Institute, observing the scene from its vantage point as an agent of organizational change, formed the opinion that no valid and durable educational reforms were possible without the willing involvement of everyone in the schools. Teachers (and their unions) would have to have a responsible role in designing and carrying out educational reform, not have reforms dumped on them.

More and more participants and observers have reached the same conclusion. The urgent needs now are (1) to furnish reliable guidance to the many urban school systems that are inclined toward alliances but are not quite sure how to form or operate them, and (2) by spelling out why alliances are essential, to galvanize into action the many other systems that have not yet gotten the message or whose leaders believe nothing can be done until management-union relations somehow become more "cooperative."

Such are the primary purposes of this book. Another is to arm parents and citizens with information that will enable them to exert steady, constructive pressure on school managers and teachers. Finally, the book seeks to persuade local, state, and federal officials to adopt policies that are conducive to the establishment and success of management-teacher alliances at every level.

Although there was little in the educational literature to go on, we felt sure that somewhere on the urban scene there must be mavericks who had begun to experiment on the industrial model, and we set out to find them and report the lessons of their experience. We reasoned as follows:

- Urban public schools are large-scale enterprises performing a critical service—the education of future citizens. Although in many respects free-standing, they must operate within larger organizational constraints.
- The most critical resource in the schools is the teaching staff, which consumes most of the budget and performs the actual work of educating.
- Teachers, like other professionals, want to do a good job. They are motivated and rewarded by the achievements of their students.
- Teachers see and feel the severe problems of urban schools, but they are rarely involved in the solutions.
- Principals must take the lead in school performance improvement, but they feel hindered by a lack of trust and authority from the district level, and they in turn do not trust teachers enough to delegate authority downward.
- Unions and management in urban school districts have operated as adversaries in a climate embittered by financial pressures, unsatisfactory plant and equipment, and low public esteem.
- No single group is responsible for the crisis in urban education, which mirrors the problems of the society itself, and no single group can reform it. The three key parties—management, teachers, and unions—must work together to turn

the schools around. Reforms imposed by legislative or executive edict impede cooperation and therefore have little lasting effect.

- Breakthrough examples of labor-management cooperation in industry have demonstrated that great qualitative advances can be achieved through employee involvement in problem-solving and decision-making teams.
- The political dynamics of large, unionized industries resemble those of urban public school systems enough to suggest that industrial models of labor-management cooperation may be adaptable to educational needs.
- The art of creating and sustaining employee involvement is difficult but can be learned. If urban school systems can be found that have already experimented successfully with labor-management cooperation and employee involvement, their experiences should be published, analyzed, and set forth as models.

To help us track down such examples, in December 1985 we sought the advice of acknowledged leaders in the field of education: Ernest Boyer, president, The Carnegie Foundation for the Advancement of Teaching; John Goodlad, professor of education, University of Washington; Clark Kerr, president emeritus, University of California; John Merrow II, "The MacNeil/Lehrer Newshour," Merrow Productions, Inc.; Bella Rosenberg, associate director, public relations, American Federation of Teachers; Theodore Sizer, chairman of Brown University's Education Department; and Gary Watts, assistant executive director for professional and organizational development, National Education Association. They recommended the following criteria for cases to be included in the study:

1. Schools to be studied should be urban public schools, preferably but not necessarily high schools.
   - "Urban" need not mean "inner city" as long as the student body is representative of local demographics and not so elitist as to be unreplicable.
   - No more than a few "special mission" schools should be included.

- "Creaming" cases—that is, using cases in which students and teachers are so carefully selected as to be unrepresentative of local population—should be avoided.
2. Schools to be studied should be equally drawn from the following four geographic regions: the Northeast, South, Great Lakes, and West.
3. In schools to be studied, administrators, teachers, and unions should have been working together on schoolwide problems and creating the infrastructures to sustain such collaboration. If parents have been involved, too, so much the better.
   - It is not essential for a union to be present in all cases.
   - Administrators, teachers, and parents should be involved, but parent involvement is relevant only if teachers are involved in school management.
   - Cases in which teacher involvement is based on delegation of power from superintendent to principal are of particular interest.
4. In schools to be studied, collaboration should have contributed significantly to the school's improved performance and community recognition.
   - Each case should have been in operation long enough to prove continuity—probably at least three years. The case will be even more useful if it has survived a change in leadership.
   - Performance improvement should be tangible, but not necessarily measurable by standard statistics.
   - Performance improvement should be assessed against goals the parties have set for themselves. These may include absences, dropouts, teacher turnover, and so on. Measures should be flexible and responsive to local conditions.

The experts also identified forty urban schools or school systems that, by reputation, might fit the criteria. On closer examination by the authors, only a few of these schools met the rigorous criteria outlined above. However, by extending the search far beyond the original list and scaling back the criteria, we were able to find eleven cases that were solid examples of worthwhile educational reform. Had additional time been available, we believe that other innovative programs might also have emerged.

Those we selected for this study are diverse with respect to geography, urban and demographic characteristics, size of district and schools, substance and procedure of reforms, mechanisms for teacher involvement, relations between managers and teachers, and so on. We believe that these examples of school reform present a credible case for the efficacy of reform through alliances between administrators, teachers, and parents. They are presented, in full, in the second half of this book.

The laborious search for cases left us more convinced than ever of the urgent need to adapt the industrial model of labor-management cooperation to urban public schools, and of the feasibility of doing so. More important, we learned that labor-management cooperation and employee involvement work well in all sorts of school systems.

Concurrent with the search for cases we convened a national advisory committee to help us think through some of the basic questions of educational reform and to criticize the drafts of case reports. The committee (see pp. xxxi–xxxv) was drawn from many branches of the public school establishment, from academia and from business, labor, and government. At four meetings, between June 1986 and June 1987, the members provided invaluable information, insights, and advice, although the Institute alone is responsible for the contents of this report.

The following background papers, commissioned by Work in America Institute, were discussed by the national advisory committee and provided the empirical base for this report:

- "Education—A Shared Responsibility: The Case for Business-School-Community Partnership," by Melanie Barron, educational consultant
- "A Matter of Balance, Power, Control, and Decision Making in the Individual School," by Melanie Barron, educational consultant

- "An Assessment of Common Models of Teacher Participation in Public School Decision Making," by Thomas B. Corcoran, educational consultant
- "Principles of Participation: Lessons from Industry," by Robert H. Guest, professor of organizational behavior emeritus, The Amos Tuck School of Business Administration, Dartmouth College
- "Teachers as Policymakers: The Role of Collective Bargaining in School Reform," by Susan Moore Johnson, associate professor of administration, planning, and social policy, Graduate School of Education, Harvard University
- "Finance and Governance Implications of School-Based Decisions," by Henry M. Levin, professor of education and director of the Center for Educational Research, Stanford University
- "Reflections on School Reform: A Position Statement," by Vito Perrone, vice-president, Carnegie Foundation for the Advancement of Teaching
- "The Connecticut Experience: A More Flexible Approach to State Educational Reform," by Arthur E. Wise, director, Center for the Study of the Teaching Profession, The Rand Corporation

In addition, the committee reviewed the following case reports:

- "The Schenley High School Teacher Center," by Janet L. Bourdon, formerly codirector of training, JobSearch, Work in America Institute
- "Case Study of a School Improvement Process in the Hammond, Indiana, School District," by Jill Casner-Lotto, research editor for policy studies, Work in America Institute
- "Hope Essential High School: A Sketch of Reform in an Urban School," by Thomas B. Corcoran, educational consultant
- "Collaborative Reform in the Cincinnati Public Schools:

A Case Study,'' by Susan Moore Johnson, associate professor of administration, planning, and social policy, Graduate School of Education, Harvard University

- "Teacher-Principal Cooperation in School 'Reform,'" by John Merrow II, "The MacNeil/Lehrer Newshour," Merrow Productions, Inc.
- "Samuel Gompers Vocational-Technical High School," by Joan L. Sickler, vice-president, Work in America Institute
- "School Renewal Through Teacher Empowerment: A Case Study of the ABC Unified School District, Cerritos, California," by Joan L. Sickler, vice-president, Work in America Institute
- "Report on Coral Gables High School," by Mary L. Tenopyr, AT&T

Audience and Overview of the Contents

This book is directed toward all who have a stake in reforming urban public school education: citizens; parents; local, state, and federal government; teachers and their unions; and school administrators, at all levels, and their associations. It is organized in two parts: the first part, written by Jerome Rosow, Robert Zager, and Jill Casner-Lotto, consists of a report on the Work in America Institute policy study of *The Teacher: Ally in Educational Reform* and a series of twenty-one recommendations; the second part, written by twelve contributing authors, consists of eleven case studies of schools and school districts that exemplify the best in educational reform in the United States.

The report in Part One guides decision makers in educational management and in teachers' unions, step by step, through the building of new labor-management alliances for urban public schools. Examples from the cases presented in Part Two have been woven into the text. They not only illustrate and support the findings and recommendations, but they also link theory to practice and offer realistic hope for making great changes with low risk and high returns. Although the cases stand alone, their full significance emerges when they are read in conjunction with the report.

Chapter One argues the need for labor-management alliances in the schools and serves as an overview of the report.

Chapter Two rebuts the popular and political belief that teachers and their unions stand in the way of educational reform.

Chapter Three describes, with numerous examples, the simple, practical steps by which teachers and administrators can begin to alter the relationships that have so long immobilized urban public school districts.

Chapter Four sets out the procedural lessons that urban districts can profitably learn from industrial experience in labor-management cooperation and employee involvement.

Chapter Five warns that the slogans of educational reform can impede real change in the schools.

Chapter Six points out that state legislators and local boards of education are part of "management," and therefore should also enter into alliances with teachers and their unions.

Chapter Seven offers some concluding remarks and introduces the case studies.

Chapters Eight through Eighteen describe the cases in full.

Acknowledgments

The study that led to this book was supported by a lead grant from Metropolitan Life Foundation and additional grants from ARCO, AT&T, Columbia Broadcasting System, the Ford Foundation, and the Rockefeller Foundation. The Institute wishes to thank those who made the study possible and to note that they bear no responsibility for statements made in this volume.

The Institute also wishes to express its thanks and appreciation to the countless individuals—teachers, principals, administrators, union officials, and educators—who provided extensive information in interviews and written materials. Their assistance proved invaluable in the preparation of our manuscript. We also wish to thank the members of the national advisory committee, who generously shared with the Institute their ideas and insights on the issue of educational reform, and the writers of background papers and cases, whose labors sparked the informative—and often exciting—discussions at committee meetings.

Robert Zager, vice-president for policy studies, was responsible for the initial planning and overall direction of the two-year policy study, as well as for the final manuscript. His creative thinking is evident throughout the pages of this book. Jill Casner-Lotto, research editor for policy studies, tracked down the cases presented here, directed the writing of the case studies, and participated in the writing of the manuscript. The Institute thanks them for their tireless efforts in bringing these significant case studies to the attention of the American public. The Institute also wishes to thank the following members of its staff for their participation in the production of this book: Adrienne Brescia, marketing coordinator; Frances T. Harte, director of communications; Carol Nardi, executive assistant to the president; and Beatrice Walfish, former editorial director.

Scarsdale, New York   Jerome M. Rosow
March 1989   President
    Work in America Institute, Inc.

The Authors

Jerome M. Rosow is the president and founder, in 1975, of Work in America Institute, Inc., a tripartite, nonprofit work research organization dedicated to the advancement of productivity and quality of working life in the United States. A graduate of the University of Chicago, he has had careers in both government and industry devoted to human resources, labor-management relations, and public affairs. He served in executive positions over a period of twenty-four years, as manager of employee relations for Esso Europe in London and, later, as public affairs manager for Exxon Corporation in New York City. In government service, he served as Assistant Secretary of Labor from 1969 to 1971 under the then Secretary of Labor, George P. Shultz. As chairman of the President's Advisory Committee on Federal Pay, from 1971 to 1984, he served as adviser to five presidents.

Rosow was president of the Industrial Relations Research Association in 1979. He has also acted as an adviser to the Committee for Economic Development and as director of the U.S. Business and Advisory Committee of the Organisation for Economic Cooperation and Development (OECD), Paris. In addition, he has served as chairman of the Conference Board Council on Compensation; chairman of the European Employee Relations Council; and adviser to the International Labour Organisation, Geneva.

Author of numerous articles on management, productivity, human resources, and industrial relations, Rosow is also editor of *The Worker on the Job: Coping with Change* (1974); chairman of the American Assembly on "The Changing World of Work"; coeditor of *Work in America: The Decade Ahead* (1979, with C. Kerr); and editor of *Productivity: Prospects for Growth* (1981), *Views from the Top* (1985), *Teamwork: Joint Labor-Management Programs in America* (1986), and *The Global Marketplace* (1988).

Rosow has directed, with Robert Zager, the following policy studies for Work in America Institute: *Job Strategies for Urban Youth* (1979), *The Future of Older Workers in America* (1980), *New Work Schedules for a Changing Society* (1981), *Productivity Through Work Innovations* (1982), *Employment Security in a Free Economy* (1984), *Improving the Management of Health Care in the Workplace* (1985), *Training—The Competitive Edge* (1988), and *Allies in Educational Reform* (1989).

Rosow has often appeared on the television program "Good Morning America," as well as on various network news programs. He is a frequent speaker at national conferences.

Robert Zager is vice-president for policy studies and technical assistance of Work in America Institute, Inc. He received his B.A. degree cum laude from Harvard College in 1940 and an LL.B. degree from Yale Law School in 1947. After receiving his law degree, he practiced law for five years in the state of New Jersey and was actively involved with official and volunteer groups dealing with city planning, housing, and education. From 1955 to 1975 he was a management consultant, about half the time in the United States and the other half in the United Kingdom, where he worked in the areas of management/organization development, labor relations, manpower planning, and long-range planning in numerous industrial companies and hospitals.

After returning to the United States in 1975, Zager served for two and a half years as consultant to the National Center for Productivity and Quality of Work Life, primarily on studies of productivity and job security. He was appointed vice-president for policy studies and technical assistance of Work in America Institute in May 1978.

Zager's writings have appeared in newspapers and professional journals in both the United Kingdom and the United States. He has directed, with Jerome M. Rosow, eight policy studies: *Job Strategies for Urban Youth* (1979), *The Future of Older Workers in America* (1980), *New Work Schedules for a Changing Society* (1981), *Productivity Through Work Innovations* (1982), *Employment Security in a Free Economy* (1984), *Improving the Management of Health Care in the Workplace* (1985), *Training—The Competitive Edge* (1988), and *Allies in Educational Reform* (1989).

Jill Casner-Lotto is research editor for policy studies at Work in America Institute, where she manages the research, on-site investigations, and writing of case reports in connection with the Institute's national policy studies. Formerly an editor of the Institute's monthly newsletter, *Work in America* (formerly *World of Work Report*), she has written extensively for the Institute and for others on such topics as managing new technology, productivity innovations, job training, labor-management cooperation, and other human resource issues.

Casner-Lotto received her B.A. degree from Johns Hopkins University and her M.S. degree from the Medill School of Journalism at Northwestern University. She served as a news and feature writer for Cornell University and also produced public affairs films. At St. Johns University she coordinated the research and production of nationally televised educational programs. She also worked as a documentary producer for public television in Phoenix, Arizona. Casner-Lotto is the author, with associates, of *Successful Training Strategies: Twenty-Six Innovative Corporate Models* (1988).

Melanie Barron, formerly an assistant professor in the Center for Science, Mathematics, and Technology Education at the State University of New York at Stony Brook, is currently an educational consultant. Her areas of research include implementation of school reform in public schools, particularly school decentralization, and changes in teacher education, focusing on prospective teachers in science. She has been a teacher and administrator in both the New York City and Boston public school system.

Janet L. Bourdon most recently was codirector of training for Work in America Institute's JobSearch Program, a hands-on approach to teaching high school students in the Philadelphia School District how to find a job. Previously, she was a job search supervisor for the San Mateo County (California) Job Search Workshops, Inc. She has also been a teacher in the St. Paul public school system and has held positions in the State of Minnesota Department of Education and in the administration of federal education programs.

Thomas B. Corcoran is a private consultant involved in research on teachers' working conditions and in assisting school districts with reform and improvement projects. He was formerly the director of school improvement for Research for Better Schools, Inc., an educational research and development organization in Philadelphia, and executive assistant to the Commissioner of Education in New Jersey. He has published extensively on research regarding effective schools, teachers' working conditions, and school improvement.

Charles Donaldson teaches journalism and English composition at Santa Monica College, Santa Monica, California, and is a student of higher education at the Claremont Graduate School, Claremont, California. He has been a reporter and editor for twenty years, including eight years at the *Los Angeles Times,* where he covered education and county government.

David C. Helms is a senior research associate at Research for Better Schools, Inc., and has directed several large-scale educational development projects. He has spent ten years in educational administration and teaching and has also held marketing and sales positions in industry.

Susan Moore Johnson is associate professor of administration, planning, and social policy at Harvard University's Graduate School of Education in Cambridge, Massachusetts. She has been a teacher and administrator for nine years and has done extensive research on teachers' unions and school reform. She is the author of *Teacher Unions in Schools* (1984) and is currently writing a book on the school as a workplace.

Charles T. Kerchner, professor of education at the Claremont Graduate School, has done extensive research over the past ten years on labor relations in education. He is the coauthor of *The Changing Idea of a Teachers' Union* (1988) and is currently working on a project with twelve school districts involved in reshaping labor relations and teachers' work lives.

Wendy Kohli is assistant professor of educational studies at the State University of New York at Binghamton and a research associate with the Kettering Foundation. She has consulted for over a decade with the Ford Foundation, the Academy of Educational Development, and the Institute for Educational Leadership. She has coauthored several articles for educational journals and is a contributing author to *On Competence* (1979). Her current research focuses on teachers' working conditions.

Eugene F. Provenzo, Jr., is professor of education at the University of Miami and is a specialist in the history and sociology of education. He has written several books on such topics as the impact of computers on society and education, the history of education, and the history of American schools. He is currently engaged in a long-term project studying teachers' attitudes toward work.

Joan L. Sickler is vice-president of Work in America Institute. She was formerly director of the institute's Productivity Forum, an organization for business, labor, and government agencies. Previously, she was director of a three-year project on improving college teaching for the Council on Learning and *Change* magazine. She has written for the Institute and others on labor-management issues and productivity innovations.

J. Lynne White is a research consultant for the Institute for Educational Leadership and the Academy for Educational Development. She has been involved in projects focusing on urban education issues, particularly teachers' working conditions, school improvement programs, and at-risk youth.

Work in America Institute

National Advisory Committee
for
Allies in Educational Reform

Anne S. Alexander
Vice-President
Education Programs
AT&T Foundation

Alberta B. Arthurs
Director, Arts and
   Humanities
The Rockefeller Foundation

Eva Bacal
Chairman of the Council of
   Urban Boards of
   Education
National School Boards
   Association

*Melanie Barron
Educational Consultant

Paul E. Barton
National Assessment of
   Educational Progress

*Janet L. Bourdon
Formerly Codirector of
   Training
JobSearch
School District of Philadelphia

Irving Bluestone
University Professor of Labor
   Studies
Wayne State University

Ernest Boyer
President
The Carnegie Foundation
   for the Advancement of
   Teaching

*Sol C. Chaikin
President Emeritus
International Ladies' Garment
   Workers' Union

Thomas B. Corcoran
Educational Consultant
Formerly Director of School
   Improvement
Research for Better Schools,
   Inc.

Alonzo Crim
Superintendent of Schools
Atlanta Public Schools

Robert W. De Sio
Retired IBM Director of
   University Relations
IBM Corporation

*A. Kenneth Ferguson
Assistant to Executive Vice-
   President
Communications Workers of
   America

*Associate member

*David Florio
Director of Policy
  Development
American Federation of
  Teachers

*Chester A. Francke
Formerly General Director
Joint Education Activities
UAW-GM Human
  Resource Center

*Paul Gounaris
Principal
Hope Essential High School
Providence, R.I.

*Robert H. Guest
Professor Emeritus
Amos Tuck School of Business
  Administration
Dartmouth College

John J. Gunther
Executive Director
U.S. Conference of Mayors

Thomas F. Hartnett
Commissioner
New York State Department
  of Labor

*Victor Herbert
Drop-out Prevention Program
New York City Board of
  Education

Marion Holmes
Executive Director
Career and Vocational
  Education
John F. Kennedy Center for
  Vocational Education

Dean Honetschlager
Research Associate
National Governors
  Association

Roy B. Howard
Vice-President
Industrial Relations and
  Benefits
BellSouth Corporation

Sol Hurwitz
Senior Vice-President
Committee for Economic
  Development

Sibyl Jacobson
President
Metropolitan Life
  Foundation

Jack Jennings
Staff Director
Subcommittee on Elementary,
  Secondary and Vocational
  Education
House of Representatives

*Susan Moore Johnson
Associate Professor of
  Administration, Planning,
  and Social Policy
Graduate School of
  Education
Harvard University

Clark Kerr
President Emeritus
University of California

Casey F. Koziol
Vice-President and Director
Personnel Administration
Motorola, Inc.

*Henry M. Levin
Professor of Education
Stanford University

*Marsha Levine
Associate Director
Education Issues Department
American Federation of
  Teachers

Harry Litchfield
Manager, Education and
  Training
Deere & Company

*Val Markos
Operations Manager
BellSouth Corporation

Floretta McKenzie
Superintendent of Schools
District of Columbia Public
  Schools

*Richard McMillan
Executive Co-Director
UAW-GM Human
  Resource Center

John Merrow, II
"The MacNeil/Lehrer
  Newshour"
Merrow Productions, Inc.

*Virginia Millan
Program Associate
Metropolitan Life
  Foundation

*Tom Mooney
President
Cincinnati (Ohio)
  Federation of Teachers

*Albin Moser
Head Teacher
Hope Essential High School
Providence, R.I.

Joe Nathan
Coordinator, Education
  Project
National Governors
  Association

M. E. Nichols
Executive Vice-President
Communications Workers of
    America

*James B. Northrop
Director of Workforce
    Planning
New York State Governor's
    Office of Employee
    Relations

*Patrick O'Rourke
Hammond (Indiana)
    Teachers' Federation
Local 394

Paul Ostergard
President
General Electric Foundation

*Wayne Pecher
Hammond (Indiana)
    Teachers' Federation
Local 394

*Vito Perrone
Vice-President
The Carnegie Foundation
    for the Advancement of
    Teaching

*Michael Roberts
Director, Technical Support
    Programs
IBM Corporation

Bella Rosenberg
Assistant to the President
America Federation of
    Teachers

Santee Ruffin
Director of Urban Services
National Association of
    Secondary School
    Principals

Samuel Sava
Executive Director
National Association of
    Elementary School
    Principals

Patrick Scollard
Chief Administrative Officer
Chemical Bank

*Neil J. Shipman
Executive Intern for Programs
National Association of
    Elementary School
    Principals

*Mary L. Tenopyr
American Telephone and
    Telegraph Company

*Charles Vernon
Retired Deputy
    Superintendent
ABC Unified School District
Cerritos, California

Gary Watts
Assistant Executive Director
  for Professional and
  Organization Development
National Education
  Association

*Arthur E. Wise
Director, Center for the
  Study of the Teaching
  Profession
The Rand Corporation

PART ONE

Educational Reform Through Management-Teacher Alliances

Allies in Educational Reform:
Some Key Characteristics

If the goal is to improve education, management, teachers, and unions must form genuine, workable alliances at the school and district levels.

Teachers and unions are willing and able to take part in alliances for reform and have demonstrated the following characteristics:

Teachers	Unions
• Are capable of contributing much more than they are now permitted to contribute.	• Support reforms when involved.
• Are ready to respond to the process of participation and to devote the necessary time.	• Have sometimes initiated the formation of an alliance.
• Support reform when involved as equal partners with management.	• Are increasingly in the vanguard of the movement for school reform.
• Do not expect a financial quid pro quo for each reform undertaken but should receive some form of compensation for time spent on school improvement teams.	• Want to be involved as partners in the change process and respect the final decision-making power of management.
• Represent the principal underutilized resource in most schools.	• Require training and education in conjunction with management in order to break the ice and sustain confidence and progress.
• Are indispensable to any reform in the schools.	• Know they cannot unilaterally create an alliance, since management has the responsibility to manage.

Management is eager to move toward educational reform, and need only seize the opportunities presented by the readiness of teachers and unions to help them:

Principals and District Officials	Principals	District Officials
• Can stimulate change, reduce conflict, and sustain commitment by inviting teachers and unions to join them in alliances.	• Can enhance their own authority by delegating defined areas of responsibility and authority—especially to teachers.	• Can encourage school-based reforms by: ☐ vesting greater autonomy in schools ☐ granting principals more voice in the management of the district ☐ changing the role of central staff from prescriptive to collaborative.

1

Joining Forces for Excellence and Equity in Education

The tough job of reforming America's urban public schools will not be accomplished by fiat, threats, exhortation, or slogans. It will be accomplished through genuine alliances between management and teachers, at the district level and at every school. America's teachers are ready, willing, and able to take part, even where relations are most hostile; but though they may offer to become allies, they cannot serve until management invites them.

When a suitable invitation is extended, teachers and their unions join responsibly in planning and executing reforms of many kinds. That is the inspiring message contained in the eleven cases on which this volume is based—the innovative approaches to education of the ABC Unified School District of Cerritos, California; Central Park East Secondary School in New York City; the Cincinnati (Ohio) Public Schools; the Dade County (Florida) Public Schools; the Duluth (Minnesota) School System; the Hammond (Indiana) School District; Hope Essential High School (Providence, R.I.); Jefferson County Public Schools in Louisville, Kentucky; the Humanitas Academy of Los Angeles; the Philadelphia School District's Writing Across the Curriculum project; and Pittsburgh's Schenley High School Teacher Center.

3

This report tells why alliances are essential, what they can do, how they are created and nurtured, and what they can learn from industry.

Alliances Are the Key

Everyone who cares about education in the United States now agrees that the performance of urban public schools has to be sharply improved. The case has been made by others so well and so often that it would be redundant to repeat it here. Among the most notable reports that argue for sweeping changes and improvements in the educational system are *A Nation at Risk: The Imperative for Educational Reform* (The National Commission on Excellence in Education, 1983), *A Nation Prepared: Teachers for the 21st Century* (Carnegie Forum on Education and the Economy, 1986), *High School: A Report on Secondary Education in America* (Boyer, 1983), *Horace's Compromise: The Dilemma of the American High School* (Sizer, 1984), *A Place Called School* (Goodlad, 1984), and *An Imperiled Generation: Saving Urban Schools* (Carnegie Foundation for the Advancement of Teaching, 1988).

The stated goals of the reformers are excellence (higher standards of performance for all who graduate from the public schools) and equity (seeing to it that everyone who is capable of learning graduates). On these points also there is general agreement.

Beyond this, agreement gives way to diversity of opinion, almost to the point of confusion, not only among politicians and the general public but within the educational establishment itself. Formulas for achieving excellence and equity vary considerably, and no one really knows which formulas—if any—will work. Experts even disagree about how to identify and measure the performance of schools.

In the long run, the voters of the district and the state decide (often by default) the standards of excellence and equity to be pursued, and the criteria by which improvements should be measured. The opinions of the voters may be influenced by employers, postsecondary educational institutions, parents, teachers, and students. But no one of those groups has the clout to overrule the voters. Even parents, it must be borne in mind, constitute a small proportion of the urban electorate, a fact that underlies the generation-long neglect of the public schools. School administrators and teachers disregard voter decisions at their peril.

The odds are strongly against the possibility that any one-shot reform, simple or complex, will do the job, any more than a single formula can solve the problems of industrial productivity. Aside from uncertainty about the efficacy of particular solutions, the goals of reform are moving targets. Educational needs change as society, the economy, technology, and demographics change.

In such circumstances prudence dictates a more modest, a more experimental approach to reform, one whose continuing objective is year-in, year-out improvement of performance. Each district and each school has to decide in what aspects of excellence and equity they fall short, and what to do about closing the gap. Since no two schools or districts will have quite the same strengths, failings, resources, or opportunities, problems and solutions will differ from site to site and from one year to the next. Some solutions will work, others will not; those that work may not produce the results sought; new ideas for action may be suggested by the experience of other schools and districts.

It would be naive to think that a regimen of continuing improvements in excellence and equity can be brought about by simply telling administrators and teachers to do a better job or by awarding merit increases to high performers. As W. Edwards Deming, a leading business consultant, has shown in the discipline of quality control, upgrading the performance of an entire organization demands systemic changes. That is, not individuals but the organization as a whole has to change its habits. It follows that an organization in pursuit of year-in, year-out improvement lives in a state of continuing systemic self-change.

How does an organization such as a district or a school sustain continuing systemic self-change without breaking down? The indispensable ingredient is agreement among administrators and teachers about the ends and means of the changes and their belief in the value of cooperation to achieve change. Agreement about ends and means comes about through discussion—open, threat-free, voluntary, unhurried—and through decision making based on that discussion. Since administrators and teachers have divergent as well as shared interests, "alliance" is the best name for a relationship of the kind described.

Management's Prerogatives

In the pages that follow, the terms *managers* and *management* will be used rather than the more familiar *administrators* and *administration* as a broader designation of those who currently bear the responsibility of running the nation's school systems. Who is "management" in the management-teacher alliances that are needed? As far as teachers are concerned, management includes everyone whose orders must be obeyed: to wit, the board of education, the superintendent, principals, headquarters staff, assistant principals, department chairs, and lead teachers. The facts confirm their interpretation. State statutes vest responsibility and authority for public education in locally elected or appointed boards of education and fix certain requirements for all schools in the state. Usually the authority includes power to levy taxes to pay the costs of the educational enterprise. Some boards prefer to think of themselves as legislative bodies concerned with making policy while the superintendent gets on with the essentials of management, but they delude themselves. The superintendent has no power other than that granted by the board. The superintendent proposes policy but the board makes the final decisions on how the district and the schools are to be run, as well as on the terms and conditions of employment for every employee from the superintendent on down.

Individual teachers have power to control only what takes place within their own classrooms, and even that power is tightly circumscribed by state and district regulations, sometimes to the point of leaving teachers as little discretion as a worker on a regimented production line. These conditions are somewhat offset by the teachers' power, exercised through their union, to shape the districtwide terms and conditions of employment.

In short, management alone has authority to decide how education is to be conducted, but teachers alone can make it happen. Each party has the power to destroy; only the two acting in concert have the power to improve.

If continuing educational improvement is the end, and alliances between management and teachers are the means, management must discuss systemic changes with teachers until a common goal is defined. Meeting this goal requires teacher involvement and regularized participation. Teachers have neither legal nor bargaining power to force management to carry on such discussions, let alone act on them. All they can do is frustrate management's goals. Most managements, but fortunately not all, seem to prefer stalemate to sharing prerogatives.

As this report demonstrates, teachers' unions sometimes take the initiative and pressure management into forming alliances with them. More often, the first move comes from management or from both sides working together. But management has the burden of making the decision that enables an alliance to be formed and sustained.

Teacher's Responsiveness

The case studies featured in this report demonstrate that when teachers and their unions are invited, they play responsible parts in educational reform. In every case both managers and teachers claimed that genuine alliances had been formed and that worthwhile improvements had resulted; and their observations matched those of our reporters. In several instances the union took the lead in initiating reforms, by focusing attention on needed school improvements and pressing for joint labor-management mechanisms to carry them out. Union involvement often put the stamp of legitimacy on labor-management alliances that teachers would otherwise have considered mere passing fads. In general, union officials asserted that the reforms or innovations being carried out were supportive of, and consistent with, the union agenda to improve the professional opportunities and working conditions of teachers. Though reservations were expressed—particularly when salary was an issue at the bargaining table—union leaders and members saw no conflict between the goals of collective bargaining and school reform. In fact, they were willing to bend the rules and amend bargaining agreements in order to allow reforms to proceed.

Our judgment that teachers' unions do not represent an obstacle to educational reform is also supported by other reports and field studies. The most recent report, by the Rand Corporation, while finding varying responses toward reforms on the national, state, and local union levels, concluded that "in no case did the organizations wage an all-out campaign to block reform proposals . . ." (McDonnell and Pascal, 1988, p. viii). The research was based on data from a representative sample of 151 collective bargaining contracts and from interviews with more than 600 policymakers and educators in six diverse states.

The cases in this report are diverse in most other respects— they are drawn from many parts of the country and districts differ in size and demographic mix. Some cases involve changes at a single school; others involve changes at the district level; still others call for simultaneous changes at several schools and/or across the district. The substance of change ranges from team teaching to inservice development, from writing-across-the-curriculum to the creation of a restructured school-within-a-school. The mechanisms include joint problem-solving teams, quality circles, professional development schools, districtwide labor-management committees or task forces, and other types of innovative governance structures in which teachers and management play active roles in school reform.

The events leading to alliance in each case were also diverse. In a large proportion of the cases involving district-level changes, alliances grew out of long-standing hostility between management and teachers rather than out of harmony, as one might have expected. Alliance became a means of moving from all-out conflict toward civility. This should give us hope, since management-teacher conflict is so characteristic of the urban public school scene. In one instance, the teachers' union practically cornered management into starting a dialogue; but once the conversations got underway, the parties quickly discovered that they shared many opinions about the need for, and the means of, improvement. In all the cases, mutual efforts on the part of management and teachers were rewarded with the creation of new avenues for communication, cooperation, joint participation, and problem solving that grew over time.

We have stressed that an acceptable invitation is essential to launch a new alliance between management and teachers. What makes an invitation acceptable?

1. It spells out the task the alliance is to undertake.
2. The task is one that both parties consider worth doing.
3. The invitation makes clear what the teachers are to contribute, and how their contribution will be put to use.
4. It acknowledges the ability of teachers and their union to make a valuable contribution to the task in question, and does not blame them for the fact that improvement is needed.
5. The proposed alliance includes all parties whose agreement is indispensable to performance of the task.
6. The alliance proposes to reach decisions by consensus.

We have yet to hear of such an invitation being turned down. Conversely, an invitation lacking any of these features is not worth having, because its chances of improving school performance are minimal. Yet, objectively considered, none of these features, singly or in combination, require management to give up anything they cannot afford to lose.

Why, then, are alliances so rare that their occurrence makes news? Many causes act as barriers:

-   The reflexive impulse common to managers, to regard as a threat any redrawing of the lines of "prerogative."
-   The custom and practice of identifying teachers with their current classroom duties, instead of seeing them as professionals capable of contributing to the improvement of the school as a whole. The habit is aggravated by the history of legalistic collective bargaining agreements, which seek to define every small detail of each side's rights and duties.
-   Each side's conviction that the other will take unfair advantage unless restrained by a legal document.

- The skepticism with which management, on the one side, and teachers and their unions, on the other, regard the sincerity of each other's interest in education. Much of this is due to their never getting together to talk about the subject and the history of relationships.
- The authoritarian relationships at every level of urban public school systems, which are at odds with an alliance's need for decisions by consensus and for a reasonable degree of decentralization of authority.
- Teachers' assumptions that teacher involvement is just another fad or "program" and therefore need not be taken seriously.
- The scarcity of successful alliances to serve as models.

Breaking the Ice

Although most urban public school districts face similar obstacles to the formation of alliances, some, like those described in these eleven cases, have broken through. Their example should encourage those who are seeking an opportunity to improve and cause reexamination on the part of those who believe that progress is blocked by "the other side." *The thesis of this report is that it is within the power of every school in every urban district to improve performance with respect to excellence and equity, whatever the circumstances may be.* Neither side has the right to blame the other until it has made every effort to break the ice.

At this point it is necessary to belabor the obvious, because the current stalemate results from refusing to look at the obvious. The fact is that one party or the other, or both, have to break the ice. The steps required are simple, requiring only a modicum of courage, ingenuity, patience, and open-mindedness: someone with authority on one side approaches someone with authority on the other; they talk tentatively about improving the schools; they enlarge the group with representatives of both sides; they keep the talks going until they agree on concrete joint actions.

The first precondition for talks is a desire on both sides to improve school performance. Although the desire is usually strong among both teachers and managers, it often takes a few risk takers from either or both sides to step forward and begin discussing school improvement in a cooperative spirit, instead of one side attempting to fix blame for problems on the other side. In several of the cases, the alliance between teachers and managers came about because both sides perceived that problems in their school or district had reached such a crisis that the status quo was no longer acceptable; a new way of working together was essential, not just for the improvement but for the continued survival of the institution.

It is unimportant whether talks are initiated at the school level or at the district level—what is necessary is that, at some point, effective representatives of both teachers and managers are brought into discussions. In some cases, at the outset of this ice-breaking stage, union leaders and district officials feel more comfortable discussing initial plans and strategies for change in informal settings, such as breakfast or lunch, rather than at bargaining sessions or other formal meetings. Breaking the mold of old relationships and building a foundation of trust and shared responsibility requires a period of courtship, sustained effort to persuade one another that the benefits outweigh the costs. During this period the parties may engage in joint learning experiences with off-site visits and site visits to school districts with effective alliances. They explore new ideas based on the belief that cooperation is better than conflict.

In some cases, the initiative for forming alliances comes from an outside group—a private foundation or a university, which can provide such substantial resources as money, training and research assistance, and the opportunity to network with other schools engaged in similar reforms. A potential problem in having an outside group launch an alliance is that the key participants may not develop a sense of ownership of the improvement process. In the examples cited here this problem was averted because a special effort was made to involve all key participants from the beginning. No decisions were reached or discussed without their input. Ideally, it is best for the interested parties to start talks themselves and, together, determine when and for what purposes outside help is warranted, so that neither side fears a "hidden agenda."

In several of the cases talks about joint problem solving began within the collective bargaining framework. The parties were able to discuss common interests, agree on goals for improvement, and formulate plans to meet those goals, without undermining the collective bargaining process. In fact, union and district officials often noted that collective bargaining had become less adversarial and more of a problem-solving process as a result of alliance. Similar effects occur in industry, but in those instances the most successful cases have evolved as parallel to, rather than as part of, the collective bargaining process. Whether talks are conducted within the bargaining context or not, the agreement to discuss and pursue educational reforms must be voluntary rather than mandated.

Most industrial practitioners have concluded that collective bargaining is not flexible enough to serve as a vehicle for experimentation and innovation with respect to the work an organization performs. In addition, if one tries to codify in advance the new and unfamiliar relationships (between principals and teachers, between management and union) that accompany employee involvement, the results may chill the enterprise. Employee involvement does not deal with ''quid pro quo,'' but with shared interests. The parties need freedom to work, learn, and innovate together for their mutual benefit and the benefit of the students, in an atmosphere of growing trust. The whole point is to stretch the imagination and creativity of the participants. Since the learning curve parallels the levels of trust and achievement, and since the parties can back out whenever they feel an alliance no longer serves their purpose, the contract need only establish the alliance and set its limits.

Some degree of mutual trust between the parties must be established if talks are to bear fruit—particularly in districts with a long-standing tradition of hostility and mistrust between teachers and managers. Often an outside consultant helps to build confidence by working with each side to focus on common interests, goals, and ideas about school improvement. Another means of alleviating fears is to issue a written agreement in the form of either a policy statement or a contract provision, which spells out the intent of such an alliance and its impact on teachers' and managers' roles and responsibilities.

No matter how well intentioned teacher-management alliances may be, they require an up-front commitment of time and money. For example, in several of our cases, teachers were provided with release time in order to meet regularly during the school day, or they received compensation for meeting after hours. Other resources include substitutes to enable teachers to take part in improvement efforts, training and technical assistance, funds for special workshops and planning retreats, or travel expenses for out-of-town meetings and conferences. In addition, key managers must be prepared to invest their own time, to make the alliance work.

Fortunately, the amounts of money required are a tiny fraction of the school budget, although they are not negligible. The time and energy to be committed will far exceed the budget costs, but the investment can generate unprecedented returns. Nothing ventured, nothing gained.

Training in team building, joint problem solving, conflict resolution, and related skills is particularly important because in successful alliances decisions are reached by consensus. Decision by consensus is unfortunately the exception, not the rule, in urban school districts; therefore, without some assistance in consensus building, many teachers and managers feel ill equipped to take part in joint projects.

Launching and Sustaining Change

Once discussions are under way, the parties have to manage the process of continuous improvement to ensure that it takes root and grows for the long term. Much can be learned from the few urban districts in this volume that have paved the way. More can be learned, in addition, from the by-now extensive experience of employee involvement in such industries as automotive, steel, and communications. The industrial experience is pertinent because (1) the size of management and employee forces is comparable to those of urban schools and districts;

(2) the unions in both situations are sophisticated, strong, and well entrenched, and have a history of conflict with management; (3) management attitudes toward the decision-making process are comparable; and (4) the external pressures to form working alliances are equally strong in both.

During the last twelve years, Work in America Institute has studied workplaces in which traditional authoritarian modes of management were replaced by more participative forms. The organizations we have examined usually employ a large work force, have demonstrated productive and enduring uses of employee involvement (EI), and are generally unionized. The following characteristics of successful EI efforts in industry are particularly relevant to school districts:

- Union partnership with management is essential because the union's countervailing force lends credibility to joint efforts. Moreover, unions receive a greater measure of trust from their members than managements do and this encourages participation.
- Employee involvement, encompassing day-to-day relationships in which managers and employees work together on common interests, is pursued on a separate track from collective bargaining, in which the parties wrestle with permanently adverse interests.
- A joint, well-publicized statement of intent outlines the philosophy and goals of EI and declares how it will serve each side's interests as well as common interests and goals.
- A joint central steering committee composed of top management and union representatives oversees the EI process, encouraging joint activities, providing advice upon request, and ensuring that intentions are translated into acts.
- Intermediate levels of management are appropriately involved at an early stage in order to ensure that changes are implemented throughout the organization. This affords first-line supervisors and mid-level managers a voice in determining whether and how EI should be established.
- Starting the EI process at a few initial pilot sites, rather than attempting to change everything at once, improves the

chances for early success, which is vital for the continued growth of EI.

School districts should pay special attention to the joint management-union steering committee, the statement of purpose and philosophy, and the involvement of all levels of the organization.

The actual work of problem solving and, in some cases, implementation of solutions is best carried out by task groups whose members serve on a voluntary basis. Facilitators trained in the dynamics of group decision making help task groups learn how to reach constructive consensus; ensure that personalities do not interfere with the process; and attend to such logistics as minute keeping, scheduling of meetings, and making sure that recommendations receive prompt responses from top management. Task-group members determine their own agenda, on the condition that contract issues are avoided; hold meetings on a regular basis during working hours; and inform nonmembers of the group's progress and seek their input in devising solutions to problems. The task group's function is to identify and define practices, to present detailed solutions, and to implement solutions within delegated areas of authority. If a group's solution is not adopted, members should understand the reasons it was not accepted so that they can reshape or redirect their efforts and sustain their trust in the process.

Hazards

The road to educational reform is paved with slogans and buzzwords, well intended but dangerous. Phrases such as teacher empowerment, participation, school-based management, and the like are attractive, but putting these ideas into practice can as readily frustrate as advance the attainment of jointly desired goals.

Understandably, these slogans have helped to mobilize teachers, whose sense of powerlessness has been pronounced in an educational system where decision-making authority is so heavily concentrated at the top. Buzzwords such as *teacher*

professionalization and *school restructuring* have stimulated serious
discussion about the problems that hamper teacher and local-
school initiatives for reform. The improvement of schools will
certainly depend on the reallocation of power within the educational system. And some degree of school-based management
and restructuring will be needed to bring about deep and lasting
educational reforms. But the fixation on slogans also distracts
attention from the central issue: *how to improve schools.*

Teacher participation, for example, can include various forms
and degrees of consultation and/or delegation, ranging from
a voice for teachers in management decisions before they are
adopted, to full-fledged semiautonomous teams in which teachers determine the problems to be solved, design their own solutions, and then implement them. The case studies in this book
describe participation in a wide variety of teacher-management
governance structures, encompassing such issues as curriculum
redesign, introduction of nontraditional staffing techniques, professional development, hiring of principals and faculty, budgeting, instructional strategies, and scheduling, to name a few.
However, given the limitations of experience, time, and other
resources, teachers and managers have to determine the form,
degree, and areas of participation that will best advance school
performance and concentrate on these.

Another oversimplification that can lead school reformers
astray is the notion that teachers should be involved in making
decisions about their jobs because they are ''the experts'' with
respect to their jobs. They are experts, but this should not
preclude help from other experts, who can provide the information and technical advice they need in reaching sound solutions to problems. In industry, the most successful employee
work teams regularly consult with other experts in the organization—engineers, accountants, and personnel specialists, for
example. Similarly, as teachers embark on school reform projects, they will require guidance and technical assistance from
both in-house and outside sources. Staff experts at district headquarters are a repository of valuable in-house assistance. The
evidence suggests that teachers, as much as possible, avoid central staff specialists, whom they view not as aids but as obstacles
to school reform because they promulgate rules and regulations

that thwart teaching efforts. However, the cases show another side of the story: teachers and district staff specialists who collaborate to solve difficult problems in education, coming together as equal partners rather than as superior and subordinate.

At the school level, principals are pivotal in forming alliances and carrying out their reforms, but for the most part they have felt threatened by calls for teacher participation and empowerment, fearing that any degree of power sharing undermines their own authority. In the cases reported here some principals are still "feeling their way" in forming alliances with teachers, honing new skills in consensus building and teamwork. The successful ones find that the likelihood of school improvement increases and that their roles are enhanced, with more time available for long-term planning, recruitment of outstanding teachers, and keeping in touch with students, parents, and the community. But as several of the cases demonstrate, principals are more likely to encourage participation by teachers in schoolwide decisions if principals themselves have had the experience of being invited by the superintendent to take part in districtwide decision making.

Support from Politicians/Managers

Education ultimately takes place in the interaction between student and teacher at a school. Nevertheless, the operation of urban public schools is inseparable from the functioning of the school districts that govern them, and the districts are creatures of the state. Whether they like it or not, school boards, state governors, and legislators are charged with managing the public schools. As managers, they are bound by the same need as lower-level managers to work through alliances with teachers and their unions. As politicians, they are accountable to the electorate and, therefore, function as politicians. Confusion between these dual roles has often led politicians/managers into trying to reform through legislation without consulting teachers. But, substantial school improvement will require them to form partnerships with the teachers, in which the parties recognize their common interests and prevent their differences from blocking collaboration on educational reforms.

Local school boards have the responsibility of pursuing alliances with teachers and their unions, even while conflict continues on traditional bargaining issues. They must also persuade voters that they are pushing for the right reforms.

Educational reforms depend on systemic changes at both the school and district levels, with improvements at one level reinforcing and stimulating further advance at the other. School boards can facilitate the formation and operation of alliances at the district and school levels by (1) assuring greater equity among schools in the allocation of dollars-per-pupil and teaching skills, (2) providing financial resources by budgeting for teacher involvement, (3) encouraging collaborative relationships between central staff personnel and teachers and principals, and (4) inducing principals to manage participatively by including shared decision making as part of the job description, rewarding them for their efforts to share decision making, and providing training in consensus-building skills.

The frequently changing composition of school boards due to elections, appointments, and retirements threatens the flow and momentum of the district's and schools' experience with alliances. In order to preserve continuity, efforts should be made to orient all new board members and candidates as to the nature and benefits of such alliances.

State governments, like local boards, must form statewide alliances with teachers if they hope to bring about educational reform. They should also encourage teacher alliances with districts and schools, by setting standards for excellence and equity, establishing criteria for measuring progress, and encouraging local experimentation within agreed boundaries to meet the standards. Some states, such as Connecticut, Massachusetts, and Washington, are already taking steps in this direction. Another move to further local alliances is the granting of waivers to legislation that may be blocking locally initiated reforms. School districts such as Philadelphia, Dade County (Florida), and Hammond (Indiana) are seeking such waivers whenever possible.

The lack of equity in state funding among districts—and the resulting disparities in allocation of dollars-per-pupil—impedes alliances as much as disparities among schools of a district. While it is not within the scope of this report to detail the extent of such disparities or recommend how to correct them, it is clear that the uneven distribution of teaching experience and talents can threaten the effectiveness and duration of whatever improvements come out of local alliances.

Recommendations

Recommendation 1.　Alliances between management and teachers are the only way for schools and districts to make the continuing systemic changes that will move them toward excellence and equity. Representatives of school management, teachers, and the public should do everything in their power to establish and nurture such alliances.

Recommendation 2.　Since management alone has the authority to run the schools, teachers have no voice in proposing or designing systemic changes unless management allows them to do so. Therefore management should take the initiative and invite the teachers to become allies.

Recommendation 3.　Where management-teacher relations have been hostile, the parties should not put off alliance pending the return of harmony. Hostility does not hinder, and indeed often stimulates, a search for common ground between the parties.

2

The Role of Teachers
in Forging Change:
Myths and Realities

Until recently (within the past five years), the conventional wisdom implicit in public opinion, federal pronouncements, and state legislation has been that urban educational reform is blocked by (1) teachers' incompetence, (2) teachers' opposition to reform, and (3) unions' opposition to reform and their obsession with the "bread-and-butter" issues of higher wages and better benefits. As a union leader in the Cincinnati public schools has said, proposals for merit pay are "based on the assumption that most of us aren't really trying or that most of us are incompetent."

Our cases, and the field research of other observers, prove that the charges are generally unfounded. They are only a lame excuse for avoiding alliances.

Competence

The issue of teacher competence is a red herring. Of course, the more skill and knowledge teachers have, the greater the potential for school improvement. But even today's teachers are capable of contributing much more than they are now permitted to do, both in the classroom and as members of the school community. Nor can school improvement wait until changes such as those proposed by the Carnegie Forum (for example, adding a new category of lead teachers, creating a National Board for Professional Teaching Standards for teacher certification, restructuring schools to provide a professional environment for teachers, and so on) become the norm (Carnegie Forum Task Force on Teaching as a Profession, 1986, p. 55). A minimum of five to ten years will be needed for these changes to take place. In addition, the salary increases now being granted in many districts are already attracting more highly qualified people into the profession.

Teachers' Opposition

The cases in this book and other research demonstrate that teachers willingly become allies in educational reforms of many kinds, so long as the reforms make sense to them. What they oppose are ''reforms'' imposed on them by fiat; and even then they have sometimes gone along when given an opportunity to reshape them.

Teachers have taken part in initiating and implementing a wide variety of school- and district-level reforms affecting both the content and structure of education, such as curriculum development and revision, peer evaluation and mentoring programs, instructional strategies, budget planning, alternative scheduling, and professional development. Two cases describe how teachers are creating totally new schools and, in the process, redefining the educational mission and the role of teachers: both Hope Essential High School and Central Park East Secondary School belong to the Coalition of Essential Schools, a national network of schools working with Theodore Sizer and Brown University staff to enhance student learning by restructuring school organizations. Each school has adapted the coalition's general principles to fit its particular needs. Teachers at both Hope and Central Park East have developed new curricula, created new grading standards, and reorganized the school day to enhance student learning. The traditional model of the teacher as the giver of education and the student as the passive recipient has been replaced by one in which teachers serve as academic coaches, moving among students and working with them on an individual basis, while students are viewed as workers: the emphasis is on problem solving, group discussions, and teamwork.

Teachers have joined in far-reaching district-level changes and school-based reforms in such major urban districts as Dade County (Florida) and Jefferson County (Kentucky), as well as in mid-size districts, such as Cincinnati, Ohio, and smaller urban districts, such as Hammond, Indiana.

- A School-Based Management/Shared-Decision Making Pilot Program, in Dade County, is an attempt to professionalize teaching and decentralize the district, shifting decision making and management roles and responsibilities to the school community members: teachers, principals, other building administrators, and parents. Eighty-two schools have participated; innovations have been proposed in such areas as curriculum, staffing, hiring decisions, and instructional techniques, and have focused on such problems as student motivation, attendance, and achievement.
- In Jefferson County, a massive reform effort, still in the embryonic stages, is attempting to restructure the school system, focusing on both districtwide policies and school-based reform, and on the teaching profession. One key element of the plan provides for Professional Development (PD) Schools, envisioned to serve the school system in much the same way as teaching hospitals serve the medical profession. So far, the faculty and principals of twenty-four schools have agreed to become PD schools and to set school goals and establish participatory governance structures to carry out these goals. In certain middle schools, where team teaching has existed for ten years, lead teachers have considerable authority in curriculum issues and teaching.
- District personnel and union representatives in Cincinnati are jointly taking steps to allow teachers to assume greater responsibility in educational policymaking. Joint committees at the district level, with equal union and administrative representation, are considering such matters as teacher allocation in understaffed schools, selection of consulting or

mentor teachers as part of a Peer Assistance Program, and implementation of career development and training programs.

- School-based improvement teams in Hammond, Indiana, made up of teachers, administrators, parents, and students (in high school), are solving problems and are involved in curriculum development, hiring decisions, instructional strategies, staffing needs, scheduling, and professional development.

Union Opposition

Another myth is that teachers' unions oppose reform and generally refuse to support change. In every one of our cases teachers were represented by a union [more often by the American Federation of Teachers (AFT) than by the National Education Association (NEA) because AFT is more heavily represented in urban districts], and union attitudes toward reforms range from acquiescence to enthusiastic support to actual initiation of reform proposals. The degree of support generally matches the degree to which teachers and unions were involved in designing and carrying out the reforms.

In one case, the union position consisted of not opposing reform and taking no action to block change:

- The teachers' union in Los Angeles has no direct relationship with the Humanitas project, an interdisciplinary humanities program designed and run by teachers. However, many of the teachers involved are active union members, and the program operates with a kind of tacit union approval.

In many more cases, the union is supportive of reform and may even be involved in the earliest stages of planning and getting projects off the ground:

- In the Philadelphia public schools, for example, teachers and administrators are collaborating on the Writing Across the Curriculum project to develop teachers' skills in writing instruction and to use writing as a tool for learning other subjects. The Philadelphia Federation of Teachers, concerned with improving staff development opportunities for teachers and giving them a greater voice in policy decisions that affect the classroom, actively supports the WAC project and views it as consistent with union goals. The executive assistant to the union president sits on the board of directors of the Philadelphia Alliance for Teaching Humanities in the Schools (PATHS), the private organization that oversees the project.

- The Jefferson County Teachers Association has been in on the restructuring of the Louisville school district from the very early planning stages. Its support has been tempered by reminders that the state ranks forty-eighth or forty-ninth in teacher salaries and that meaningful participation cannot occur without attention to the issue of pay. Several teachers active in both the union and the restructuring effort see no conflict of interest between union goals and those of the new organizational culture, which stresses professionalism. Nonetheless, many note that without some compensation for their extra efforts in implementing innovations, their continued participation is unlikely.

- Union support and cooperation facilitated the creation of Central Park East Secondary School. The union provided input to program design and, through the close working relationship between the president of the United Federation of Teachers and the principal, agreed to bend many work rules in the contract to accommodate the experiment. The union's most recently negotiated contract with the New York City Board of Education encourages flexibility and innovations to enhance teachers' professionalism throughout the city school system.

- In Providence, before the Hope Essential High School program was launched, the president of the Providence Teachers Union held meetings with faculty at the high school to answer their many questions and concerns—implications for teachers' roles, the impact on their jobs, and so on. An amendment to the bargaining agreement, drawn up by the union with a faculty committee and the administration, addressed the selection process for EHS teachers, teachers working outside of their content areas, and teachers assuming duties as administrators. The two-thirds faculty vote needed to initiate the program would not have been reached, most teachers agree, had it not been for the union's efforts.

- Similarly, the Pittsburgh Federation of Teachers negotiated a very progressive agreement with the district that helped make the Schenley High School Teacher Center a success. Teachers throughout the district may participate at the center without giving up teaching rights at their home schools. The union continues to work closely with the district in developing and implementing the program.

- The ABC Federation of Teachers was instrumental in bringing about many of the reforms in the ABC Unified District. Through its efforts, teachers developed the state-funded mentor program, proposals for the California Classroom Teachers Instructional Improvement Program, and teacher evaluation instruments. The 1986–89 contract provides that a monthly budget printout and chart of accounts will be made available to individual schools. The union sees itself as a full partner with the administration in bringing teachers into the decision-making process and carrying out reforms.

- In Hammond, Indiana, where the Hammond Teachers' Federation is actively involved in school improvements, the 1985–89 contract has become an important vehicle for facilitating the School Improvement Process (SIP). Not only does it explicitly endorse the principles of school improvement and shared decision making; it also provides a procedure by which individuals may deviate from the contract in order to carry out a school-level improvement plan. Union support has also helped boost teacher support, convincing many of them that SIP is more than a passing fad.

- In Duluth, the union proposed the idea of a participative management model for the district. Together, the Duluth Federation of Teachers and management have developed a joint committee to improve their working relationship and facilitate Participative Management/Quality of Work Life

(PM/QWL), a process designed to open up decision making in the district to members of the school community and bring about educational improvements. In addition, joint problem-solving teams operate at school level. The union views PM/QWL as reflecting its own goals to enfranchise teachers in decision making and to improve their professional opportunities. The district committee is now considering a major plan for teachers' internship, mentoring, and peer assistance evaluation.

- The School-Based Management/Shared-Decision Making pilot program in the Miami schools was jointly conceived, initiated, developed, and implemented by the United Teachers of Dade and administration. Since 1973 the district and union have employed joint task forces to reconcile differences that could not be worked out at the bargaining table. The most recent contract endorses the professionalization of teachers and recognizes the value of teacher input in educational policymaking. It specifically includes provisions for a Joint Professionalization Teaching Task Force and for the current pilot program. Thus, the collaborative model established in Miami has emerged within the collective bargaining framework on a gradual basis.

- The Cincinnati Federation of Teachers took the lead in initiating reforms in the school district. Its president surveyed members to identify key issues in the district, going beyond salary and benefits. In a carefully orchestrated press campaign, he publicized the union's interest in increasing teacher professionalism and improving schools, and successfully shaped the direction of contract talks to focus on education as well as economic issues. The union proposed several changes that increased the teachers' voice in decision making and improved the educational process: peer assistance, union appointment of teacher representatives on committees, higher standards for student promotions. As a result, the contract established joint committees to review and recommend policy. The union also developed a ten-point proposal to improve neighborhood schools with high percentages of at-risk students; recommendations included all-day kindergartens, preschool programs, reduction in class size, expansion of visiting teacher services, training in social skills, the appointment of counselors in elementary schools, increased parent involvement, maintenance of k-6 or k-8 elementary schools, in-school disciplinary measures, and clerical assistance for teachers. A joint planning committee of teachers and administrators was established to oversee the program.

The experiences cited in our cases are consistent with the findings of major field studies on the role of collective bargaining in educational reform. The research shows that collective bargaining, while an imperfect forum for solving complex educational issues, has led to positive changes in school districts, improving the conditions of teaching and pupil-teacher ratios, establishing teacher representation on committees, and expanding the process of teacher evaluation. The process does have flaws—unions negotiate unwise work rules; school boards try to undermine teachers' status through narrow interpretations of legislation; and because collective bargaining is an adversarial process built on demands and compromises, the parties are often unwilling to take risks or experiment within the formalized bargaining process. Despite these drawbacks, the findings of four major field studies (McDonnell and Pascal, 1979; Kerchner and Mitchell, 1981; Johnson, 1984; and Jessup, 1985) confirm that the effects of collective bargaining have been more beneficial than harmful to educational reform.

Even under current state labor laws, there is room to negotiate over educational policy issues, provided that the parties want to. Despite state mandates regulating the issues to be bargained, many districts have established broad interpretations of such mandated subjects as "working conditions," resulting in contracts that include, for example, provisions about the length of the school day, the teaching and nonteaching duties assigned to staff, the rights of teachers to exclude disruptive students, and maximum class size. Some districts have ventured even further, negotiating such far-reaching provisions as the school-site management program in Monroe County (Florida); a peer review plan to replace a traditional teacher evaluation process in Toledo, Ohio; a requirement that teachers hold a major or a minor with recent teaching experience for any subject they teach in a suburban Detroit district; a detailed student discipline code in Youngstown, Ohio; and a progressive discipline plan in a rural California district.

In some states, legislation requires negotiations concerning certain educational reforms. For example, the distribution of additional state incentive funds is a negotiated issue in Massachusetts school districts; in California and Florida, school boards and teachers negotiate the implementation of reforms directly affecting the terms and conditions of teachers' employment—a mentor teacher program, counseling program, career ladders, financial incentives for increasing the length of the instructional day and year.

Despite the difficulties of bargaining about the terms of programs that did not yet exist, "negotiation enabled the parties to better anticipate the practical implications of reform initiatives, to adapt them to local conditions, and to devise processes and procedures by which they might be implemented," according to field research conducted in two of these districts (Johnson, 1987, p. 5).

In other districts experimentation with less adversarial and more conciliatory processes of problem solving has resulted in written agreements. In these so-called "win-win" bargaining agreements, the participants, frustrated with the limitations of positional bargaining, are reshaping the collective bargaining process, making it more open, flexible, and creative, conducive to problem solving and generation of ideas rather than bartering. Unlike traditional collective bargaining, the process is accepted as a cooperative venture, based on mutual trust, good intentions, and the recognition that both sides are genuinely committed to educational reform (Johnson, 1987).

In short, the evidence is clear. Neither teachers nor their unions stand in the way of educational reform. Examples from various types of districts in all parts of the country show them supporting and carrying out the broadest imaginable array of reforms.

3

Breaking the Ice:
How to Initiate
Management-Teacher Alliances

If urban teachers and unions do not oppose educational reforms, why are there so few successful alliances? What does it take to create a workable alliance? For answers, one must look at the present constellation of forces in the educational system.

Everyone in the educational establishment accepts that reforms can be brought about only if teachers support them. The problem is that, by and large, those who direct the establishment believe teachers' support can be commanded (or purchased).

This belief is embedded in the organizational structure of most urban districts. School districts, like all other management agencies, have three major functions: planning and design, implementation, and evaluation. Almost all planning and design are carried out by the local school boards and states, which set guidelines determining curriculum, resource allocation, personnel selection, school organization, and the many other details of school policy. For the most part, decision-making authority rests in the central district office, while implementation is left to the individual schools, which have had little or no say in formulating those decisions or evaluating their outcome.

While the school principal is responsible for administering district policy and coordinating the logistics of the school, classroom teachers are primarily responsible for implementa-

29

tion of those policies. Class size, length of class periods, curriculum, materials, attendance and discipline policies, and evaluation of student achievement are determined exclusively or largely without teacher input, except insofar as teachers' unions, through contract negotiations, have influenced policy decisions.

This organizational structure undermines educational effectiveness and efficiency. First it causes a lack of responsiveness to the variety of student needs and characteristics in different schools. District administrators have little or no day-to-day contact with students and teaching. The resulting standardization of textbook selection, curriculum, and evaluation criteria leaves little room for teacher discretion concerning these matters.

Second, teachers feel no responsibility or accountability for educational outcomes, since they have been excluded from decision making and evaluation. Teachers view educational outcomes as resulting from factors beyond their control, a perspective that only reinforces an unwillingness to face actual student needs and a sense of powerlessness to change conditions.

Third, talent is underutilized in the schools. Educators who have worked with teachers have found that they have a wealth of productive ideas and suggestions. However, the present organizational structure actually stifles initiative and creativity rather than creating opportunities for teacher input concerning organizational design, curriculum, and educational strategies (Levin, 1987).

The only practical way to gain teachers' heartfelt support of change is for management to give them a responsible part in selecting, designing, and executing the educational reforms. Given the force of inertia, it takes a mighty shove to start the process of improvement.

In order to get started on teacher-supported reforms, the following conditions are essential:

1. Management and teachers want to improve school performance.
2. One side approaches the other and proposes talks about school improvement.

3. The other side agrees to talk.
4. The parties talk until they agree on the desirability and achievability of one or more improvements.
5. The two sides establish enough mutual trust to enable the agreed-on projects to go forward without unacceptable personal risks.
6. Both sides commit time and resources to achieve the agreed-on improvements.
7. All decisions relating to jointly adopted projects are made by consensus.

1. *Management and teachers want to improve school performance.* This should be the easiest of all conditions to fulfill. Criticism of school performance and of teachers has been rife for many years, and no one likes to be the butt of criticism. On the positive side, there is a widespread desire among teachers and managers to see improvement take place. Whenever a real opportunity to improve the schools is presented, at least a few teachers and managers come forward. Many more would like to take part, but will wait until events prove that the efforts are genuine and likely to be fruitful.

In some cases, it takes a crisis to jolt both sides to the realization that there must be a better way to work out problems in the school system.

- In the Hammond school district, for example, the decline of the high school—slipping academic achievement, soaring dropout rates, racial tension, drug abuse, and other problems—and the sense that both teachers and administrators had "run out of solutions" galvanized them into action.
- Similarly, in Pittsburgh an innovative and nationally recognized teacher development and renewal center, based in a functioning high school, evolved from a desire not only to improve instruction and student achievement but also to save Schenley High School. Pittsburgh in the 1970s was plagued with the same problems as other large urban school districts: court-ordered desegregation, declining enrollments, declin-

ing student academic performance, and teacher burnout. School improvement was judged to be more than necessary— it was critical to the survival of Schenley, which was considered to be one of the worst schools in the system.

- In the Duluth school district, a teachers' strike had deeply divided the teachers and administrators. The real cause of the strike, according to the teachers, was their poorly respected professional status rather than salary issues. Determined to overcome the bitterness and confrontation brought about by the strike, the two parties developed a labor-management committee to improve their working relationship and joint conduct of the educational process.

2. *One side approaches the other and proposes talks about school improvement.* "One side," of course, means one or more representatives of either management or teachers, although it is easier for management to take the first step. The two sides may discuss how to improve one particular school or the entire district. Management may be represented by the principal of a school, by the superintendent, by the board, or perhaps by a member of the central staff; teachers may represent themselves or act through their union. At some point, both individual schools and the district as a whole must be involved, but the movement may proceed in either direction.

- In the ABC Unified School District, located in Cerritos, California, the superintendent who served from 1976 to 1986 is credited with initiating several of the reforms that led to teacher empowerment and the renewal of schools throughout the district, while the union exercised considerable influence in promoting these reforms and shaping their development. Two years before the state of California established its Mentor Teacher program, the superintendent had started a drive to bring teachers into leadership positions through appointment of Instructional Resource Teachers who serve as teacher leaders and partners with the principal on instructional issues. Eventually, the mentor program, though mandated by the state, became a union-directed and union-implemented program.

- The reforms and innovations now under way in the Dade County Public School System are based on strong labor-management cooperation that has evolved over a ten-year period. Joint task forces set up by the union after the negotiation of the first labor-management contract in 1973 provided the basis for the close working relationship. Equally important were the informal talks (breakfast and lunch meetings) away from the bargaining table, between Pat Tornillo, the union president, and the school superintendent, originally Leonard Britton, and most recently (as of July 1987) Joseph Fernandez. Here district and union leaders had the opportunity to candidly discuss their concerns and views regarding shared decision making, professionalization of teachers, and other reform strategies. As a result of these informal discussions, specific language, which established the foundations for the current reform experiments, was added to the contract.

- In the Cincinnati schools the person most frequently credited with initiating change is Tom Mooney, president of the Cincinnati Federation of Teachers. Despite the adversarial relationship between the union and the board, it was the close relationship and "behind-the-scenes" problem solving by Mooney and Lynn Goodwin, the deputy superintendent, that ultimately brought the two sides to an agreement. From there, the parties moved on to tackle the problem of at-risk students in low-income neighborhood schools.

In other cases reforms are initiated at the school level, usually on a pilot basis, and subsequently expanded throughout the district.

For example, the assistant principal at Hammond High School and the former assistant superintendent had become interested in the school improvement efforts initiated by an outside foundation. These two individuals approached the teachers at Hammond High, and eventually a group of teachers, parents, school administrators, and board members was formed. The first school improvement committee was established at Hammond High School; shortly thereafter, the two schools that feed into Hammond High were selected to participate in the School

Improvement Process (SIP). Impressed with the successes achieved at these pilot schools, the school board voted to extend the SIP to the remaining schools in the district and to provide district resources to make it work.

Often it has taken charismatic leaders from one side or both to break the ice, for several reasons: a history of adverse relations between the parties, lack of precedent for joint teacher-management actions, a reluctance to face problems. As information spreads about how to proceed in such matters, however, competence and confidence will prove more important than charisma.

- Bold leadership on the part of a school principal, Deborah Meier, and district officials was a key factor in breaking the ice in East Harlem's District 4. This New York City district was faced with declining enrollments and school closings in the early 1970s. Urged by the school board to make radical changes in order to improve education in the district, the then superintendent, Anthony Alvarado, asked Meier to open one of the first two alternative schools in District 4. Meier's commitment to teacher-directed alternative education and the district's willingness to bend the rules to allow the necessary changes were crucial to the school's success and to further experimentation. The climate of innovation that had been created led to the opening of other alternative schools in the district and, ultimately, to the establishment of Central Park East Secondary School in 1985. Also important in the case of CPESS was the cooperation of the union, the United Federation of Teachers, whose president, Sandra Feldman, had developed a close working relationship with Meier and District 4 administrators.
- Charismatic leadership—this time from the union side— was instrumental in starting negotiations in Cincinnati. Tom Mooney, the union president, launched an extensive campaign to increase teachers' influence in educational policymaking and building better relations with the school board and administration. His newspaper articles emphasized teachers' new professional roles and interest in educational

reforms while downplaying demands for improved working conditions. With the enthusiastic support of the press, the union negotiated several programs that increased teacher involvement in policymaking. While those bargaining talks were decidedly adversarial, the outcome—several joint committees in which administrators and teachers tackled complex problems—helped lay the basis for a collaborative relationship. The 1988 bargaining discussions were marked by cooperative problem solving rather than adversarial bartering and yielded far-reaching agreements on many educational improvements and innovations.

Occasionally, an outside agency takes the initiative to bring the two sides together, with money and technical assistance as the magnet. Such is the case in two highly successful projects, the Writing Across the Curriculum (WAC) project instituted in the School District of Philadelphia and the Humanitas Academy in the Los Angeles school system.

- The Philadelphia Alliance for Teaching Humanities in the Schools (PATHS) initiated the WAC program, a teacher-directed project that has resulted in significant improvements in students' writing and in attitudes toward writing among both teachers and students. PATHS, a private organization founded by business and school community leaders, works closely with the school district to improve the humanities curriculum. While initial seed money for the WAC project came from the Rockefeller Foundation, the Pew Memorial Trust, and a Philadelphia corporate support group, program costs are now entirely absorbed by the school district. PATHS has been able to unify teachers, principals, and administrators at all levels, by steering away from union-administration confrontation and honoring both teachers' contracts and district policies. At the same time it has emphasized the need for school-level control of the project, encouraging the input of teachers and providing the resources to allow this to happen.
- In a similar fashion, the Los Angeles Educational Partnership (LAEP), an outside independent group, introduced the

idea of an innovative, teacher-run interdisciplinary humanities program now operating in thirteen high schools of the
Los Angeles Unified School District. Smaller in scale than
the Philadelphia WAC project, Humanitas has achieved
equally dramatic results, due partially to LAEP's avoidance
of politics and bureaucracy in the district. The Partnership
oversees the Humanitas program and provides resources for
its operation. It has forged close interpersonal relationships
with district and school personnel in order to implement programs. Program costs are shared by the LAEP and the school
district.

- A major influence for renewal in the ABC school district
  was the Laboratory in School and Community Education,
  a project established by the University of California at Los
  Angeles and codirected by John Goodlad. By providing skills
  in team building, communication, and group decision making, the laboratory played a crucial role in initiating serious
  faculty-administrative discussions about how to improve
  schools. As a member of a laboratory-sponsored consortium
  involving school districts, community colleges, and county
  school offices, the ABC district had access to UCLA consultants who exposed teachers and administrators to new
  ideas and encouraged them to work together in determining goals and action for school-level improvements.

- Another national school reform network, the Coalition of
  Essential Schools, which is directed by Theodore Sizer of
  Brown University, also helped to initiate change at Hope
  High School in Providence, Rhode Island. Inspired by
  Sizer's ideas, Hope High School principal Paul Gounaris
  and other key individuals—the union president, the former
  superintendent, Sizer, and coalition staff member Paula
  Evans—engaged the Hope faculty in discussing the efforts
  of the coalition and its nine principles for restructuring
  schools. Hope Essential High School bases its program on
  these nine principles, shaped and adapted to meet the needs
  of Hope students. The Essential School faculty works in concert with Brown faculty to apply the principles.

While not the case in the examples cited above, a possible drawback in having an outside group initiate change is that the change may be perceived as imposed from without rather than owned by the key participants. Ideally, the parties start by themselves and jointly call in an outisde agency to fill a need, as in the Hammond school district, where a team of teachers, administrators, and parents went to the Kettering Foundation seeking help. The major role of the foundation was to provide technical assistance—training in consensus building and other skills needed to improve schools—rather than money. Providing money before ownership of the school improvement process occurred might have acted as a deterrent to the process, according to a consultant who worked with Hammond school officials.

- A Louisville (Kentucky) organization, the Gheens Foundation, played a crucial role in initiating the restructuring process in the Jefferson County schools. It donated $600,000 in operational start-up funds for the Gheens Academy—a human resource development center for the school district that serves as the focal point and coordinator of the many programs that make up the restructuring movement—but only after the superintendent had established his leadership and made significant changes in the district, such as winning the business community's support.

At the ice-breaking stage, it's best not to get too specific about what improvements the parties should discuss. A commonly used tactic at off-site retreats for teachers and administrators is to have the participants formulate a vision of what or where they would like their school to be in five or ten years, and then list some goals to achieve that vision. The next step is to develop a school improvement plan. But the most important prerequisite to any detailed discussions of school improvement is to get the parties used to sharing ideas and realizing that they have compatible interests and goals.

3. *The other side agrees to talk.* Agreement to discuss any kind of reform or improvement has to be truly voluntary, or

it is fruitless. Some commentators have urged that the parties should be mandated to bargain about educational policies, but neither party can be compelled to talk except in a strictly legal sense.

In some school districts, negotiations between the teachers and the school board touch on a fairly broad array of policy issues, such as scheduling, content of curricula, or student assignments, but only because both parties agree to include them.

If teachers and school boards were mandated to bargain educational policy issues, as some have recommended, the results would be counterproductive. First, there is no guarantee that concessions will be made or settlements enforced. Since the law states only that the parties must bargain "in good faith," not that concessions must be made, teachers could not depend on winning either legitimate policymaking roles or the assurance that agreements would be enforced.

According to field research of a sample of six diverse school districts, different kinds of contract provisions are enforced to different degrees. *Fully implemented* are those that are easy to enforce and, if violated, can be easily remedied, for example, class size and teachers' seniority rights. Violations of such provisions are usually redressed through the grievance procedure.

Partially implemented are those that are difficult to enforce through the grievance procedure—assurances of equitable treatment, student discipline standards, guarantees of building security or maintenance. Violations of these provisions are hard to document, and compliance depends on changed administrative attitudes or allocations of funds. Teachers' concerns about leaky roofs or unfair administrators are typically pursued through informal channels rather than through the grievance process.

Variably enforced provisions—those that are enforced in some schools, ignored in others, informally renegotiated in others—include assignment of teachers to supervisory duties, length and frequency of meetings, appropriate use of preparation periods, role of building committees. The extent of enforcement of such matters depends more on the working relationship between teachers and principals than on the contract language.

Second, if bargaining about policy matters were mandatory, principals, who are usually relegated to the periphery in contract negotiations, would be further excluded from influence over school site policies—the antithesis of school-based management.

Finally, requiring reluctant school boards to negotiate instructional policy issues might very well diminish rather than expand teachers' influence over what happens in the classroom. While some aspects of teachers' work are under close supervision, such as cafeteria duty or arrival and departure, historically they have exercised considerable discretion concerning classroom materials, lessons, and tests. Bargaining over instructional policy might invite unwelcome pedagogical demands, thereby seriously hampering teachers' autonomy in the classroom. In fact, in one California school district, the board tried to require all teachers to be trained in a teaching effectiveness program called Teacher Power—a move which was resisted by the union (Johnson, 1987).

A far better way to induce experimentation is through site visits, in which school board, management, and union officials observe and learn how their counterparts in other districts have formed successful labor-management alliances for educational reform. This approach has proved particularly helpful in the business sector. Site visits to leading plants, offices, and factories that have established innovative work practices are frequently offered by Work in America Institute. Limited to small groups, these visits have provided company and union representatives the opportunity for intensive discussions with all levels of the host organization—from workers to senior management to local union officials in organized settings—on the major challenges and roadblocks to establishing and maintaining joint work teams and other new organizational systems. Direct contact with the participants carries a degree of conviction that written and oral reports alone cannot match.

4. *The parties talk until they agree on the desirability and achievability of one or more improvements.* The improvements selected for joint attack may concern school governance procedures and/or the content and structure of teaching. High school teachers are

content oriented and tend to favor content projects, while elementary teachers are less so. The improvements selected should be modest enough to achieve in a reasonable period of time by parties who are unused to working together. Not only are managers and teachers unused to working together; teachers are unused to working with other teachers; managers of different levels are unused to working together; school managers are unused to working with central staff; and so on.

- The Duluth School District emphasizes this point repeatedly and instructs the school teams first to go for ''the small solvable'' problems before tackling the larger, more difficult issues. At one junior high school, in Duluth, Minnesota, where the improvement process is firmly in place, the principal observes that agreement on issues ''did not come easily'' and that ''considerable skill in conflict resolution from all those involved'' was required. Nonetheless, by having the opportunity to air their disagreements, the parties were able to move ahead and agree on an initial agenda for improving their school.

  At the district level in Duluth, the joint steering committee initially agreed on such proposals as an employee recognition program, a revised parent/teacher conference program and schedule, and a revised school year calendar, before moving on to tougher, not-so-easily-resolved issues such as teacher evaluation, staff development, instruction, and educational improvement.

To say that improvements selected should be modest in scope does not mean that they must be directed toward traditional educational goals. The goals may be new—for example, restructuring the school or recasting curriculum to ensure that even those who would normally drop out stay and win a valid high school diploma (as Albert Shanker urges)—but the initial steps toward such goals should be modest:

- In Dade County, Florida, the nation's fourth largest school district, the parties are seeking to professionalize teaching and decentralize decision making in the district by implementing new models for staffing, planning, and collaborative decision making at the schools. But changing the way schools operate in a district with some 250 schools has to be implemented on a gradual basis, providing time for both parties to reflect on and evaluate their accomplishments before moving ahead. The School-Based Management/Shared-Decision Making program has been implemented on a pilot basis, with thirty-two schools participating in the initial phase. A joint district-union task force monitors the program, reviewing progress and making recommendations for change.

Labor-management agreement on goals and programs for improvement has also been facilitated by the use of joint task forces, dating back to 1973, in which union and district officials have worked out contract differences. The positive working relationships that emerged out of those task forces helped both parties negotiate increasingly progressive contracts, eventually leading to the 1985 agreement, which provides for the current innovations under way in Dade County.

- The Hammond district also implemented its School Improvement Process (SIP) on a pilot basis at three schools before adopting it throughout the school system. The union president in Hammond commented that the gradual introduction of SIP in the district allowed the union some time to assess its worth before providing formal support.
- One of the first steps taken as part of the massive restructuring movement under way in the Louisville school district was the establishment of twenty-four Professional Development (PD) Schools, where teachers and administrators share decision making and a common vision for change. The most successful PD schools are the middle schools, where team teaching has existed for nearly ten years, providing teachers with considerable input into policymaking in such areas as curriculum, scheduling, counseling, budget planning, and discipline. These schools—which have experienced significant

improvements in test scores, student achievement, and attendance, as well as a decrease in the number of teacher transfers—serve as important models of change for other schools.

If the talks do not go smoothly, it may help to bring in a third party trusted by both sides. The outsider can help the parties understand each other's views; he or she can also assure each side that the other means no harm and that, in fact, the parties share common goals, aspirations, and ideas about school improvement. Again, this pattern is often observed in industry, where a private consultant, knowledgeable in the dynamics of employee involvement, is hired to serve initially as a kind of mediator, talking to each group separately, pointing out common interests, and bringing the two sides closer together. Another crucial role of the consultant is to emphasize the amount of patience needed to initiate and sustain the process. Since the two sides are not used to cooperative problem solving, they often expect miracles overnight and, without the intervention of a neutral third party, might easily become frustrated.

- In Duluth, the teachers' strike that had deeply divided the school community convinced both sides of the need for an improved working relationship. In forging a new labor-management alliance, union and administration obtained guidance from two sources: (1) the Duluth Labor-Management Council, a private organization supported by local employers and unions, which seeks to improve labor-management relations in the area, and (2) the Minnesota Educational Effectiveness Program (MEEP), a state program that provides training in team building and problem solving.
- In the Hammond School District, the consultant from the Kettering Foundation provided training in creative problem solving, consensus building, leadership, group dynamics, brainstorming, conflict resolution, and forecasting. Given the climate at Hammond High when the pilot school improvement process was initiated—low teacher morale, academic decline, gang fights, and mounting hostility and mistrust between administrators and faculty—training in these

skills was instrumental in getting the parties to work together in improving the school.

- In the Cincinnati School District, negotiators were aided by trainers from Conflict Management Incorporated, a group associated with the Harvard Negotiation Project that encourages new, more cooperative approaches to bargaining. Teachers and administrators learned to share data openly, express their views and interests in a candid manner, jointly explore alternative solutions, and eventually reach agreements based on "principles" rather than self-interests.

5. *The two sides establish enough mutual trust to enable the agreed-on projects to go forward without unacceptable personal risks.* "Trust" is not meant in a broad philosophical sense, but as a purely pragmatic phenomenon. Whenever people undertake a venture together, even if they are friends, they expose themselves to risks—not only that the venture may fail, but that another party or parties may take unfair advantage of the vulnerabilities presented. When the coventurers have a long history of hostility, as is so often true in urban school districts, the risks are magnified.

Trust is measured by the degree to which the parties feel it is safe to relax their guard. At the early stages of a coventure between parties with long-standing mutual mistrust, each will want to rely less on the other's goodwill than on objective defenses. Ordinarily, defense takes the form of a written agreement of intent—a public document issued by one party, a newspaper report of a public statement, a collective bargaining contract, or a letter of agreement.

In several cases, incorporating new language or an amendment into the contract greatly helped to dispel the initial skepticism of teachers. Even in districts such as Hammond and Dade County, where school superintendents and union presidents had discussed innovations informally and established close working relationships, the contract legitimized the effort and moved the process ahead.

- In Hammond, once the School Improvement Process (SIP) was approved on a districtwide basis, the union feared that shared decision making and the programs being considered at some schools might violate the contract. In the new three-year contract, the board and the union included language endorsing SIP and recognizing the value of teacher participation for improved educational opportunities for students. According to the union president, incorporating SIP into the contract helped win the support of many teachers.

- Similarly, in Dade County, despite the informal cooperation between union and district leaders, an amendment to the contract, establishing the practice of shared decision making, gave the parties confidence to continue and constantly improve on their efforts. Each round of negotiations produced new steps toward shared decision making—first joint task forces, then faculty councils and more joint committees, and, finally, an agreement endorsing the School-Based Management/Shared-Decision Making pilot program.

- At Hope Essential High School and at Schenley High School Teacher Center, amendments to the bargaining agreements paved the way for experiments that might have posed a threat to teachers' interests. Before launching the ''school-within-a-school'' project, the parties at Hope High School held a series of meetings with the Hope faculty, at which district leaders, the school principal, the union president, and Theodore Sizer discussed the purpose of the project and its implications for teachers. As noted in Chapter Two, in order to resolve teachers' concerns, the union worked with a faculty committee and the administration to develop an amendment to the bargaining agreement, covering teachers' roles and responsibilities, their eligibility for EHS positions, their transfer rights, compensation of department chairpersons, and other concerns. The amendment convinced the faculty to vote for the project.

- In the case of Schenley, the high school would have to be temporarily closed, Schenley teachers would be transferred to other schools, openings for the new teacher center positions would be posted, and teachers applying for these positions would need their positions at their home schools held open for them during the four years of the project. The contract amendment, by not requiring teachers to relinquish

their rights in their home schools, enabled the district to attract the best-qualified people.

- In Duluth, the school board issued a policy statement com-
mitting itself to Participative Management/Quality of Work
Life. The statement encouraged employee involvement and
participation in problem solving and called on supervisory
personnel to create a work environment that encourages participation and builds commitment to shared goals. To the
statement is appended an extensive set of rules, procedures,
and guidelines to aid in implementing the PM/QWL process.

Occasionally, trust arises from action rather than written words.

- At Central Park East Secondary School, it was Deborah
Meier's prior experience as director of the Central Park East
network of open elementary schools and her commitment
to an educational philosophy of teacher ownership that gave
teachers the security and confidence to take risks and fully
exercise their professional judgment in creating a completely
new school structure, standards, and curriculum.

Prevailing practices in the operation of urban school districts tend to stifle trust even among teachers of the same school.
Teachers picture themselves as in solitary confinement. Their
unions do not so much embody trust among teachers as erect
a common defense against management. The systematic sow-
ing of mistrust by certain political figures has intensified these
feelings. A prime function of contract provisions allowing local
deviations from the district contract is to relieve teachers' anxieties about being sold out by other teachers and/or the union.

- In Hammond a contract provision allowing local school site
deviations has enabled innovative school improvement projects to go forward without jeopardizing the rights of teachers
at other schools or without undermining the contract in any
way. When a local plan conflicts with the district contract,
teachers at the school in question go through a complex voting

procedure in which they express, on a scale of one to five, endorsement or opposition to a limited trial of the project. If the procedure is followed correctly, the union relinquishes its right to file a grievance alleging violations of the contract, but individual teachers maintain the right to file grievances. The union president believes the contract waiver protects the interests of the union and the individual rights of teachers, while simultaneously enhancing the decision-making authority of teachers in pursuing school improvement programs.

• Waivers to the district contract in Dade County have also been made on a school-by-school basis, to allow local school programs to be implemented. The waivers have had to be granted for every program proposed so far. Jointly authorized by the union and school superintendent and ratified by the school board, they have involved changes in curriculum, class size, scheduling, and job descriptions (Fiske, 1988, p. 1).

6. *Both sides commit time and resources to achieve the agreed-on improvements.* Any improvement worth pursuing requires an investment of management time, teacher time, and school district money and other physical resources. Those charged with designing and carrying out the improvement need time to think together, a place to do it, relevant information, and so on. In several of the cases described, teachers were granted release time in order to meet during the school day, or they combined release time with their own time by working after hours. Other resources have been provided: personnel to coordinate school improvement efforts and to act as trainers or facilitators, and funds for hiring outside consultants, sponsoring training workshops and weekend retreats, attending out-of-town meetings and conferences, and other activities. An unusual level of support is provided both teachers and principals in the Louisville district, where the Gheens Center operates all personal and professional development programs, with a Media Center, a Curriculum Resource Center, and Professional Library. The Professional Development Schools, in particular, have access to Gheens Center funds, which may help pay expenses for implementing a variety of innovations.

In several of the cases, foundations or special grants provided money that enabled the project to get off the ground, with flexibility to try unconventional or costly experiments. It is unwise, however, for a school board and administrators to make outside funding a *condition* for forming an alliance. To do so signals to participants that the board is only half-hearted, or that it believes little can be accomplished without outside funding. It is better to get the alliance underway with district funds— the amounts required are quite modest—and then seek outside financial help on the basis of what has already been achieved.

Teachers and managers who take part in discussions must be authorized to bind those they represent. Attendance by delegates without such authority signifies a refusal to commit time and resources. Teachers and administrators alike are cynical about "programs" that lead nowhere; they will not support decisions that emerge from groups that lack authority. Typically, school improvement teams include the principal (or a representative), one or two other administrators, and faculty members who serve on a voluntary rotating basis.

- In Duluth, for example, the building-level teams include the principal and union steward, plus faculty representatives popularly chosen or elected. The district steering committee, whose membership is determined by position or appointment, includes various administrative and faculty representatives: school board members, the district superintendent and his assistants, a high school and an elementary school principal, the union president, and other faculty members.
- The participants in Philadelphia's Writing Across the Curriculum project have devised a well-organized network of committees, operating at both the district and school levels, which assure the maximum collaboration of classroom teachers, district administrators, school principals, district curriculum specialists, school librarians, and college-based consultants. An important link between the district and the school is the School Writing Leader, a classroom teacher or department chair who serves as an activities coordinator, a resource person, and a liaison between the school and central PATHS office. Within each district, the group of School

Writing Leaders is crucial for developing school-to-school networks and for communicating district information and objectives to the school writing teams. The principal, in collaboration with the School Writing Leader, supports the team by providing regularly scheduled meeting times and other needed resources.

Whether teachers should receive additional compensation for time spent in joint ventures has been extensively debated. During the first flush of enthusiasm, teachers may put in extra time without compensation. But over the long haul they *must* receive either repayment or release time. In just about all the cases, teachers expressed concern about the lack of time within normal work hours to collaborate on school improvement projects. In several instances, teachers were working after hours on these committees, and while not insisting on compensation during these initial stages, they suggested that they could not continue at this level indefinitely.

Joint programs of employee involvement in decision making in industry typically provide pay for all hours worked on joint projects and overtime rates where applicable. This is not a salary issue. The issue is how useful and productive are the hours devoted to problem solving and teacher participation for school achievement.

Recently, foundations have come to the aid of school districts needing money to launch joint ventures. Their willingness is conditioned, however, on the understanding that once the project is fully underway and has proved its value, the school district itself will assume the funding. While the seed money to start up the WAC project in Philadelphia came from foundation and corporate groups, the School District of Philadelphia now funds the project and has allocated a budget of more than $500,000 to support WAC. Similarly, foundation support in Jefferson County and in the Los Angeles Humanitas project will eventually be replaced by school district funds.

7. *All decisions relating to jointly adopted projects are made by consensus.* Consensus is essential because decisions based on authority alone or on a vote will not convince teachers that their views are being considered on the merits. If they believe their

views are not considerd on the merits, they will simply return to the status quo. Particularly during the early planning stages, reaching decisions through consensus rather than having them mandated "from above" is instrumental in gaining the support and trust of teachers who, from past experiences, are skeptical of reforms initiated from outside the classroom.

Consensus is not to be confused with compromise. Compromise means that each of the contending parties gives up something in order to accommodate the others; no one is fully satisfied, but neither is anyone badly dissatisfied. Consensus means talking things out until all serious objections to a unified course of action have been resolved, or until all the parties are sufficiently persuaded to give the decision a fair try. Consensus usually takes longer than compromise, but decisions made by consensus are more rapidly and enthusiastically carried out; and implementation is what counts.

- At Hope Essential High School, making decisions about crucial issues—curriculum, grading, student recruitment, and so on—clearly did not come easily to this group of teachers, who were unused to the skills and responsibilities that go with consensus building; yet, they emphasized the opportunity to play a broader role in decision making and to influence policy as the main attraction of the project. Despite their disagreements, the team members reported great satisfaction and the sense of making a difference.
- At Central Park East Secondary School, consensus decision making on curriculum issues, teaching methods, classroom materials, and assignments are emphasized. Content teams and "houses" (groups of students that meet regularly and are led by a four-member faculty team) support the kind of collaborative teaching and decision making that enhances teachers'professional autonomy. Teachers plan curriculum together, observe one another, offer feedback, and help one another learn how to teach.

Consensus implies that management representatives must also be satisfied with the decision. All parties who will be affected by the decision must have a voice but not a vote in making the decision.

- Philadelphia's WAC project is notable for the degree of input from administrators at all levels as well as from teachers. The multilevel committee structure encourages the participation of district superintendents, school principals, district and school administrators, and curriculum specialists.
- The "pyramid" communication system at Hammond seeks to involve as many representatives in the decision-making process as possible. Faculty, administrative, and parent members of school improvement teams are responsible for communicating information and receiving feedback on the team's agenda from five to seven of their peers. Each of these individuals is then expected to contact several other individuals, who, in turn, keep in touch with still others outside the team.

If committees are set up to study and recommend (or implement), the committees must proceed by consensus, which takes a considerable degree of coordination, organization, and commitment on the part of the participants. A committee recommendation to set up a transitional kindergarten program at an elementary school in Hammond was preceded by extensive research and fieldwork. Committee members distributed their findings to parents, teachers, and administrators, in order to consider their responses.

Unfortunately, making decisions by consensus is foreign to the tradition of urban public schools. Authoritarian behavior characterizes relations at every level: between superintendent and principals; between principal and teachers; between teacher and students. Training in consensus forming is often requested by administrators and teachers alike when they undertake joint projects. In several of the cases examined, such as Hammond, Duluth, and Cincinnati, outside consultants provided initial training to faculty and management in consensus-forming skills, team building, collaborative strategies, and other problem-solving processes. Training is then usually handled in-house through peer training or by a specifically appointed facilitator who assumes training duties.

Recommendations

Recommendation 4.   Urban public school systems are never monoliths. In every district and in every school, without exception, there are teachers and managers who believe that educational reform can be achieved through management-teacher alliances. Those individuals should seek each other out and begin talking informally about the need and potential for school performance improvement.

Recommendation 5.   As the informal talks begin to discover common ground between teachers and managers, efforts should be made to add, if they are not already involved, individuals who can legitimately speak for the group they represent.

Recommendation 6.   The discussants should aim at agreeing to undertake one or a few improvements that both sides consider desirable and achievable.

Recommendation 7.   If agreement is reached, the parties should maximize the probability of success by ensuring that (1) the interests of neither party, and of none of the individual participants, are jeopardized by taking part in the improvement projects, (2) each party commits the time and resources needed, and (3) all project-related decisions are made by consensus.

Recommendation 8.   The school district should make an up-front commitment of adequate financing for the activities of the alliance. This will convince managers and teachers that the district takes the alliance seriously.

Recommendation 9.   Teachers should be paid for extra hours devoted to joint activities and provided with release time during normal work hours where necessary. These activities are as important as normal teaching duties and hold promise of high returns to the school.

4

Lessons from Industry: How Employee Involvement and Labor-Management Cooperation Facilitate Success

As America's urban public school systems move toward educational reform through greater involvement of teachers in decision making, they can spare themselves many disappointments and failures by studying relevant experiences in the business sector, as described in several current volumes. (These volumes include Rosow, 1986; Zager and Rosow, 1982a, 1982b; Kochan, 1984; and Siegel and Weinberg, 1982.) It is not necessary to draw analogies between schools and factories (or offices)—although many teachers complain that urban schools *are* run like factories, and indeed the obsolescent methods of "scientific management" are more prevalent in school districts than we had imagined. The point is that the basic political dynamics of decision making are similar in all large bureaucracies, whatever their end product or clientele. In the industrial model, corporate and union officials review and evaluate joint labor-management teams at the plant or office level. Similarly, some school boards and unions, as in Duluth, Hammond, Cincinnati, and Dade County, have drawn on this model by agreeing to pursue a joint improvement process carried out by teams of teachers and school administrators.

Our sources of relevant experience have been workplaces that (1) embrace fairly large numbers of employees, (2) have operated under traditionally authoritarian forms of management before undergoing transformation to more participative forms, (3) have unions representing most employees, and (4) demonstrate successful and enduring use of employee involvement. We have looked only to unionized sites because, to the best of our knowledge, every sizable urban district (outside the states that bar teachers' unions) is unionized. For the purposes of this discussion, we regard teachers as employees, albeit professional employees, despite the sometimes-heard argument that they should be regarded as supervisors of their students.

The Union as Partner

Whether employee involvement (EI) begins at district level or school level, it is essential for the union to be a partner from the inception. Union partnership makes the process legitimate in the eyes of members and encourages them to participate. If the process is initiated by management unilaterally, it never gains a solid foothold, and subsequent attempts to involve the union do not remove the stigma for a long time. The union will not risk blame for failures unless it can also take credit for successes.

By a seeming paradox, a strong union—one whose ability to stand up to management has won the confidence of employees—provides the best guarantee of effective employee involvement. The essence of EI is that employees' voices are heard and attended to. When employees raise problems or recommend solutions that managers would prefer to ignore, the union has the power to keep management honest; it cannot compel acceptance, but it can compel a reasoned response.

Another reason for union partnership is that in schools even more than in industry the union provides historical continuity, which individual managers or employees cannot. Principals, superintendents, and board members in urban districts are notoriously transient.

Employee Involvement versus Collective Bargaining

Employee involvement and collective bargaining are quite different processes and as far as possible are kept on separate tracks.

EI is a day-in, day-out set of relationships, through which the parties work together on common interests affecting the work itself. It is evolutionary, experimental, open-ended. Collective bargaining is concerned with wages, hours, working conditions, grievance procedures, and other provisions to stabilize relations for a fixed contract term.

Should talks be in the context of collective bargaining, or on a separate track? While collective bargaining has provided opportunities for teachers and school boards to negotiate substantive policy issues, it is not the ideal form for cooperative problem solving, particularly when problems are complex, multifaceted, and hard to resolve. The most successful joint problem-solving efforts in industry have evolved outside the formal bargaining process. One of the earliest examples occurred in 1973 when General Motors and the United Automobile Workers signed a Letter of Understanding that recognized the company's and the union's mutual commitment to improve the quality of work life, "thereby advantaging the worker by making work a more satisfying experience, advantaging the Corporation by leading to reduction in employee absenteeism and turnover, and advantaging the consumer through improvement in the quality of the products manufactured" (Warren, 1986, p. 122). The parties formed the Committee to Improve QWL, with equal representation of top company and union officials. The committee meets periodically and is responsible for reviewing and evaluating joint programs, developing new experiments and projects, and making regular reports to the company and the union on the results of its activities. The GM-UAW agreement also triggered action at the local plant level, where rank-and-file workers and managers have cooperated in joint efforts to improve work operations and product quality.

The pattern adopted at General Motors was followed at Ford and other major companies such as AT&T, Champion International, Honeywell, Philip Morris, and Xerox. Workers and managers are encouraged to pursue all types of decisions affecting the work environment, the only restriction being that their joint QWL or employee involvement efforts do not deal with contractual matters, such as wages, benefits, hours, or conditions of employment. Joint problem-solving efforts have thrived even when there are periods of labor-management tension at the bargaining table.

In some cases, the cooperative spirit generated by joint efforts has had the "spin-off" effect of making collective bargaining more a problem-solving than a problem-creating endeavor. For example, in 1982, in the midst of an economic depression and declining public confidence in U.S.-built cars, UAW and Ford Motor Company officials negotiated breakthroughs in employment security, income security, profit sharing, and training, in exchange for economic concessions on the part of workers (Bluestone, 1986, p. 44).

In the auto industry, both parties emphasize the separation of bargaining and joint problem solving. Alfred S. Warren, Jr., GM vice-president, notes that the "GM-UAW National Quality of Work Life Committee is not a substitute for the collective bargaining process. Rather, the committee constitutes a formal system apart from the collective bargaining" (Warren, 1986, p. 122). While GM and UAW have cooperated for years in alcohol and drug-abuse recovery programs, selection and training of apprentices, and employee orientation, "what makes QWL unique," notes Warren, "is the scope of its objectives and the depth to which it seeks to permeate the organization" (Warren, 1986, p. 122).

Few school districts have followed industry's lead in creating forums, apart from contract talks, for the purpose of addressing issues that go beyond the contract. An exception is Duluth, whose formalized districtwide Participative Management/Quality of Work Life Process seeks to achieve excellence in teaching, student achievement, community involvement, and general operations, by encouraging employee involvement in problem solving and decision making. A districtwide joint steering committee facilitates the participative process at the school level by providing guidance, direction, and training assistance to school teams and by identifying and solving problems that are of concern to employees on a districtwide basis. The eighteen-member committee includes two school board members, the school superintendent, and several of his appointees (both district- and school-level administrators), the union president, and five teachers appointed by the local's executive committee.

Unlike the industry model, Duluth's participative process—while a joint endeavor in spirit and practice—was announced as a school board policy rather than as a *joint* board-
union effort. Also, the process allows employee relations and
contract issues to be discussed at the steering committee, if they
are not in the grievance procedure or in bargaining, although
problem-solving teams in the schools may not deal with contract issues. (Both parties expressed reservations about this
limitation and hoped that it would gradually be phased out.)

By all means, the parties should avoid using EI as a pawn
in the chess game of collective bargaining, lest they undermine
the mutual trust on which EI rests. This separation may be more
difficult in school districts, where collective agreements often
include items—such as curriculum and class size—that more
properly belong on the EI track. The parties should consider
how to phase out such overlappings and sources of unnecessary
conflict.

Joint Statement of Purpose

Because EI works best with a maximum of "transparency,"
the inception of the process is marked by a well-publicized joint
statement of what the parties intend to do, how they think the
EI process will further each side's interests and goals as well
as shared goals, how EI will run on a separate track from collective bargaining, and how EI conforms to the contract but
reaches into areas outside of the contract.

Whether the statement applies to one school or to the entire district, it should be publicized throughout the district.

Joint Steering Committee

As part of the joint statement of purpose, the parties should
establish a joint steering committee for the district and one for
each participating school, whose function is to nurture and
oversee the process of EI. A steering committee encourages but
does not try to coerce EI activities. It renders advice when requested; it circulates activity reports; it makes decisions within

its range of authority; and it communicates with the outside world. The committee includes the most senior appropriate members of management and union as a symbol of the value the parties place on EI and as a means of ensuring that intentions are translated into actions. The committee may find it useful to appoint a "facilitator," that is, someone from inside or outside the district who can help its members get used to making decisions by consensus.

Involving All Levels

The most frequent source of failure in EI has been the bypassing of intermediate levels of management. Time and again the chief executive of a work site or a corporation has directed junior managers to establish the practice of EI for rank-and-file employees, without first giving the intermediate managers a voice and opportunity to participate in the launching of an EI process. Since EI inevitably alters the power relations between employees and supervisors, and thus between supervisors and their bosses, the uninvolved intermediate supervisory levels have predictably done their best to impede change. Similar disasters occur when the top leadership of a union fails to involve intermediate union leaders in the decision to establish EI.

Conversely, when intermediate levels are properly involved at all stages, the organization is able to make significant changes without supervisory resistance.

Where to Begin

As with any educational process, early successes are vital to the continuation and growth of EI. The chances for early successes improve if the joint steering committee focuses its attention on a few carefully selected pilot sites than if it overextends and broadens its attention over too many sites. The chances are further improved if the initial sites are ready and eager for change. Readiness may be present at a given site regardless of whether it is prosperous or in decline; it is present when a substantial proportion of management and the work force feel strongly that

important decisions have to be made and that the time has come
to involve employees responsibly in making them.

The steering committee will be tempted to try to change
everything at once, but the members must remind themselves
that they have limited knowledge of EI and limited time to
devote. Instead of trying to force change before management
and the work force are ready for it, they should let the first few
examples of success entice the skeptics into the fold. Participation of an individual school should be voluntary, and should
reflect both a felt need to change and management's willingness
to engage teachers in the process.

Lessons Relevant to Individual Schools

Task groups.   The actual work of proposing problems
and goals, devising solutions, and sometimes implementing solutions is carried out not by the steering committee but by joint
management-employee task groups. The steering committee
decides the structure and type of membership for each task
group. Employees serve on task groups only if they volunteer;
managers are required to serve at the direction of the work-site
manager. This latter point is crucial. EI can thrive if even a
minority of employees take part, but not if management refuses
to play.

For best results, an employee rather than a manager chairs
each task group: it is important for employees to know what
the manager thinks, but it is essential that the manager not be
able to block the free expression of employee views.

Facilitators.   Task groups, especially in the early stages
of EI, need procedural help. If a group is to escape "group-
think"—that is, a series of compromises and evasions that eventually eliminate everything of value—the members must learn
how to reach constructive consensus. Training can help, but
only practice can produce learning. A skilled "facilitator" helps
the group resist the centrifugal forces that otherwise defeat consensus. The facilitator ensures that every idea, even unpopular
ones, get a fair examination; that the group does not rush to
judgment by giving insufficient attention to controversial issues;

that personalities do not overshadow reasoning; that the group develops a solution rather than a problem statement. The facilitator also maintains momentum by ensuring that minutes are kept, meetings are held on time, supervisors make employees available to attend meetings, group recommendations reach higher management, and final decisions of the steering committee are prompt and explained.

Because of the central role played by facilitators, the work-site steering committee selects them, oversees their training, and assigns them to task groups.

Task-Group Agendas. To ensure that employee voices are heard, task-group agendas are decided by their members in two different ways. If the steering committee has called for the establishment of a task group to deal with one particular issue as its sole function, the employees accept the agenda by volunteering to serve. By contrast, the steering committee may invite the task group to decide for itself what issues to consider and resolve, almost without restriction. Both forms are common in industry. However, the EI process loses employee support when a task group of the latter type is established and management later tries to manipulate the group's agenda. The one universal restriction on a task group's agenda is that it may not encroach on the sphere of collective bargaining.

School managers should be prepared for the fact that task groups often start out by focusing on housekeeping and similar problems, and only gradually work their way into tough, substantive matters. This happens for two reasons: first, to test the seriousness of management's commitment, on the theory that if management won't act on small nagging problems, it can't be relied on to act on large ones; second, to make the point that there is a contradiction between asking teachers to behave like managers in dealing with substantive problems, on the one hand, and subjecting them, on the other hand, to such indignities as leaky and deteriorating classrooms and littered halls.

Task-Group Procedures. The best test of whether EI is intended to become a permanent style of managing at a given work site is found in the way task groups conduct their business.

Groups who believe that they are working on important questions and that their products will be put to use follow predictable patterns: they meet regularly; they do the necessary research; they keep fairly detailed, accurate minutes; they let nonmember employees know what they are doing; they try hard to sell their decisions. They meet during working hours to demonstrate that meetings are an integral part of the organization's business, and not an afterthought. Management does not permit work pressures to preempt scheduled meetings.

Task-Group Products. Task groups are rarely asked merely to identify new problems: management has all the problems it needs. The function of a task group is either to present detailed solutions on which management can act, or to implement solutions which may or may not require prior management approval. Management's responsibility is to supply information, expert advice, and technical support, as needed, and to respond promptly when a solution is presented. Due respect for the task group does not require management to adopt every solution offered, but it does require a reasoned reply on the merits, so that the task group can amend its work or start on another tack. Successful group results receive wide publicity within the organization, and sometimes beyond.

Recommendations

Recommendation 10. Successful methods of establishing and conducting employer-employee alliances have been, over the years, remarkably similar from one industry or work site to another, despite differences of technology, personnel, and tradition. Teacher-management alliances should study and profit from that experience; some have already done so.

Recommendation 11. Local boards of education, superintendents, principals, and teachers' unions should study the experience of well-developed alliances in the automotive, steel, and communications industries, with which they share the characteristics of (1) large numbers of employees, (2) an authoritarian tradition of management, and (3) representation of employees by entrenched, militant unions.

The most successful management-employee alliances in unionized settings display a number of functional characteristics in common: (1) the local union is in at the inception of the alliance; (2) employee involvement (that is, the process of carrying on an alliance) runs on a separate track from collective bargaining; (3) the more intermediate management levels are involved in the process, the more smoothly the process works; (4) the more the local union enjoys the confidence of its members, the more the alliance can accomplish.

Recommendation 12. Teacher-management alliances, whether at district or school level, should pay equal attention to (1) overall strategy, planning, and monitoring of the alliance, and (2) businesslike conduct of the task groups that carry out the substantive work of the alliance.

Recommendation 13. The separation of employee involvement from collective bargaining opens up more options for day-to-day collaboration and experimentation without the legal restraints of the written contract. School boards and unions should evaluate the two-track system.

5

Going Beyond
the Slogans of Reform

After the initial burst of educational reform programs in the early 1980s—in which fed-up politicians tried to legislate and regulate school improvements into existence—a period of slow reconsideration set in, leading to the conclusion that deep and lasting reforms can come about only through the spontaneous efforts of individual teachers, schools, and districts. Several educational thinkers had advocated such an approach well before the politicians were ready for it, but almost overnight their ideas became the new conventional wisdom. The slogans of the new wisdom are: professionalization, participation, teacher empowerment, school-based management, and restructuring.

These words, falling on an educational establishment in which power is so densely concentrated at the top, appeal to the powerless but arouse anxiety and fear among the rest. As rallying cries, the slogans have the virtue of stirring into action large numbers of previously despairing teachers. However, they make productive action more difficult, because they divert attention from the main issue.

Advocates tend to seize on a word or phrase, "define" it, and then try to deduce practical policies from the definition. For example, educators become persuaded of the importance of *empowerment*. Then comes the argument: since the word *em-*

powerment has various connotations, we cannot be truly in favor of empowerment unless we are in favor of all of its connotations. These may range from each teacher's deciding his or her own curriculum to teachers collectively running schools and determining the district's budget. By a similar logic, the phrase *school-based management* has been proved to *require* specific revolutionary changes in the governance of districts and schools, as if preordained. As for *restructuring,* many educators have complained that the term is so broad that it is often misunderstood and that it leads to confusion and inertia among decision makers, rather than stimulating concrete policies or changes (see " 'Restructured' Schools: Frequently Invoked, Rarely Defined," 1988, p. 1).

Fixation on slogans diverts attention in this sense: argument becomes centered on the terms *empowerment, school-based management,* or *restructuring,* instead of on the central question of *how to improve the performance of schools.*

It is almost certain that, in order to improve school performance, teachers will need more power sharing and opportunities to enhance their professional status than they have had until now. And certainly some degree of school-based management and restructuring is necessary to bring about and to sustain educational reform. But it does not follow that if a small dose is good, a big dose is better. In each case, the people involved must ask themselves: How much, when, what kind, will enable us to accomplish practical changes that will produce improved school performance? And even this form of question rests on the assumption—a large assumption, indeed—that the people involved can agree on what constitutes improved school performance.

Practical Participation

What does it mean when one says that teachers are "involved" or "participate" in making decisions? At a minimum it means that someone in management drafts a decision and invites teachers to voice their opinions before it is put into effect. At the other extreme, management and teachers agree on the statement of a goal to be met or a problem to be solved, whereupon management says: "Okay, figure out how to do it, then do it, and tell me what you've done." Between those points lie many possible forms and degrees of consultation and/or delegation. Each expert has his or her own favorite definition: some insist that the only "true" participation is complete delegation, as in the case of semiautonomous work teams. But why must participation be "true" in that sense? The best way to begin is to use whatever approach feels most natural to the managers and teachers involved. As the participants gain experience and mutual trust, their approach will evolve of its own accord. A good example of evolution is Ford Motor Company's engine transmission manufacturing plant at Sharonville, Ohio, which in the early 1980s changed from authoritarian rule to a system of consulting hourly employees about immediate problems, and which now delegates authority to joint management–hourly worker teams to plan and execute major technological projects.

In what kinds of issues is it feasible for teachers to be involved? Researchers have developed the appended list of procedural and substantive issues, which are extensive but not exhaustive (Table 5.1). However, participative management is an art that does not come naturally to people raised in the old tradition. It has to be learned by doing, and that takes time. If a superintendent or principal decided to manage participatively and, as evidence of sincerity, began at once to require *all* decisions to be made participatively, the organization would quickly disintegrate. No organization has the time or resources to cope with a sudden change of that scope. The available resources have to be concentrated on a few areas of learning. The parties should elect, preferably by consensus, areas in which teacher involvement will best promise school achievement, and the form and degree of involvement appropriate to each area.

For example, among the thirty-two schools in the Dade County pilot program a wide variety of innovations were proposed for joint action, as well as governance structures to carry them out. At one elementary school an existing quality circle program was expanded to include several teams for teachers, as well as for office staff, cafeteria workers, and custodians.

Table 5.1 Types of Organizational Decisions.

1.	*Instructional Coordination*	6.2	Determining criteria for selecting personnel
1.1	Determining activities for multiple classrooms	6.3	Selecting personnel
1.2	Determining activities for teaching teams	6.4	Determining criteria for removing personnel
1.3	Selecting instructional materials for more than one classroom	6.5	Removing personnel
		6.6	Assigning and reassigning personnel
2.	*Curriculum Development*		
2.1	Determining curriculum outcomes or goals	7.	*Rules and Discipline*
2.2	Selecting curriculum content	7.1	Determining school rules
2.3	Selecting an organizational format for content	7.2	Determining consequences for rule-breaking
		7.3	Resolving conflicts concerning student behavior
3.	*Professional Development*		
3.1	Determining professional needs and goals	8.	*General Administration*
3.2	Planning professional development activities	8.1	Determining how to allocate space
3.3	Determining preservice needs and goals	8.2	Determining how to allocate time (scheduling)
3.4	Planning preservice educational activities	8.3	Determining school calendar
3.5	Selecting professional development personnel	8.4	Determining public relations priorities
		8.5	Settling employee grievances
4.	*Evaluation*	8.6	Determining public relations priorities
4.1	Selecting methods for evaluating curriculum, programs, professional development activities, teacher effectiveness, etc.	8.7	Approving extracurricular activities
		8.8	Determining organizational rewards
4.2	Determining how to react to evaluation results	8.9	Determining budget
		8.10	Determining student placement
5.	*School Improvement*	9.	*Policymaking*
5.1	Determining areas in need of improvement	9.1	Determining how policy is to be made
5.2	Planning school improvement	9.2	Determining local goals for education
5.3	Identifying resources for school improvement	9.3	Determining how to comply with external mandates, legislation, etc.
6.	*Personnel*	9.4	Determining rules for employees
6.1	Determining personnel needs	9.5	Determining program priorities

Source: Duke, Showers, and Imber, 1980, p. 14.

Teachers are involved in developing a bilingual curriculum and a science/reading program; introducing nontraditional staffing techniques; and devising a plan for reducing absenteeism among teachers, with the financial savings applied to special school programs. At another middle school, the administration, the faculty council, and student-teacher teams are concentrating on problems concerning student attendance, motivation, and achievement; while at a senior high school, committees within the school's departments are recruiting and hiring new teachers and proposing new scheduling procedures.

Another elementary school is experimenting with the way it teaches Spanish: rather than hiring a regular teacher, it has engaged the Berlitz School of Language to provide instruction. If this method doesn't work, the teachers and principal will try something else. Teachers at this school have also given up their planning time in order to reduce class size during basic-skills instruction. Teachers and administrators at another school district—Hammond—have implemented a variety of changes, depending on the particular needs of the individual schools. For example, in one elementary school a transitional first-grade/kindergarten program was developed for students having problems in kindergarten and in need of more preparation before entering first grade. At another middle school, faculty and administrators are using a special rotating schedule that adapts to the learning characteristics of middle school students. And at several high schools, teams of teachers, administrators, parents, and students are involved in screening, interviewing, and making recommendations on the appointment of school principals.

The Use of Staff Experts

As the schools move toward adopting or adapting parts of the private sector's experience in employee involvement, it would be well to avoid another dangerous oversimplification. Industrial managers have gotten into the habit of saying that the reason employees should be involved in making decisions about their jobs is that they are "the experts" with respect to their jobs. The statement is true only up to a point, as employees themselves know. Yes, they are in the best position to test and decide on the best solutions to the problems they face, but they are far from knowing all the facts about their problems or all the possible solutions from which they can choose. To make sound decisions, they need information and advice from numerous other "experts"—accountants, industrial engineers, mechanical and other brands of engineers, personnel specialists, and so on.

By the same token, when teachers are offered the opportunity to recommend or carry out decisions regarding in-service training, curriculum, textbooks, new forms of instruction, and so on, it should not be assumed that the transfer of power also conveys the knowledge of what needs to be done. They, like employees in the private sector, will need information and technical advice from other experts. Currently, such guidance comes unasked from staff experts at district headquarters, who, in fact, are charged with making the actual decisions embodying their expertise.

There is evidence that teachers, given a choice, prefer *not* to rely on central staff for expert advice. They view central staff as responsible for the application of raw bureaucratic power and rules that hobble rather than facilitate teaching. Even when administrators try to "sell" ideas through lectures followed by question-and-answer periods, the stigma remains because teachers lack the time and self-assurance to turn question-and-answer sessions into genuine debates that might lead to consensus. Teachers would rather make their own mistakes and receive advice of their own choosing.

- In Philadelphia and Boston, for example, groups of teachers from schools without formal EI, wishing to thrash out their own ideas about how schools should be run, have organized continuing forums where they discuss their classroom experiences, methods of making them more fruitful, and the advice of outside experts. Occasionally they take public

stands on educational policies in their districts. For example, in Philadelphia, one such group became involved in the
district's attempts to standardize the curriculum. For the
most part, however, the groups fulfill the needs of individual
members who have complete control over the meeting agendas (Olson, 1987c, p. 1).

Properly designed joint teacher-management projects,
however, can encourage mutually advantageous relations between teachers and central staff advisers and, at the same time,
reach out to university researchers or consultants in order to
extend the knowledge base. And this can occur without the
dissolution of district headquarters. Teachers and staff advisers
can come together as equal partners, rather than in a superior-
subordinate relationship, and share the responsibility of solving difficult problems through consensus.

- During the planning stage for the Schenley High School
  Teacher Center, for instance, technical support personnel
  developed recommendations concentrating on such issues
  as orientation and follow-up, content areas, staff selection,
  and public relations. Their recommendations became important resources to the core planning group. In addition,
  the committees surveyed 805 secondary school teachers in
  the district to determine professional development needs.
  All subsequent program development efforts were based on
  this needs assessment.
- Though emphasizing the "teacher as trainer" model, the
  Schenley Teacher Center recognizes the contributions of district representatives and school administrators in shaping the
  teacher's training experience. Central office personnel are
  called on to run seminars for teachers on current district initiatives. During the program's orientation and assessment
  phase, the teacher, principal, and other staff specialists select
  the training and development activities considered to be most
  beneficial. During the actual training phase, a content area
  supervisor helps the teacher plan activities designed to update

the teacher's knowledge in his or her specialty. Teachers are also encouraged to organize their own seminars, select outside speakers, or visit outside organizations, in pursuit of their professional goals. Preparation for reentry into the classroom once the training is completed is a collaborative effort: the teacher, principal, content area supervisor, and teachers' peers are all involved in the review of goals and objectives.

- The Writing Across the Curriculum project in the School District of Philadelphia draws on the expertise of teachers, district administrators, curriculum specialists, school principals, college-based consultants, and librarians. Committees are structured at both the district and school levels to bring these participants together in an exchange of ideas on how to improve writing instruction and performance in the schools. The district-level teams provide advice, assistance, and resources to individual schools and initiate training workshops for teachers and administrators, who then train others in their school.

    Within each of Philadelphia's seven districts, the WAC project is coordinated by the district supervisor of reading/English language arts. For example, in one district this individual meets every month with the language arts teachers from participating schools to plan staff development activities. Another district sponsors "miniconferences"— in-service sessions focused on a particular topic or technique of interest to teachers and principals. Attendance is optional, but each school participating in the WAC project agrees to send representatives to some of these organizational and information exchange meetings held throughout the school year. This district has also developed a writing resource center, which offers videotapes, professional journals on writing, various samples of school publications, and classroom writing lessons. Materials can be checked out by teachers who are planning in-service sessions.

- The Gheens Professional Development Academy in Jefferson County, Kentucky, supported by the school district and the Gheens Foundation, sponsors professional development programs that encourage collegial interaction and support. Support groups of principals and teachers meet regularly, discuss books and selected topics, and share their ideas and concerns. A Media Center, Curriculum Resource Center, and Professional Library are among the facilities at Gheens. Teacher representatives from the Professional Development (PD) Schools attend monthly meetings at Gheens to share their experiences and report back to their schools. Gheens also provides staff, consultants, and financial resources to PD schools.

- In the Cincinnati schools, joint committees of union and centrally appointed administration representatives are involved in the selection of consulting teachers, new teacher allocation methods to relieve overcrowded classrooms, new grading and promotion standards, in-service training, and development of an implementation plan for a Career in Teaching program including four promotional steps leading to the position of lead teachers. Though viewed with initial skepticism, several of these committees have proved to be effective problem solvers. For example, the Teacher Allocation Committee, consisting of three union members and three administrators from the Department of Curriculum and Instruction, successfully tackled the problem of understaffed schools by assigning additional teachers or aides from a reserve pool and disbursing additional funds to compensate teachers for overload.

No Participation Without Principals

Calls for participation and teacher empowerment have annoyed, worried, or frightened principals and, in at least one instance, in Rochester, New York, have led to litigation. However, principals have less reason to be upset by the possibilities of teacher empowerment than by the vagueness of their own job descriptions. Educators hold widely varying opinions as to what the job of a school principal is or ought to be. Instructional leader? Administrator? Manager? By what standards should a principal's performance be evaluated?

Whatever the principal's responsibilities may be in any given instance, the support of teachers in carrying them out should be counted a blessing, not a burden. A teaching staff that pulls together with the principal increases the likelihood of school achievement and makes the principal look good to those who judge his or her performance; it also enables the principal to devote more time to advance planning, attracting outstanding teachers, and extending his or her influence beyond the schoolyard.

But clearly that is not the way it looks to most principals. Like traditional managers in industry, they believe that their organizations need to be kept firmly in check. The superintendent has granted each principal a fixed amount of authority with which to maintain control. Any sharing with teachers is perceived as exposing the principal to danger. Any power sharing that is requested by teachers, or urged by the superintendent, must therefore be opposed with whatever stratagems come to hand.

Since no significant empowerment at the school can take place without the principal's support, the prospects for improvement are not favorable. A school here and a school there may move ahead, but the mass will scarcely budge. Teachers and other educators are convinced of that, and that is why they long to see a new breed of principals. They recommend that all new principals have the self-confidence to share power, the patience to work with teachers until consensus is reached, and the courage to let teachers make occasional mistakes as they experiment with reforms. They recommend training courses, perhaps given by industry, which will equip principals to behave in these ways.

In industry, as in education, there are always a few visionaries with the requisite personal attributes who learn to manage participatively in a traditionally authoritarian context. Most managers, however, stick to the old ways (although they may adopt the new rhetoric) until the context leaves them no choice. As for training, results appear only when the organization compels and rewards the application of newly learned methods.

Teachers often wish aloud that principals would try to put themselves into teachers' shoes and understand what they are up against. Perhaps teachers should try to put themselves into a principal's shoes. Most principals have never experienced participative management, either as teachers or as administrators. Assurances by teachers or outsiders to the effect that participation benefits the manager as well as the managed, carry very little weight. Orders to empower teachers, issued by a superintendent, carry weight but do not persuade; principals may go through the motions, but little of lasting value will happen on the ground. In industry, as in education, chief executives find it much easier to instruct subordinates to manage participatively than to manage their own subordinates participatively.

Sharing power with subordinates can feel very threatening to a manager whose boss keeps him or her under tight control. Inviting teachers to help make decisions that affect the operation not merely of the classroom but of the school as a whole doesn't make sense to a principal who has never been invited by a superintendent to participate in decisions about the district. In short, the strongest impetus toward teacher involvement in the reform of schools would come from superintendents treating principals as full-fledged team members in managing the district.

- For example, in the ABC Unified District, the move to empower teachers was part of a broader decentralization effort to involve staff at all levels. A streamlined management organization improved communication between the district and the schools and freed more funds for local school initiatives. Decentralizing the budgeting process gave schools and principals more leeway over allocation of school funds. Seven management associations of elementary school principals, secondary school principals, assistant principals, and other groups of administrators meet monthly, and each group meets three times a year with the district superintendent. In addition, the chairperson of each group forms a Management Team Administrative Council, which also meets regularly with the superintendent.
- The principal's support of the participative management process in the Duluth School District is said to be the key fac-

tor in its success, according to several sources interviewed. School principals are represented on the QWL steering committee, thus permitting them a voice in district-level decision making as equal partners with other district administrators and with union and teacher representatives. The district superintendent is also committed to hiring administrators who are supportive of participative management and demonstrate skills that would enhance the process.

- The Schenley High School Teacher Center was developed as part of a broad staff development effort that initially focused on principals and vice-principals. A team of principals developed PRISM (Pittsburgh's Research-Based Instructional Supervisory Model), a tool to help principals become successful instructional leaders. Principals learned how to work in teams and were involved in decision making and in delegating responsibilities. The experience gained in working on PRISM helped shape attitudes that supported teacher involvement. Principals also taught teachers the PRISM model, which included such tenets of good teaching as teaching to an objective and monitoring learners.
- In Dade County, principals have been involved in various types of school-based management procedures since 1974. One such experimental program in the district increased school principals' control over the allocation of financial resources at their schools. Though the program was eventually dropped, the experience contributed to the current district superintendent's interest in school-based management and prompted him many years later, as the deputy superintendent, to attempt to resurrect parts of the program. A committee of principals and other administrators focused on the problems of inner-city schools and the need for maintaining good relations between principals and faculty as a way of reducing teacher turnover and improving the work environment. The discussions that ensued gradually focused on enhancing professional opportunities and eventually led to the district-union agreement to establish a task force on teacher professionalization—a major component of Dade County's pilot program in school-based management.

Teachers, in their own interest, should lobby the super-intendent and/or the board to expand the districtwide responsibilities of principals.

Collective Principalship

The Carnegie Forum report *A Nation Prepared* (1986) sparked controversy by suggesting that one possible solution to carrying out the difficult responsibilities of a principal might be to vest them in a group of senior teachers, who would jointly manage both instructional leadership and business administration for the school: the fullest expression of teacher empowerment. Many principals are still incensed by the proposal, which jaundiced their reaction to other, less controversial parts of the report.

Can collective principalship work? In theory, there is no reason why it should not—depending, in part, on how one defines *work*. Would it work better than individual principalship? Only experimentation can provide an answer. However, one should not try the experiment in the hope of saving money. No matter how the job is carved up, it demands a certain number of person-hours of effort, and it is hard to believe that senior teachers will permanently invest the hours (and experience the anxieties) without suitable compensation. Moreover, any time they put in on managerial affairs must either be taken from or added to their classroom hours. If taken away, some other person must replace them. Nor should one assume that teachers have more managerial talent than principals. In fact, some educational researchers have suggested that schools "recognize existing resources and use them to the fullest—specifically, the management skills of principals and the instructional leadership of master teachers" (Rallis and Highsmith, 1986, p. 304). They point out that the dual role of the principal—as manager and instructional leader—encompasses such different duties and responsibilities and requires such diverse skills that it is impractical for any one individual to handle it. They suggest that the principal's position be divided into two jobs, with a group of master teachers handling the instructional leadership role and the principal carrying out management duties.

At any rate, one should not assume that senior teachers will want to permanently spend a large portion of their working hours in making schoolwide management decisions. Experience at Hope Essential High School and at Central Park East Secondary School suggests that teachers would much rather have a voice in formulating policy than responsibilities for executing it day-by-day. Teachers at Central Park East were interested and involved in determining schoolwide policy matters, and, in some instances, were responsible for implementing policy decisions such as hiring faculty and running staff development activities. However, according to several teachers interviewed, their primary interest lies in the classroom—deciding curriculum, interacting with students, and helping one another teach. They had neither the time nor the inclination to take on the detailed responsibilities for policy implementation in such areas as budget, school resources, and liaison with the district office. Similarly, teachers at Hope Essential focused their time and energies on curriculum and classroom issues, while the head teacher, Albin Moser, carried out administrative duties, such as day-to-day scheduling, student recruitment, and dealing with both the district office and the Hope High School administration.

School-Based Management

A key districtwide item for joint consideration by the superintendent and principals is how to expand principals' authority and responsibility for reform within their own schools. Such expansion has sometimes been labeled school-based management, but that phrase needs to be guarded against, because it is too often interpreted as requiring almost total autonomy for the schools at once. The principals' sphere of influence should be enlarged step by step, in line with increases of responsibility for school reform and only as fast as the principal learns to involve teachers in making decisions. If principals' authority is expanded faster than they can manage it, their failures may do severe damage to the valid purpose of school-based management. The purpose is not to embarrass those who are slow to learn new methods of management, but to help all principals improve the performance of their schools.

James W. Guthrie, professor of education at the University of California at Berkeley, points to four major components of school-based management:

1. *Principals* who function as chief executive officers, meaning they are held accountable for the effectiveness of their school.
2. *School advisory councils* that serve as the vehicle for eliciting feedback and encouraging participation of parents and faculty members. The purposes of such a council include: providing advice to the principal on such issues as disciplinary policies, program planning, hiring new faculty, and allocation of school resources; helping to shape district and state policies to the needs of individual schools; and aiding in the preparation of annual school performance and planning reports.
3. *School-site budgeting and accounting*
4. *Annual planning and performance reports,* which include information on student performance, future goals, school assessments by parents and professional staff, and budget information. In addition to these school performance reports, which are directed to parents, local employers, and district officials, state-administered performance assessment systems, currently in use in seven states, let state policymakers and the public know how well the school is meeting its goals [Guthrie, 1986, pp. 306–308].

Dade County's approach to school-based management, originating with a 1971 Citizen's Committee on Education, identifies the school as the primary center for educational decision making, with allocation of funds for instruction, setting of educational objectives, and organization of instruction to be determined by members of the school community, including parents. The principal is recognized as a major player in school-based management; according to guidelines for the pilot program, he or she is provided "with the utmost flexibility and freedom to enhance current programs, initiate new programs and to work in concert with teachers and community to provide an exemplary

program'' (Office of School-Based Management, Dade County
Public Schools, 1987, p. 9). The guidelines also state that training for administrators and faculties is to encompass all aspects
of school-based management, including school-level performance
objectives, curriculum, student services, reporting, public relations, budget, personnel, and learning-centered schools.

Understandably, the process of determining how to share
authority is not easy; mistakes have been made; and, in some
cases, Dade County union and district officials have gone into
schools to help principals and teachers work out problems. But,
in an environment that encourages experimentation and risk
taking, mistakes—even failures—are an expected part of the process of reform: ''We wanted to remove that threat from hang-
ing over their heads . . . ,'' said Joseph Fernandez, the district
superintendent. ''If we see something that is not working, we
can go and try to correct it. Let's not continue as we often do
in education: We put things in, and we leave them there whether
they're good or not'' (Olson, 1987b, p. 19).

To begin with, the board and the superintendent have
to decide what they will hold each school and its principal accountable for achieving. If they want, in essence, to maintain
the status quo, with strict conformity to district directives, and
with minimum exercise of initiative and imagination, there is
no point in enlarging the authority of principals; all decisions
about personnel, budgets, curriculum, textbooks, and so on
should continue to emanate from headquarters.

If, on the other hand, principals are to be accountable
for improving school performance, they need whatever degree
of authority it takes to make the desired reforms. For example,
''No teacher [should] be assigned to a school without the principal's approval,'' because it is impractical and unfair to hold
a principal responsible for the effectiveness of a school if he or
she has no control over who is assigned to teach in that school,
even in those districts that continue to centralize their teacher
recruitment activities (Guthrie, 1986, p. 307).

Similarly, if the board and superintendent want principals
to function as chief executives, principals will need discretion
over school resources as well as accountability for the way they

allocate them. Each school will need a given sum per pupil, consistent with the state funding formula. A standard amount should be taken off the top to pay the expenses of the district's central office, says Guthrie; but beyond that percentage, the aggregate amount a school generates by virtue of its enrollment should be under its control (Guthrie, 1986, p. 309). For example, "The principal and staff of a given school might decide that the district's division of curriculum and instruction could adequately meet their needs for technical information and advice, and they would elect to 'purchase' curriculum and staff development services from that division. However, if the principal and the school staff believed that private consultants, institutions of higher education, or corporations could better meet their needs, they [should] be free to contract instead with those agencies" (Guthrie, 1986, p. 309).

Recommendations

Recommendation 14.   School managers, teachers, and unions should take care not to fall into the trap of believing that any single concept of reform, followed to its "logical" conclusion, will of itself lead to the desired goal—that is, continuous advances in the excellence and equity of school performance.

Recommendation 15.   An alliance should not dissipate its resources by trying to apply participative methods to every facet of school management at once. It should determine which few systemic changes now and in the near future will contribute most to the improvement of school performance, concentrate attention on them, and achieve them participatively, before setting its next round of goals.

Recommendation 16.   Boards of education have impeded school reform by giving central staff experts authority to prescribe teaching activities in detail without holding them responsible for the consequences; principals and teachers, on the other hand, are held responsible although they have no such authority. To rectify the situation, boards should restore appropriate authority to principals and teachers, and enable staff experts to take part as equals in the work of alliance task groups.

Recommendation 17. If local boards and superintendents wish to persuade principals that involving teachers more fully in school management is helpful and nonthreatening, they should allow principals to share the analogous experience of being involved in managing the district.

Recommendation 18. If a local board and superintendent wish to expand significantly the responsibility and authority of principals, they should do so one step at a time, not all at once. Each step should be accompanied by (1) changes in the job description and the related criteria for assessing performance, (2) provisions for making available the additional information and advice the principal will need, and (3) training programs directed specifically to the expansion. These accompaniments should be designed and executed jointly by the board, the superintendent, and the principals.

6

Managing the Politics
of Change:
How Local Boards and
State Legislators Encourage Reform

State governors and legislators, along with local boards of education (whether elected or appointed), wear two hats. First, they are answerable to the electorate, so they must behave like politicians. Second, they are directly in control of public education, so they must behave like managers. Likewise, public school teachers are part of the electorate, but they are also *employees* of the politician/managers.

Confusion between these dual roles often leads politician/managers into the erroneous belief that they can improve the operation of schools merely by writing laws, issuing regulations, and manipulating budgets, with little regard for the opinions of front-line employees. The heads of America's largest private corporations have learned that they can no longer manage in that fashion. It is time for the politician/manager to catch up. Teacher bashing may, in a perverse way, win votes for a while, but it is guaranteed not to make the schools function better. The legislators are responsible not merely for writing laws, but for operating the public schools. Conversely, manager bashing and politician bashing may help teachers to win union office when the relationship is sour, but it improves nothing.

Improvement requires alliances between groups whose interests are common in part and adverse in part. In successful alliances there can be no heroes and no villains. Everyone involved—especially those in exposed positions—must have an opportunity to share credit for achievements.

Local Boards

The local board, being closer to the front line, has more visible managerial duties than the state but must still respond to the voters. If the board hopes to improve the schools, it must press for reforms that are realistic and have the support of managers and teachers. It must also persuade voters that it is pursuing the right reforms, which is sometimes more difficult than persuading the teachers. Politicking and disagreements among the board members add to the difficulty. A reform-minded board has no choice but to form alliances with the teachers and their union, even as conflict continues on other bargaining issues.

The new conventional wisdom holds that educational reform comes down to improving the way each school operates, and ultimately to the interaction between teacher and students. Work in America Institute took this formula as a working hypothesis. We have since come to the opinion, however, that in an urban district it is unrealistic to try to divorce what happens in the individual school from what happens at the district level.

To begin with, state laws and regulations, which establish the framework of public education, are applied through the district. Second, principals, administrators, teachers, and students frequently move from school to school within the district. Successful performance by administrators (and sometimes by teachers) is usually rewarded by promotion out of the school. Third, from the teacher's standpoint, every manager in the district (that is, anyone who can give orders to the teacher) derives power from the board and superintendent. Teachers defend themselves against the arbitrary exercise of power by forming a union, which is organized on a districtwide basis to ensure equity in all schools.

For these reasons it is unlikely that reforms initiated at one level, whether school or district, can have a lasting effect unless related changes take place at the other level. Which level comes first matters little; that is usually a result of where the ice is broken first. The allies have the task of designing change so that improvement at one level reinforces improvement at the other.

- In the ABC Unified District, initiatives to renew the schools emanated from the district level but have spurred changes at the local level, resulting in a variety of participative structures at the schools. Teachers who have participated in the district's curriculum committees have pointed to the unprecedented opportunities for interaction and mutual reinforcement among different schools, across grade levels, and between subject areas.
- The district-union agreement in the Dade County Public Schools to initiate the School-Based Management/Shared-Decision Making program has provided the impetus for actual change in thirty-two pilot schools. Implementation of school-based management—in terms of the reforms proposed and the types of structures to carry out those reforms—is in the hands of the principal and teachers, who determine what is best for their individual school. The district and union have been committed to monitoring and evaluating the progress and problems experienced in the pilot schools before the program was extended to other schools.
- In Cincinnati, reform initiatives were implemented first at the district level through the formation of joint committees to oversee district policy issues such as teacher allocation in schools and peer evaluation and assistance. Soon after, experiments were launched to improve learning opportunities for at-risk students at two demonstration schools, where teachers and principals work together in designing and carrying out improvement programs. These experiences helped stimulate further district-union agreements to seek improvements both at the district and school levels.
- In Philadelphia, the Writing Across the Curriculum project was initiated and conceived as a districtwide program, but implementation is left entirely up to the individual school, which accounts for the wide diversity of writing im-

provement programs among schools. A recently instituted proposal process, in which teachers and the principal from each school jointly submit a written proposal indicating goals and planned activities to meet those goals, indicates the gradual decentralization that has occurred in the WAC project. The proposals, which are reviewed by the district committee that oversees the school programs, have helped shape the district agenda by indicating the types of resources WAC schools need to implement their programs and suggesting new ideas for other schools that might be interested in joining the project.

- The radical changes that have occurred at Central Park East Secondary School, which literally is being created from the ''bottom up'' by a team of teachers and a principal, would not have been possible were it not for the long-standing tradition of experimentation and innovation supported by the district. District-level initiatives to introduce alternative education were carried out by principal Deborah Meier, who started one of the first two alternative schools in the district, Central Park East Elementary School. Today, there are thirty alternative schools in the district, including CPESS, one of the only two high schools in the New York City school system that is cooperatively run by a district and the central office.

The board can facilitate the formation and operation of alliances at district and school levels by allocating money more equitably among the schools, by paying teachers for time spent in alliance task groups, by changing the relationship between central staff and the schools, and by helping principals make the transition to employee involvement.

Equity. Self-improvement by schools is never easy, but it is hardest for inner-city schools because allocations of dollars-per-pupil and teaching skills are tilted against them (Chavez, 1987). In theory, all schools in a district receive equivalent allocations of both resources. However, the theory often does not work, because experienced, higher-paid teachers, by dint of seniority, assign themselves to schools where their skills are least critically

needed, while schools with the greatest need get the least experienced teachers.

Allocation of dollars-per-pupil is based on districtwide
averages of teacher salaries, not on the actual salary mix of each
school. Since the least experienced teachers receive the lowest
salaries, and the number of teachers in a school is budgeted on
the basis of districtwide average salaries, the actual number of
dollars-per-pupil in the least effective schools is far below the
actual dollars-per-pupil in the best school.

The financially poorest schools get not only the least experienced but also the least competent teachers. Teachers who
perform least well are pushed out of the better schools in one
way or another, and percolate to schools that have to make do
with less. In addition, the poorest schools suffer the highest turnover, which weakens teacher interaction with students, ensures
that teachers have less to learn from one another, and tends to
shorten the life of whatever improvements are made.

Budgeting for Teacher Involvement.   When alliances are
in their early days, teachers usually volunteer the time they spend
in task groups, but once the novelty has worn off they may well
feel put upon. Justifiably so, since they take that time from normal work hours, from rest hours, or from after-work hours. If
a school or district is serious about alliances, and considers that
work on task groups is real work, not a sop, it will prove it by
paying for teachers' time, thus increasing the number of voluntary participants and the quantity and quality of results.

The additional cost of such teacher-time in any school is
unlikely to exceed 1 percent of the school's salary budget. Alliance task groups in a large organization typically involve less
than one employee in five, at any given time. The other four
out of five employees feel involved because the membership of
task groups tends to rotate and because nonmembers receive
a continuous stream of information from, and pass along their
suggestions to, those who are directly involved. A task group's
meetings usually consume one to two hours a week, although
some employees volunteer additional time (for study on or off
the premises) because they consider it in their interest to do so.

Two hours a week is equivalent to 5 percent of the workweek. Five percent (of the individual workweek) multiplied by 20 percent of the work force (one in five employees) comes to 1 percent of the salary bill. Every system has waste or misdirected funding far in excess of 1 percent. If the board cannot find that amount of money for alliances, it does not value alliance very highly.

Central Staff.   As teachers view it, the district's central (or HQ) staff are the long arm of the board and superintendent. Staff are accustomed to issuing rules and instructions unilaterally, but alliances require that advice be rendered in the form of consultations, leaving the task groups to decide what use to make of it.

Staff people exercise power because the board and superintendent give them the authority. Therefore, the relationship between staff and teachers will change only if the board and superintendent say so. Today, relations are so strained that it is not unusual to hear demands for the utter dissolution of HQ staff.

Until HQ staff are proved to be monsters by nature, we are inclined to believe they are as human as teachers, and certainly not less competent (since many were promoted out of the ranks of teaching). The bitterness with which teachers regard them is the product of faulty organizational design. Similar conditions are common in business, too. When staff talents are correctly deployed, a healthier relationship comes into being.

The best examples, as previously noted, include the Jefferson County School System, where the district's Gheens Center—fully equipped with staff facilitators, curriculum resource materials, and library—functions as a human resource development center for teachers and principals; Philadelphia's Writing Across the Curriculum project, where a network of school and districtwide committees invites participation and draws out the expertise not only of teachers and principals, but of district leaders and curriculum specialists as well; the Duluth school system, where a district steering committee assures ongoing input and advice from central administration representatives as

well as faculty and school administrators; the Schenley High
School Teacher Center, where, in addition to the peer training
and evaluation that occur, district staff members play an active
role in training and advising teachers; and the Cincinnati schools,
where joint committees consisting of union members and district-
appointed representatives are dealing with a variety of issues
to improve teaching and learning conditions in the school system.

As pointed out with respect to teachers, the board should
not expect to change the established behavior of staff people by
issuing a memorandum. The change has to be talked through,
as between allies of equal dignity though different degrees of
power. Previous commitments to security, pay, and respect have
to be honored. The parties have to redesign the staff job jointly
to make it more consistent with teacher involvement. The new
job should be viewed as desirable because it can achieve more
of substance, and because it enhances the relationship of staff
to principals and teachers.

Principals.   The fate of an alliance at a school depends
on the principal's (1) job description, which determines the limits
of the powers that can be shared with teachers, (2) willingness
to involve teachers in decision making, and (3) skill in working
by consensus. The board, through the superintendent, can make
a significant difference in all three aspects. It can redefine the
principal's job in a way that leaves room for teacher involvement. It can reward principals for their efforts to form alliances
with teachers. It can provide financial resources to stimulate
change. It can provide training, coaching, and—most important—role models to help principals develop skill in consensus
building.

Continuity.   In the foregoing discussion we have discussed
the board as if its composition were static. Clearly it is not. Elections, appointments, and retirements change the membership
of the board at frequent intervals. With each change, knowledge
of the district's and schools' experience of alliances is attenuated
and momentum is lost. Provision must be made to orient new
members and make them aware of the benefits that have resulted

from such faculty-administrative alliances. In Hammond, for example, the school superintendent was credited with building board support of the district's School Improvement Process. In fact, it might be wise to orient all candidates for election to the board, lest they prejudice the fate of alliances in the district by campaigning in ignorance. Since the union is the strongest element of continuity, self-interest should induce it to take responsibility for such orientation—preferably, but not necessarily, in conjunction with the surviving members of the board.

State Governments

In the years leading up to the National Commission on Excellence in Education's *A Nation at Risk* (1983), and even more so afterward, state governments enacted educational reform measures that teachers interpreted, with justification, as insults to their competence and sincerity. Merit pay legislation added the affront of putting more power into the hands of school managers, whose behavior the teachers already considered arbitrary.

Understandably, when these measures reached the districts for implementation, teachers did all they could to block or at least soften their impact. A similar fate is likely to befall future measures that set teachers up as scapegoats for America's long neglect of urban public schools. There is no way that governors or legislators can apply "reforms" that offend teachers' dignity and common sense, short of placing a spy in every classroom—the antithesis of democracy.

What is the alternative? Should the state abdicate its educational role in favor of the teachers? Obviously not, any more than it should abdicate in favor of local boards, superintendents, or principals. But if state officers hope to produce actual improvements in school performance, as distinguished from short-lived political triumphs, they will have to form alliances with the teachers, just as the districts must. They must go through the same process of open discussion with the teachers until a broad consensus is reached. Reaching consensus does take longer than the traditional method of legislation, but it vastly increases the probability of actual school improvement.

The state can also encourage improvement at the district level by facilitating alliances and by funding more equitably.

Facilitating Alliances.   While the state government sets the ground rules for public education and its reform, the detailed systemic changes that translate rules into results take place at district and school levels. State legislation, therefore, should aim to facilitate the formation and success of local management-teacher alliances. The state should lay down standards for excellence and equity, and outline criteria for measuring progress. Then it should encourage local experimentation, within agreed boundaries, to meet the standards.

- In Connecticut, a state Education Enhancement Act—based on the recommendations of the Governor's Commission on Equity and Excellence in Education—seeks to help local districts explore the usefulness of such innovative personnel practices as career ladders, differentiated staffing, and professional teacher evaluation systems. The act provides incentive grants to districts interested in designing such programs, subject to approval by a newly established state commission. In addition to adopting regulations concerning local evaluation and career incentives plans, the state commission provides training and technical consultants for participating school districts and disseminates information on career incentive and evaluation plans to all districts (Governor's Commission on Equity and Excellence in Education, 1986).
- Massachusetts has allocated an estimated $1.5 million to support a "Carnegie Schools" grant program aimed at schools interested in designing innovative governance structures, which promote shared decision making among school faculty and administrators and improve student learning. During the first year of the program, school teams will receive grants to develop comprehensive three-year plans, subject to the approval of the board of education and any other local school committee having jurisdiction over the school. Provided annual progress reports are approved by the board and local

committee, additional grants for implementation and administration of programs for up to three successive years will be available to schools. The state has agreed to provide technical assistance to participating schools. In addition, any state or district policies or contract provisions that hinder implementation of the Carnegie school plan will be waived.

- The state of Washington is expected to implement a pilot program to encourage school-based change by awarding funds to twenty schools and one school district to explore new management systems. Schools will be granted waivers to certain regulations, but in return will be expected to develop their own evaluation plans and will be held accountable ("'Restructured' Schools: Frequently Invoked, Rarely Defined," 1988, p. 7).

- In Minnesota, attempts are under way by the legislature to promote school-based management by allowing school boards to delegate any of their powers and duties to school-site management teams.

Pending the amendment of legislation to make it more favorable to local alliances, states can mitigate the harmful effects of existing laws by granting waivers, as in Washington and Massachusetts, wherever they will assist the desirable work of local alliances. Some educational specialists have said that waivers are, in fact, simpler to obtain than local managers and teachers make them out to be; inability to get a waiver may be, they suggest, a handy excuse for inaction.

Some school districts are actively seeking waivers to state regulations that impede locally initiated reforms. In Philadelphia, for example, the superintendent established a regulatory reform task force that includes members of the teachers' union, administrators, university representatives, and other public officials. The task force is making impressive headway by identifying regulations that stifle local programs, initiating discussions with state representatives, and negotiating changes in existing laws in order to encourage implementation of reforms at the local level. In Dade County, district and union officials have agreed not only to grant waivers from school board policies and union rules in order to promote local experimentation, but also to seek such waivers from the state whenever possible. And in Hammond, district and union officials have also expressed a commitment to secure waivers from state rules that impede local progress.

Equity in Funding.   Gross disparities among districts with respect to the availability of dollars-per-pupil for education hinder alliances as much as disparities among the schools of a district. For example, studies carried out for the state of Connecticut in the early 1980s found that "the typical high-spending district spent $3,215 per pupil compared with $1,988 spent by the typical low-spending district in 1981–82. Not surprisingly, the typical high-spending district also has a more highly paid and more highly experienced staff and provides 24 percent more staff to its pupils. These differences in staff levels and salaries accounted for the greatest portion of the variation in expenditures among school districts. . . . The gap between the state's richest and poorest towns grew wider between 1977 and 1981 because the tax base grew faster in wealthier towns. . . . The wealthy towns have been able to increase the gap while lowering their tax rates. In short, wealthy districts have a growing advantage as they compete with poor districts for highly-qualified teachers" (Governor's Commission on Equity and Excellence in Education, 1985, p. 6).

Such disparities are common in urbanized states. Although they do not preclude the possibility of school-by-school performance improvement, the maldistribution of experience and talents that results from uneven funding makes alliances more difficult and less rewarding than they should be.

Recommendations

Recommendation 19.   State governors and legislators, like local boards of education, are charged with responsibility for successfully operating the public schools, not for passing statutes, issuing regulations, or criticizing employees. If they wish to improve the operation of the schools through systemic changes, they, as managers, should form alliances with school administrators, teachers, and their unions. In addition, they should foster alliances at district and school levels by (1) waiving the application of laws and regulations that impede the establishment and conduct of alliances, and (2) ensuring that schools attended by the children of low-income families have enough budget to pay for competent principals and teaching staff.

Recommendation 20.   In urban districts the fate of the individual schools is tightly bound to the fate of the district. If a board wishes to foster continuous improvement of the schools, it should form a districtwide alliance with the teachers and their union to ensure that district policies and actions stimulate and reinforce systemic changes at the schools.

Recommendation 21.   An acid test of how seriously a board regards alliances is its willingness to pay teachers for the time they spend participating in task groups. Since 1 percent of the school's budget for teacher salaries is more than enough to pay for such time, even in the most intensive alliance, the board should not allow this minor cost to stand in the way of a decision to proceed.

7

Sustaining the Partnership:
Toward a New Era
in Educational Reform

It is within the power of every school and district to make the continuous improvements in excellence and equity that add up to educational reform.

Continuous improvements require systemic changes in the ways that schools and districts operate—changes made with the active support of management, teachers, and teachers' unions.

Alliances

Teachers and their unions actively support changes whenever management involves them responsibly in selecting, planning, and executing the changes, under the aegis of a formal alliance. The parties to an alliance do not always have the same interests. They cooperate on shared interests, but this does not inhibit them from competing on divergent interests. Cooperation on shared interests, however, often facilitates the negotiation of differences over competing interests.

School management, teachers, and unions, therefore, should not put off the formation of alliances until harmony sets in. Some of the most successful alliances have sprung directly out of labor-management hostility, and their successes have helped to mitigate the hostility.

The first step in forming an alliance is to break the ice. One or more people on management's side have to start talking—as informally as possible—to one or more people on the teachers' side, on the subject of improving the schools. Either side can make the overture, and charisma is not necessary. The talks should focus on what unites the parties, not on their differences. The parties should talk until they agree to make one or a few modest changes which, in their opinion, will improve educational performance and are within the parties' capacity to achieve.

While the parties are making up their minds whether, and how, to form an alliance, they would do well to visit sites where successful alliances are already in existence. Management and the union can visit jointly or, to conserve time, each party can conduct its own visits. Firsthand, on-site discussions with people who have had actual experience of alliance convey more learning, and more valuable learning, than any number of written or oral reports.

The greatest mistake that management or the union can make regarding an alliance is to picture it as a machine that runs itself while the business of the schools goes on as usual. An alliance does not run like a machine; it is a way of life for everyone concerned. Both management and union leaders have to invest a substantial amount of time and energy to make it work. They do so, experience shows, only if the alliance tackles important projects and succeeds. In addition, management must be prepared to invest money to cover the cost of running the alliance: relatively little in proportion to the district's overall budget, but not negligible. But the potential for achievement far exceeds the risks.

Union Participation

The cases in this book indicate that it makes little difference whether the earliest joint projects are districtwide or specific to one or more individual schools. Before long, however, changes must be under way at both levels, and the changes at each level must reinforce those at the other. Otherwise the school-based projects will wither for lack of support, and the districtwide projects will fail to improve educational performance. This relationship, above all, makes the union, as the teachers' district representative, an essential party to any durable alliance.

The necessity of union participation, however, has led to the dubious inference that alliances must be conducted as part of collective bargaining. Industrial experience challenges this notion. Alliances, being concerned primarily with improving the ways in which organizations do their work, rather than with the terms and conditions of employment, need flexibility to experiment, to innovate, and to modify tactical goals and methods when the unexpected happens. Since collective bargaining does not fit this prescription, industrial alliances are established and given their limits by the contract, but all joint projects and employee involvement efforts are conducted through parallel structures entrusted with a good deal of autonomy. School districts should do likewise.

Industrial experience provides some other lessons:

- The stronger the local union's standing with its members, the more fully it can enter into alliance with management.
- Union participation from the start gives an alliance legitimacy in the eyes of its members.
- Every level of management, not only the top, must have a part in forming and carrying out an alliance. Those omitted feel no commitment.

New Relationships for Teachers

If teachers are to play a responsible part in educational reform, their relations with principals and staff experts will have to be redesigned.

Teachers have only as much voice in the operation of a school as the principal allows and encourages. Principals reared in the authoritarian tradition of urban public schools tend to hold teachers' voice to a whisper. In large measure that is because the principals themselves have had no experience, as teachers or administrators, of being involved in decisions affecting the larger organization of which they are part. To help them change behavior, principals need: a job description that includes teacher involvement; rewards based, in part, on success in teacher involvement; training in the art of involving teachers; and, most of all, a role model provided by their superintendent.

Urban public school teachers have almost no voice in many decisions that directly shape day-to-day conduct of the classroom—selection of textbooks, curriculum design, in-service training, discipline. Such decisions are made and imposed by staff experts at district headquarters, often over the objections of principals and teachers who must carry them out. If teachers are to be involved in these matters, the staff experts will have to give up their right to prescribe. Instead, they will serve as coequals with teachers and principals in joint decision-making teams. Since the board is responsible for the current anomaly, it is up to the board to involve the staff experts in rectifying it.

Managers/Politicians

When state legislators and members of local boards of education take office, they acquire authority over public education, but they also accept responsibility for the excellence and equity of school performance. It is impossible to discharge that responsibility by legislation (that is, statutes and regulations) alone or by micromanagement. With respect to equity, they have to ensure that every school has enough money to purchase the talent and physical resources required to give every student an excellent education. With respect to management, they should encourage the formation and continuation of local management-teacher alliances. With respect to state and local legislation, they should seek consensus with the legitimate representatives of all elements of school operation—including the teachers' unions—in forming educational policy.

Our confidence in the foregoing remarks, as well as the other findings and recommendations of the report, is bolstered by the eleven cases that follow. The cases have been referred to throughout the first part of this volume. They are presented in full in the following pages. In addition, a summary of the types of reforms initiated in each of the eleven cases is presented in the appendix.

The cases were selected as examples of successful alliances for educational reform. How do we define *successful?* First, in the opinion of the participants and neutral observers, they led to improvements in educational excellence and/or equity. Second, the improvements resulted from joint management-teacher efforts that, in the eyes of both parties, were based on genuine consensus. The latter test may be more important than the first: although the parties' judgment about particular improvements may alter with the passage of time, their experience of alliance will enable them to continue undertaking new and more ambitious changes.

The cases are marked by a wide diversity of geography, educational content, form of alliance, and evolutionary path. Work in America Institute designated the districts and schools to be studied, then asked the authors to visit the sites and seek answers to the following questions:

- What are the areas of policy decision making in which teachers are involved?
- When did the process of teacher involvement begin? How?
- How are teachers involved? What are the mechanisms or structures used? Are there teams or committees? How often do these meet?
- What part does the union play in the process? Is there any language in the contract providing for teacher involvement?
- How has the principal's role changed as a result of this process? To what extent has the principal shared the decision making? (For example, are there responsibilities that were formerly carried out by the principal and are now joint faculty-administration responsibilities?)
- How much real effect has the process had on the school, in terms of teachers' impact or influence on decisions made and the impact on student performance (achievement scores, attendance rates, drop-out rates, and so on) or any other measures used to evaluate the process?
- How have the teachers themselves measured the effects of participation? That is, do they feel they are being treated more professionally?

- Is there support for this process on the district level? Does the process occur at one school or at several schools in the district?
- How have the district superintendent's role and responsibilities changed as a result of this process? Have responsibilities been delegated to principals to a greater degree?
- What role has the school board played in the process of teacher involvement?

Within those parameters each author was free to follow his or her own insights, so there is also a diversity of form and style. Unless otherwise noted, all quoted material was obtained from on-site and/or telephone interviews.

For ease of understanding and for purposes of comparison, the cases have been organized into three categories: (1) those in which the educational reforms were pursued through district-wide alliances, (2) those in which the alliances were limited to individual schools, and (3) special content-oriented programs that required reforms at both district and school levels. The cases, according to this organizational framework, are as follows:

School Districts

ABC Unified School District of Cerritos, California
Cincinnati (Ohio) Public Schools
Dade County (Florida) Public Schools
Duluth (Minnesota) School System
Hammond (Indiana) School District
Jefferson County Public Schools in Louisville, Kentucky

Schools

Central Park East Secondary School (New York City)
Hope Essential High School (Providence, R.I.)

Special Programs

The Humanitas Academy of Los Angeles
Philadelphia School District's Writing Across the Curriculum project
Pittsburgh's Schenley High School Teacher Center

These eleven cases represent the real world since they are urban schools drawn from a cross section of cities, all of which face serious education problems. They can teach us a great deal if we study them closely and if we want to consider their hard lessons and achievements as a guide to future innovations. The existence of these models of excellence confirms that it is feasible to change schools by engaging the knowledge and commitment of all the parties involved, especially the teachers.

As important is the fact that these novel alliances should inspire many others in similar situations to raise their expectations in the clear knowledge that it can be done, that it works, and that the participants—teachers, unions, and management—are proud of their achievements.

The real truths and lessons to be drawn from the cases will allay many doubts and dispel the stereotypes, half truths, and myths that deter any effort to reform institutions. They can build confidence in the change process and in the open-ended opportunities at hand.

PART TWO

Educational Alliances in Action:
Eleven Models of Excellence

Reform at the District Level

ABC Unified School District
Cincinnati Public Schools
Dade County Public Schools
Duluth School System
Hammond School District
Jefferson County Public Schools

Improving Individual Schools

Central Park East Secondary School
Hope Essential High School

Achieving Excellence
Through Special Programs

Humanitas Academy
Writing Across the Curriculum Project
Schenley High School Teacher Center

8

School Renewal Through
Teacher Empowerment:
The ABC Unified School District
of Cerritos, California

by Joan L. Sickler

The empowerment of teachers in the ABC Unified School District in suburban Los Angeles has been an evolving process over the past decade and has resulted in a highly participative structure for individual schools and for the district as a whole. Through a combination of internal and external influences over the ten-year period—the commitment of top leadership to teacher involvement, creative union initiatives for change, financial and philosophical support targeted by the state for the professionalization of teaching, and a university intervention program—the ABC District made significant changes in its structure and method of operations and experienced substantial improvements in its results.

In the ABC Unified District, teachers control curriculum development and textbook adoption; teachers participate in the determination of teaching assignments and participate in assigning students to classes; teachers help to set student routines and determine discipline policies; teachers participate in the selection of in-service staff development topics; teachers select and evaluate their peers for leadership positions as mentor teachers; and teachers helped to create an evaluation procedure for all certificated employees.

In the ABC Unified District, management has significantly reduced its ranks through attrition to allow for more direct communication between schools and the district; used the reduction in overhead to move more funds into the classroom; decentralized the district budget, giving control over expenditures to each school; and worked with the union to substantially raise teacher salaries.

This chapter will present the developments across the district, examining changes in the roles of the superintendent, principals, teachers, and the union leadership, as well as the outside influences of the state and the university. Profiles will be presented of three schools within the district—Artesia High School, Killingsworth Junior High School, and Aloha Elementary School—in which teacher involvement in decision making is especially strong.

Located thirty minutes southwest of central Los Angeles, the ABC Unified School District serves a racially and ethnically diverse student population. Its twenty-nine schools have a total enrollment of 21,526, with a student body of approximately 60 percent black, Hispanic, and Asian and nearly 40 percent Caucasian. The current student population represents a shift for the district since 1976, when the white population represented 53 percent. Today, whenever the district prepares a major informational piece for parents, it is issued in four languages: Korean, Mandarin Chinese, Portuguese, and English. In all, forty-six languages are represented among the students. The district employs some 950 teachers and has a certificated administrative staff of 67; classified support staff number just over 900. The district budget for 1986–87 was $82.2 million, 77 percent of which was allocated to salaries and benefits. The ABC Federation of Teachers, an affiliate of the American Federation of Teachers, is the bargaining unit for the ABC District teachers.

While considerable data on the individual sites show the most significant gains (see school profiles), districtwide statistics also reflect improvements. In 1970, ABC students were scoring below the 15th percentile of standardized achievement tests. By 1975–76, districtwide scores on the California Assessment tests reached 62 percent in mathematics, 66 percent in spelling, 59 percent in written expression, and 60 percent in reading.

In 1985–86, gains were reported in each subject: up to 72 percent in math, 71 percent in spelling, 64 percent in written expression, and 62 percent in reading. Excused absences declined from 178,358 in 1983 to 170,969 in 1986. In addition, teacher absenteeism in the district declined from 1981 to 1986.

The move to empower teachers in the ABC District with responsibility for decision making has been an evolving process that was initiated a decade ago by Eugene Tucker, who served as district superintendent from 1976 to 1986 and who is now superintendent of the Santa Monica/Malibu Unified District. The move was based on Tucker's own broad commitment to involve staff at all levels in the management of their work. Three steps taken during that period greatly influenced the process of change across the district:

1. *A new management organization.*   District administrative staffing was streamlined with a goal to reduce the number of management levels between the superintendent and the principals to one—a district director for elementary or secondary education. From 1981 to 1986 twenty-two district management and secretarial positions were trimmed through attrition and retirement. "We haven't had to lay off anyone in the ABC District," noted retired Deputy Superintendent Charles Vernon, who worked closely with Tucker during this period. Having fewer personnel at the district level also served to free funds for more direct support of local school initiatives. Kenneth Moffett, who took office as the new district superintendent in August 1986, underscores that commitment. One of his goals is "to keep management lean at the district and keep the funds out in the schools."

To increase communication and professional interaction among administrators, seven management groupings, or "associations," were created—of elementary principals, assistant principals, and so on. Each group meets twice a month to discuss issues of common concern, and each meets three times each year with the superintendent in a breakfast meeting. In addition, the chairpersons of each of the groups form the Management Team Administrative Council, which meets regularly with the superintendent to exchange information. "We took steps to open up the organization and cut through the lack of trust across the district as to how decisions are made," recalls Tucker.

2. *Teacher control of curriculum.*   For teachers, one of the most meaningful changes in the ABC District has been the complete transfer of the control of curriculum into their hands. In the early 1980s, a long-standing informal tradition of teacher involvement in curriculum development was formalized into a structure of ten districtwide Subject Area Committees and a Curriculum Master Plan Council, both of which met monthly. A representative teacher from each school served on each subject area committee, and the Federation of Teachers checked committee membership for duplication. A management facilitator served on each committee, and each group elected a chairperson to serve on the Curriculum Master Plan Council. The 1985–86 chairperson of the council was an administrator; the 1986–87 chairperson was a teacher. Budget cuts in 1987–88 have reduced the number of committees, but teachers are still closely involved in the committee's work.

When a new curriculum is prepared, the work is done by district teachers, who work for three weeks over the summer and receive compensation of $16 per hour. Subject to the approval of the Board of Education, the council makes the final decisions on new curricula after circulating draft versions to all teachers in the district for comments and recommendations for changes. Additional responsibilities of the council are to examine curriculum issues across the district, deal with cross-curriculum issues, and evaluate and approve proposals for grants from teachers.

The benefits of the structure are many, according to ABC teachers. First, the end result is a far more useful product because it has the ownership and professional stamp of the teachers who will use it. The former state-mandated curriculum "was put on the shelves," according to Wade Austin, Killingsworth Junior High School science teacher and member of the Curriculum Council. "Now the emphasis on curriculum is ongoing, year in and year out, and it's based on the needs of the students," he notes. "And the exciting thing is that teachers are making the decisions."

Second, the committees and the council have created an unprecedented opportunity for interaction among different schools, across grade levels, and between subject areas. "It's the first time I've ever seen elementary teachers talking to secondary teachers," said Cherie Vela, Artesia High School social science teacher and chairperson of the social studies curriculum committee. "There's a whole new respect for each other we never had and a whole new communication link. We never even talked to the feeder schools before."

3. *Teachers as school leaders.* Two years before the state established the California Mentor Teacher Program, in the 1984–85 school year, the ABC District, under Superintendent Tucker, began a drive to bring teachers into school leadership positions. The vehicle was through the appointment at each school of Instructional Resource Teachers (IRTs), who would provide leadership for teachers and work in partnership with the principal on instructional issues. For skeptical principals threatened by the idea of sharing power with teachers, Tucker recalled, the IRTs were a practical demonstration of how teachers "could enhance and give strength to the leadership role." Initially selected solely by the principal, the IRTs today are chosen through a somewhat more formal application procedure. IRTs receive a salary bonus for their additional responsibilities.

In contrast, the ABC Federation of Teachers negotiated the selection of mentors in the ABC District by the teachers themselves. The program at the ABC District receives $250,000 in state funding annually. To be chosen as mentors, teachers must complete an application and submit a videotaped lesson; applications are screened by the committees of teachers elected at each site. State funding provides mentors with a $4,000 salary bonus and $2,000 that can be spent within a wide latitude to buy release time or materials. Mentor teachers conduct staff development workshops at their own schools and others.

The mentor teachers, IRTs, Curriculum Committees, and council are "pieces of the overall puzzle in improving the teaching profession," notes Wade Austin. Former Superintendent Gene Tucker estimates that close to 30 percent of the nearly 1,000 teachers in the district have been drawn into roles of responsibility. "We developed a tremendous cadre of teacher leaders," he said. "Over the last three to four years, we increased tenfold the number of teachers involved in a significant leadership role with administrative responsibility and as partners to management."

The Role of the Union

Collective bargaining began in the ABC District in 1977 when the California Teachers Association, an affiliate of the National Education Association, won a membership vote on a slim 52 percent to 48 percent margin. The California Federation of Teachers unseated CTA three years later by a split of 51 percent to 49 percent. Today, the ABCFT has a growing membership of around 520, which represents a 30 percent increase since the beginning of the 1985–86 school year.

From the start, the ABCFT worked steadfastly to establish the principle of a "partnership for education" between the union and the district management, with the shared goal of achieving what was fair for teachers and best for the children. Former ABCFT President Dennis Cox recalls emphasizing their goals very clearly to the administration: "We take the partnership very seriously. We expect to work with you. We don't want to be forced into a public stance." Although just over half of the teachers in the district are officially ABCFT members, the union believes its charter covers the welfare of all district teachers, and it acts accordingly.

The ABCFT, in fact, has had a strong influence on the development of each of the steps to bring district teachers into roles of responsibility. Upon presenting proposals for the third consecutive three-year contract with the district to the ABC District Board of Education in February 1986, current ABCFT President John Ennes reviewed the progress to date and urged the continuation and formalization of many of the developments in the district: "With some prodding from the ABCFT, this district began some years ago involving teachers in the decision-making process, recognizing that without their whole-hearted efforts, little of lasting value could be accomplished. The obvious achievements of this working partnership have put ABC in the forefront of the professionalizing movement and brought us recognition as a thinking person's district. . . . ''

Ennes continued, ''The facts go on and on: in sharp contrast to other districts, in ABC the mentor program itself was developed by teachers; the high quality CTIIP proposals were developed by teachers unfettered by administrative restraints; the evaluation instrument now being piloted was developed in conjunction with teachers; an evaluation tool for principals will probably be developed in cooperation with teachers; and a possible internship program is currently being studied by teachers. Enough of the facts. What they boil down to is this: the steps toward a full partnership between unit members and administration taken thus far in ABC have been far from tentative. . . . ''

''Now,'' Ennes observed, ''lest we allow vanity to get the better of us, we need to remember that we used the word 'expand' earlier. Obviously, there are laggards who have yet to fully adopt as their own the current direction of efficiently utilizing unit members' expertise. Just as clearly, there are honest differences of opinion that must be worked through. In short, though the past bodes well for the future, unless we take positive steps to bring this future to fruition, it will not come to pass. . . . ''

Many, though not all, of the ABCFT proposals for the 1986–89 contract were finally adopted. A proposed ''budget council'' at each school to oversee and direct site budgets was not approved, but agreement was reached that schools were to make available to teachers a monthly budget printout and chart of accounts. Ennes would like to see many of the current innovations—which have become standard, though informal, procedure at nearly all of the district schools—become codified in the contract as a means of pushing change forward in the less progressive schools in the district. ''Our goal,'' said Walter Zvaleko, Ennes's predecessor as ABCFT president, ''is getting at all sites what we have at some sites.'' Those chances are good, he says, assuming the basic leadership approach at the district level remains the same. ''The track record is set.''

Teachers agree that the union has been ''very instrumental'' in bringing about improvements in the district. ''Instead of being adversarial,'' notes Wade Austin, junior high science teacher, ''they are working through problems and seeking creative solutions.''

ABCFT is proud of its part in the substantial salary increases the ABC teachers have received over the period of their representation. With leadership and backing from the superintendent and the district school board, a deliberate drive was made to pull up district teachers' salaries from their standing below the median in 1977, when compared with salaries in ten area districts, to their current position in the upper quartile. Since 1980, teachers in the district have averaged in excess of a 9 percent increase each year. Even in 1987, when the district was facing its first major cuts in seven years, the union negotiated a 5 percent salary raise. ''Salaries are important as a sign of commitment,'' noted Charles Ledbetter, assistant superintendent for personnel and employee relations and negotiator for the district. The salary range for teachers in the district is $21,278, for a beginning teacher with a bachelor's degree, to $40,195, for the highest-level seniority step, with bachelor's and master's degrees required.

The district and the union work ''diligently'' on management of the contract and on maintaining good labor relations, according to Ledbetter. A working committee of two representatives from each of the three unions in the district—the Civil Service Employees Association (CSEA) and American Federation of State, County, and Municipal Employees (AFSCME) represent the clerical and custodial workers—meets monthly with two management negotiators, and both sides ''talk about a win/win philosophy and we mean it,'' Ledbetter said. The ABC District has had eight grievances in ten years, he reports. School Board Chairperson Peggy Lee has characterized union relations with the district as ''excellent.'' ''We are reputed throughout the county as having labor peace,'' she said.

External Influences

In 1980, the Graduate School of Education of the University of California at Los Angeles established through private funding a project called the Laboratory in School and Community Education, which was codirected by John Goodlad. The Partnership, one of four major efforts of the Laboratory, was a program to develop a collaborative network among educating institutions. Involved in the consortium with the university were twelve area school districts, two community colleges, and five county school offices. The ABC District was one of the participants in the Partnership.

While not the most critical factor in many of the developments in the District during the 1980s, the Partnership clearly influenced and encouraged change to take place. "The Partnership initiated a philosophical and process change," noted Paul Gonzalez, Special Programs Coordinator at Artesia High School. "But the schools were left alone to make their own decisions." One of the greatest contributions of the Partnership, according to former Deputy Superintendent Vernon, who retired in August 1986 after thirty-eight years in education, was to give people "exposure to new ideas." The Partnership helped as well in another key step in the development process identified by Vernon—"to nurture the resource and idea people and get them to interact." "They get excited and transmit enthusiasm, and then you develop a critical mass," Vernon said. "You must make sure a critical mass is developed to keep the renewal process moving." The Partnership served to educate ABC District teachers and staff on theories of organizational change, to give them a common vocabulary on renewal, and to encourage them to share practical ideas for change at their own schools.

Through commissions and special funding programs, the state of California endorsed and supported school improvement in general and the professionalization of teaching in particular. During the 1980s, the Mentor Teacher program was approved by the state, the California Classroom Teachers Instructional Improvement Program was initiated, and the School Improvement Program was begun. The California Commission on the Teaching Profession recommended involving teachers in a team effort to manage the schools and defined the role of the principal as the leader and facilitator of that effort.

All of these influences combined to encourage and support change at the school level. But the implementation still remained the responsibility of the schools.

Artesia High School

Built in 1952, Artesia High School is the oldest high school in the ABC District. It has a student population of 2,100, 34 percent of whom are Hispanic, 18 percent Asian, and 41 percent "other." Predominantly from lower middle-income families, a significant percentage of whom are on welfare, the students are a migrant, transient population drawn from five different area cities. There are approximately 100 teachers, counselors, and administrators at the school.

Between 1979 and 1983, Artesia students' scores on the California Assessment Program achievement tests rose dramatically: in math, from the 21st percentile to the 78th percentile; in spelling, from the 14th to the 83rd percentile; in written expression, from the 17th to the 58th percentile; and in reading, from the 16th to the 62nd percentile. In addition, the number of students continuing their education after graduation rose from 50 percent in 1980 to 82 percent three years later. Also, in 1983, enrollments in math increased 60 percent, eleven new sections were added to biology, five sections were added to chemistry, and physics was taught for the first time.

The earlier reputation for gang fighting at the school is gone today, although it continues to exist within the community. Vandalism is "drastically reduced," and parent involvement has increased. While only 100 parents attended the fall 1985 back-to-school night, the October 1986 event—"Artesia Lights Up the Night with Pride and Hope"—drew 1,500 people.

The change process began at Artesia in 1980 under the leadership of then principal, Mara Clisby, with the support of the Partnership Program of the UCLA Graduate School of Education. An off-site retreat was organized and thirty people—or roughly 30 percent of the staff—volunteered to attend. The focus was to identify the strengths and weaknesses of Artesia and the

Artesia students. Staff were encouraged to answer the question: What do you need to be a better teacher?

The structures developed to maintain the momentum of renewal and empowerment of teachers at Artesia have included the following:

- Formation of a Dialogical Forum of ten to fifteen representative volunteer teachers from various departments who meet monthly with the principal to discuss personnel issues and basic needs. Once termed "the Diabolical Forum," the meetings can sometimes serve as a gripe session, according to social studies teacher Gene Hawley. "But there's a need for that, too," he notes.

- Off-site retreats were organized twice each year for five years; nearly every staff member has now participated at least once. Teachers at Artesia cite the retreats as "the single, most unique" step in improving the school. Usually a 60/40 mix of teachers/administrators, the retreats at first focused on the basic improvements needed to improve teaching and moved on to an examination of what the ideal Artesia student would be like and how to achieve that goal. Tightened budgets districtwide have meant cutbacks in the number of retreats.

- Staff development sessions, which focus on topics chosen the previous spring by the staff, are held monthly. On-site teachers are the primary resource for staff development; Artesia's principal, and former assistant principal under Clisby, Joseph Quarles, has given responsibility for staff development to the school's MIRT team—Artesia's five Mentor Teachers and four Instructional Resource Teachers. Hawley, who is both a Mentor Teacher and Department Chairman, sees staff development as critical to the process. "You must have an avenue to work through the change," he said.

- Teacher representatives sit on the school Site Council, which in 1987 controlled $128,000 in state funds through the School Improvement Program (SIP). Artesia and the other schools in the ABC District that are eligible for the SIP monies set up local Site Councils in accordance with state requirements for administration of the funds. The Council is composed of fifteen members—five teachers, five parents, and five students from the school. As Artesia student Alan Bone, a council member, explained, every member has equal voting power. "Teachers prepare their proposals and list the objectives for the project," he said. The committee then votes by secret ballot to set priorities for the projects, and "there are no revotes." The principal also requests funds, but he has no special influence. "Last year he didn't get any," Bone noted. Membership on the council is an elected position; six parents were running for two open positions.

Among the top-priority SIP projects of the thirty-one funded in 1985–86 were an English curriculum revision, English Department student helper, and support for the calculus program; the funded item with the lowest priority was a series of fine arts field trips. For 1986–87, the science/math equipment bank, a $10,738 item, is top priority, followed by clerical assistance for the SIP program and additional funding for the school's Wilderness Program. The Council will fund twenty-four projects during this school year. But state funding of the SIP program is expected to "sunset" this year. "The money is put in and then pulled out," Gene Hawley comments. And such dramatic changes in funding are "disruptive."

But the renewal of Artesia nonetheless appears to be institutionalized. A "critical mass" of the school's teachers and administrators—30 percent by Hawley's estimate—understand the process well and have adapted it as their normal mode of operation, teachers have a common vocabulary about "empowerment" and change, and the Mentors and IRTs have been in place for so long that they have adopted school renewal as their own responsibility. "Change is continuous," notes Paul Gonzalez, special programs coordinator. "We are constantly slaying a dragon. Renewal is ever constant. It takes an empowered staff to realize that change is possible."

Gonzalez cites a number of key steps Artesia has gone through thus far in its renewal process: first, to bring the school

environment under control and "straighten out the students";
second, to encourage teachers to work as professionals by helping them set higher goals, providing the resources to make their
jobs easier, and making them—and all school staff, from the
principal to the custodian—accountable for their work; third,
to empower teachers with the control and ownership of their
own work; fourth, to involve parents in making their children
accountable as students; and, finally, to hold and believe in a
vision that change is possible.

The role of administrators in that process, notes Principal
Joseph Quarles, is to serve as facilitators. "Their purpose is
to serve the 'customers'—the students—and to serve those who
serve the customers—the teachers," he said. "Their purpose
is to clear the way for things to change."

Killingsworth Junior High School

"Killingsworth students are high-need kids. They hurt emotion-
ally and physically." That description by Killingsworth Junior
High Assistant Principal Yvonne Contreras sums up the characteristics of this 560-student site. Predominantly from working-
class families, 60 percent of whom are on Aid for Dependent
Children, the students suffer from family problems of unemployment, drug abuse, alcoholism, and child abuse. Sixty-five percent of the students are Hispanic, and one-third of the population is transient. Fifty percent speak English as a second language,
and 70 to 80 of the students have only limited English. Killingsworth serves a group of special education students as well.

"Killingsworth has all the traditional characteristics of
a school that should fail but doesn't," notes the newly appointed
principal for Killingsworth, Pat Moscorro. The 1979–80 school
year was the low ebb for the school. In that year, only 4 Killingsworth students were able to pass the district proficiency exams; the following year, 73 students passed; the year after that,
140 passed. In each consecutive year, the number has increased.
In the 1970s, there were 130 requests for transfers out of Killingsworth each year; this year there were 3. Student absenteeism
has been cut by two-thirds, from 120 per day to 40 per day,

and disciplinary referrals to the principal's office have dropped significantly: comparative figures for September 1985 and September 1986 showed a decline from 27 to 12. In the late 1970s, morale was "horrible," according to one teacher; today, new hires are attracted to Killingsworth because of its reputation for teacher participation. The teaching staff numbers approximately 30.

The change process at Killingsworth began in 1981 with the arrival of a new principal, Nadine Barretto, and the simultaneous influence of the UCLA Graduate School of Education Partnership Program. It was a time when there was room in the budget to commit funds for professional development with support from the district superintendent, to draw on the services of an outside consultant in communication skills, and to set up two-day, off-site retreats for teachers and staff. Eight teachers volunteered in the first year to develop a plan for the renewal of the teachers and the school as a whole.

The staff decided to move to a core teaching format to provide greater structure for the children and build closer relationships between them and the teachers. In core teaching, a selected number of teachers—one from each of the disciplines—is responsible for a group of students throughout the year. Today, all teachers at Killingsworth work in core groups, with eight teachers responsible for 150 students each. Originally established only for the academic subject areas, the core staff now includes elective teaching staff as well.

Each core group teaching staff has a one-hour "articulation period" each day to review plans and share information on individual student development. The teachers are committed to the core structure for its value for the students. "Our kids need structure; the core program gives them that," notes Contreras, who taught in the core program before being chosen for the assistant principal position this fall. "Without cooperative groupings, we can't accomplish what's best here for the kids," agrees Principal Moscorro.

With the articulation period, core teaching adds an additional $45,000 to the school's budget, funds that are likely to become more difficult to allocate as budgets tighten. But when the structure was first established, five Killingsworth teachers went directly to the superintendent to argue the need for the articulation period. According to one Killingsworth teacher, teachers can accomplish more in the core approach to teaching than in the traditional format, where, he said, they "are not as productive as they can be in the team approach." And the new principal is supportive of the concept: "The amount of problem solving that occurs during the articulation periods is very exciting," said Moscorro.

The core structure has also provided a means of standardizing disciplinary procedures, as all teachers within each core work to set the same standards for classroom behavior. The schoolwide disciplinary procedure was set at a two-day process at Killingsworth that allowed for teacher input. "We could have written it ourselves more quickly," noted Contreras, "but we wouldn't have had the buy-in and the long-range benefits."

One day this fall, a group of eight Killingsworth teachers—including three of the school's six Mentor Teachers—and three administrative staff offered their opinions on the key elements in the change process at their site. First, leadership is critical in cultivating participative management, they observed, and principals need training in the appropriate skills to act in that role. It takes "strong individuals to put their egos aside" and move to a participative style, said one teacher.

Second, teacher "empowerment" and commitment require a "critical mass" of teachers willing to spend extra time and energy. But the experience of participation is very powerful, they noted. "Teachers who know the power of participation and what exciting things can occur will work toward it," said one.

Staff development is another critical factor. Training in communication skills, conflict resolution, and team building are especially important, as is the inclusion of elective staff in all skill-building sessions. "We keep opening doors for ourselves," one teacher commented. "When we started to plan how we could achieve our vision, we found that we needed more skills," said another. "We're learning more."

Trust among teachers and administrators is the beginning step in the empowerment of teachers, according to the group. "If the teachers perceive a lack of trust, even if the perception is inaccurate, it will kill the process," said one teacher. The building blocks needed to create that level of genuine trust include open, two-way communication, the creation of methods to ensure that input is gained from all teachers, the encouragement of risk taking, and the patience to wait for consensus among all those involved.

Examples of teacher empowerment at Killingsworth include participation in the selection of the new principal. The entire teaching staff met in a brainstorming session to list the characteristics needed in a new principal. The list was delivered to the Board of Education, the Superintendent, and the District Director of Secondary Education. Those characteristics included commitment to change and renewal, commitment to participation and empowerment, commitment to the core program, and experience working with high-need students. In the selection of the assistant principal, four representative teachers interviewed all candidates and recommended the final two, from which Yvonne Contreras was chosen.

Discussing the role of the principal in a participative environment, Principal Moscorro enumerated a number of characteristics: to "set the tone" for the school, to be a facilitator, to explain district procedures and provide information, to "let the group go" and to allow teachers the freedom of decision making, and to be visible in the classroom. There is time for more classroom observation, Moscorro noted, because the participatively managed school "runs itself." "Here we are at 9:00 A.M.," he said during a morning interview, "and it's quiet here in my office!" Teacher control translates into far fewer disciplinary problems "that eat the average administrator up."

"The principal must be more willing to relinquish power," said Moscorro. "Ultimately it's a labor-saving device. You're increasing the size of the brain trust."

Moscorro also admitted, however, that "Personally, often times it's easier to make decisions yourself." And, in fact, two months into his first school year at Killingsworth, he was embroiled in a dispute with some of the teachers over a staffing decision he had made unilaterally. Under pressure from the district office to make staffing cuts to meet fall budget pressures caused by overstaffing, Moscorro had moved ahead on his own to determine where cuts should be made. "This wouldn't be a crisis for a school in a traditional mode," he said. "But now I need to deal with the consequences."

When he presented his decisions to the entire teaching staff, Moscorro was met with both reprimands and compliments. Why didn't you use staff to brainstorm ideas for the cuts? he was asked. Because of time pressures. "I know it wasn't right," Moscorro told the teachers. "It won't happen again." But another teacher told the principal: "I think you're to be commended," for showing "outstanding leadership, courage, and grace under pressure."

The meeting moved on to discuss more likely budget cuts in the long term and the specter of future pressure to cut out the core group teaching structure. Teachers recommended setting up a group, perhaps made up of the Mentor and Instructional Resource Teachers, to look ahead to the next three to four years and make long-term projections and recommendations for programs. Suggestions were made to document the strengths of the core program and the reasons why teachers believe it is important. "We finally have a foundation," said one teacher. "We're finally starting to reach the kids and make a difference." Would the principal support the teachers if they decided to "take their causes to the district?" "If that is the staff's plan of attack," Moscorro responded, "I would support it 100 percent. There's nothing like being face to face with the folks."

Aloha Elementary School

One-half of the 477 students at Aloha Elementary School are eligible for the free lunch program. Fifty-six percent are Caucasian, 25 percent Korean, and a high percentage Hispanic. Today's student population at Aloha represents a substantial change from the early 1980s: In 1982, there were 7 Korean students; eighteen months later there were 126. The teaching staff includes sixteen regular education teachers and two specialists; there are six part-time district support personnel, as well as the administrative support staff. Since the initiation of the change process at Aloha, considerable improvements have been evident, according to Principal Decla Johnson and teacher Darylene Schreiber. They include: a greater sense of professionalism among teachers; more student learning; improved school morale; fewer discipline problems, with referrals cut in half each year since 1984; a dramatic reduction in vandalism; greater community concern; and an enthusiastic, motivated, and more productive staff.

For Aloha, involvement in the UCLA Partnership program provided the impetus to begin the process toward participative management of the school. In 1983, under the auspices of the program, eight of Aloha's sixteen teachers, together with the principal, voluntarily attended a weekend retreat and jointly formulated a value and mission statement for the school. An outside consultant conducted the program for the retreat and focused on team building for the staff, with exercises in communication skills and group decision making. Today, the teachers and principal continue to hold off-site meetings three to four times each year.

The opportunities for communication and development are numerous: Staff meetings are held three times monthly. Three times each year, the teachers and principal hold "Quality Time Days," consisting of a two-hour staff development period during the school day; the teacher committee selects all in-service training topics. A staff development committee of teachers conducts a needs assessment among the staff and offers corresponding activities to meet those needs. Staff development is optional and takes the form of retreats, dinner meetings, Saturday workshops, after-school sessions, and "quality time" meetings within the school day. In addition, Aloha teachers have ninety minutes weekly during school hours for Individual Planning Time, a luxury "unheard of" for most elementary teachers.

Aloha has created its "quality" free time by developing an extensive network of eighty-six volunteers—parents, grandparents, and community members—who commit one hour each week to "support classroom instructional programs." For a two-hour staff development session this fall, for example, eight parents took over in the classrooms, an all-school assembly was scheduled, and physical education activities were added to recess to extend the time outdoors, all adding up to two free hours for teachers without drawing on additional funds. This fall parents raised $6,500 for the sixth-grade students to attend a summer outdoor education program, and a recent parent-organized Festival of Friendship drew an attendance of 700. The Back-to-School Night this fall had 300 participants.

Around the same period as the UCLA Partnership, all teachers throughout the ABC District participated in a Professional Development Program, which emphasized theories of cooperative learning in the classroom. These theories have been very influential in the renewal of the district. In cooperative learning, the teacher becomes less directive toward students, encourages students to share the responsibility for learning among themselves, and takes on the role of facilitator in the classroom. The commonality between the notion of empowering teachers and that of empowering students has helped to establish a unified theme throughout the Aloha community—and most of the district—linking the principal, teachers, students, and parents.

Cooperative learning in action in the classroom is reminiscent of employee involvement groups or quality circles in business and industry. The students at Aloha study together in small groups to achieve a joint solution to a common problem. In one sixth-grade class, students moved into their cooperative learning groups for a section on mathematics. After completing a sheet of math problems, each student in the group was required to check over and approve the work of the other group members. Any errors found were to be discussed with the student and the correct answers worked out. The first group to complete the process—in this case with the additional burden of being polite and kind to one another—would be the winner. The sixth-grade teacher Cathy Green has been using cooperative learning techniques for the past three years. "The students really help each other learn," she observed. "I get better projects, better ideas. The biggest adjustment is to the noise level!"

Thus the students learn how to work together, how to achieve consensus, and how to maintain discipline within their groups. During the first month of school, students are trained in the skills necessary for group interaction—communication, trust building, giving and taking criticism and compliments, and identifying individual skills.

The majority of teachers at Aloha and across the ABC District use cooperative learning techniques to some degree in their teaching. At Aloha, the process has been in use for the past four years. Parents are introduced to the concepts as well; a recent evening meeting drew 150 Aloha parents who were divided into small groups and given tasks to accomplish as an experiential demonstration of the principles of cooperative learning. Thus the role of leader as facilitator is reinforced throughout the system.

For Decla Johnson, the role of principal as facilitator has meant changes in what she sees as her responsibilities. She is now a manager of statewide requirements, a liaison between teachers and the district office, and an instructional leader. As the key support person for the staff, she has ordered business cards for all teachers and special school notebooks for their professional development materials. To maintain open communication and exposure to new ideas, Johnson issues a weekly bulletin to staff, maintains a daily sign-in sheet with information on statewide conferences, and stocks the teachers' lounge with professional journals.

Another of this principal's responsibilities is "valuing opinions: asking for them, accepting them, reacting to them, and doing something with them." A newly hired Aloha teacher commented to a colleague: "I can't believe your staff meetings. The principal really listens to us—and acts on it!" Johnson also considers high visibility in the classroom important, and among her posted goals for the school year includes teaching in a classroom a minimum of once a month. She has taken the teacher training in cooperative learning and used it in the classroom. Top district leadership is supportive here as well; newly hired Superintendent Moffett encourages principals to be in the classroom: "Don't pull principals out of classes if I call," he has said.

Nearly half of the Aloha teachers responded to a last-minute, informal announcement of the opportunity to discuss the Aloha work environment after school with a visiting researcher. Their comments focused on a number of issues: first, trust and patience. It is important to remember, they noted, that "the process takes time"; in the case of Aloha, it had been five years. "You must be prepared to give a five-plus-year commitment," noted Decla Johnson.

Building trust with one another and with the principal has been another key step in the process. "The word is trust. We trust enough to ask each other for help," said another. "We've had it for the last two to three years. We're not threatened by each other's strengths and weaknesses." These changes came only after teachers were able to break out of the traditional mode: "You forget how isolated a teacher can be and how hard it is to open that door," one teacher said.

The process began, according to the teachers, when the district was decentralized and the "superintendent was willing to give up power." Discussing the school budget together and setting priorities cooperatively is one of the new responsibilities for teachers. "We know the budget choices. We give input, prioritize, and decide," said one. "We decide, 'Is it a school priority?' and we set a stipend for it." Equally as meaningful are the "little things," noted another teacher, such as an open supply room. "We feel comfortable, always included, and we share responsibilities. It's our job to make the school work better."

Prospects for the Future

Three developments since the spring of 1986—appointment of a new district superintendent, changes in the composition of the ABC Board of Education, and significant shifts in special state funding for education—are all beginning to have an effect on the outlook for the ABC District. To what extent they will cause changes in policies, attitudes, and practices remains to be seen, but certain responses have already occurred.

At the end of the 1985–86 school year, the district lost $2 million in state funding and, for the first time in seven years of surpluses, the district will face the need to balance its budget. While the district has begun to receive state lottery monies, those gains are offset by a reduction to 2.5 percent of the state budget's cost-of-living allowance.

"The public is lulled into thinking that the current period is a gold mine and that the lottery will solve all the problems," noted ABCFT President John Ennes. In fact, it is "a continued battle on the state level for funds," according to ABC Board of Education Chairman Peggy Lee. "Every year we fight crazy battles." In an attempt to establish a "secure formula for educa-tion funding," Lee and her colleagues across the state have begun a new grass roots campaign—called "Initiative 88"—for a ballot initiative to achieve a stable funding source.

"Education is not going to get massive infusions of money for general funds," according to Charles Vernon. "Most new money is going to be earmarked, and there will be no general monies for release time for professionals. So we need to have creative ideas for new programs."

Participative management is even more critical in a period of tight budgets, Vernon said, because people at all levels will better understand the reasons behind the need for funding cuts. Also, Vernon noted, in an $82 million budget, "there is always some discretion, some places to set priorities. The district should never say there's *no* money."

Adjusting to the subtleties of a new leadership style at the top takes time, and while the ABCFT and Superintendent Mof-fett have had some disagreements, the opportunity for construc-tive collaboration does exist. "We must create an honest dialogue and be clear about the bottom line," Moffett said. "It takes more time when there's no money." But he is clear in his belief in teacher involvement: "You have to empower teachers," he said. "If they are not part of the process, they certainly won't go along with the content."

The most surprising development in the district for both teachers and administrators appears to be the changes in the positions taken by the Board of Education since the installment in late 1985 of two newly elected board members, both of whom the ABCFT campaigned vigorously for. Elected following the controversial closing of three schools in the district because of declining enrollments, the new members reflected community distrust of the district bureaucracy and a concern for increasing the influence of parents in decision making. Their opinions have swung the board toward a more authoritarian stance and a more conservative view of teacher empowerment.

When the board called for the involuntary transfer of teachers among schools to accommodate a special curriculum at one site, five teachers filed grievances and the issue went into binding arbitration. In December 1986 the issue was decided in favor of the board's position. Another proposal—which was developed without teacher input—called for the creation of a hotline for parents to report their concerns about education in the district. When some board members wanted to allow complaints to be filed anonymously, the union protested, and it required nearly a year of discussions before the decision was changed.

"We had gotten used to collaboration," John Ennes said. "The administration understood that we cared about the kids, but the board was bound and determined to have its own way." Helen Fried, director of elementary education for the district, does not see changes in the outlook of the board as a serious roadblock. "School boards are not the stumbling block to teacher participation. A lot can be done without threatening the board," she said. "I do not see a major change in direction in this district in the future." And according to Charles Vernon, the process of renewal is irreversible: "Once people become educated and committed in a personal way, it doesn't go away."

9

Bargaining for Better Schools: Reshaping Education in the Cincinnati Public Schools

by Susan Moore Johnson

There is change afoot in Cincinnati. Serious change. Homegrown change. Change that could reshape the work of teachers and the education of children in the Cincinnati Public Schools. Although many might expect teachers' unions to act in self-serving ways, ignoring educational concerns in their pursuit of higher wages and better benefits, the Cincinnati Federation of Teachers (CFT) is building a collaborative relationship with the school board and administration that would enable teachers to assume greater responsibility for educational policy in the school district.

The course of change in Cincinnati deserves close attention by educational policymakers and analysts throughout the country, for the initiatives there—consulting teachers, demonstration schools, increased responsibility for teachers in administration—are much like those recently proposed by the Carnegie Forum and Holmes group for the reform of the teaching profession. By understanding the origins of collaborative efforts in Cincinnati and by analyzing the accomplishments and challenges that educators there face, we can pursue change elsewhere more realistically and responsibly.

The City and Its Schools

Cincinnati, located on the Ohio River, has a population of 368,712, making it the thirty-second largest city in the nation.

The city's economy, which is stable and diverse, has not suffered the severe decline that other Midwestern cities, dependent on the auto industry, have experienced. The city is historically a company town, with large nonunionized companies such as Procter and Gamble and Cincinnati Milacron employing many citizens and influencing local public priorities.

The Cincinnati Public Schools enroll 52,000 students in eighty-three schools. An extensive magnet school program offers parents the choice of enrolling their children in either neighborhood schools or one of twenty-eight specialized programs, such as Montessori, creative and performing arts, and physical education. Communities within Cincinnati take a serious interest in their schools. At some, Local School Advisory Councils (LSACs), composed of teachers, principals, parents, and community members, have been active and influential in setting school-site policy and in budgeting funds since 1982.

Despite what many would regard as a progressive and decentralized approach to schooling in Cincinnati, labor relations in the district have historically been formal, centralized, and adversarial. In 1967, the CFT called a strike to initiate collective bargaining, which was not then required by state law. The school board agreed to negotiate with teachers, but the CFT lost the representation election to the Cincinnati Teachers Association, an affiliate of the National Education Association. The CFT subsequently gained the right to bargain through a challenge election in 1977, a right that they successfully defended in a second challenge election in 1982. Currently, 2,600 of Cincinnati's 3,200 teachers (about 80 percent) are CFT members.

Historically, the Cincinnati Board of Education assumed a conservative stance toward the union, seeking to protect the rights of management and husband the resources of the district. A bitter nineteen-day strike in 1977 over salary left teachers disillusioned and the labor relationship in disarray. As one union leader recalled, "We fought them to a bloody draw." The school administration, too, maintained an adversarial relationship with the teachers and their union. The superintendent during those years is widely said to have exerted little leadership in the schools, while his assistant held tight control of a traditional line organization. One central office administrator said that the superintendent had been "apathetic. There was a leadership void. He let a lot of things happen."

Moreover, the district was unusually inbred. Between 1974 and 1987, no principal was hired from outside the district and, reportedly, "those who worked their way to the top took a hard line with the union. [The assistant superintendent] sent the message to the principals: 'Don't empower teachers.'" As a result, a sharp division developed between teachers and their principals, with teachers believing that their values and purposes differed markedly from those of administrators. There were repeated complaints that principals changed teachers' grades or promoted students who failed a majority of their courses. Teachers saw the principals as illegitimate interlopers in their instructional domain.

Except for the community-based LSACs, school improvement efforts in the district were decidedly top-down initiatives from the school system's Office of Research, Planning, and Development. As one teacher explained, "Teachers were the recipients of R&D wisdom." Another said, "Whatever R&D wanted, R&D got. Things were piped down." A union leader argued that "the bureaucrats had turned teachers into drones." Although teachers held seats on planning and policy committees, they generally did not think that their efforts finally mattered, and they believed that the school officials eventually did what they had intended from the start.

Today, those on both sides of the bargaining table are working toward more cooperative relationships. Union leaders are directing their members' attention to instructional policies and practices. The central office is promoting more meaningful involvement of teachers in decision making and is planning to hire principals who will work collaboratively with their staffs. Moreover, the school board and administration are looking to the teachers for new ideas and understandings about how to improve the schools.

What is behind these changes? Those teachers, administrators, and board members interviewed for this research generally offered three explanations. First, members of the school board have gradually come to believe that a more cooperative relationship with teachers would be good for the schools. During the late 1970s and early 1980s, the school board exercised a more traditional managerial approach toward Cincinnati's teachers. One union leader recalled: "They thought of teachers as employees to be seen and not heard rather than as professionals to be consulted." When the current school board president joined the board in 1983, he had a good relationship with the union president and teachers and "didn't share the view that the teachers' union was an evil force." Over time, a majority of members came to share this view.

In the board's view, a hard-line stance by central administrators toward teachers and their union stood in the way of more cooperative relationships. When the superintendent died suddenly in 1985, the board sought a replacement who would build more constructive relationships with teachers, and in 1986, appointed Lee Etta Powell, an experienced administrator from the Montgomery County Public Schools, who advocated strong and collaborative roles for teachers and principals. Powell is widely seen as being supportive of teachers and is expected to redefine how the central office will do business with the schools.

Although most respondents credited the school board and the superintendent with supporting new roles for teachers, it was the CFT president, Tom Mooney, who most said was primarily responsible for the changed approaches and attitudes. Mooney, a long-time union activist and president of the CFT since 1979, had experienced the strike that divided the schools in 1977 and he recognized the need for a new approach to bargaining. In 1983, he initiated a carefully designed plan to increase teachers' authority over educational decisions and to build better relationships with the board and administration. He addressed his members, school officials, and the public through the press. Writing as a guest columnist in the *Cincinnati Enquirer,* Mooney asserted that popular proposals for merit pay were wrongheaded because they were "based on the assumption that most of us aren't really trying or that most of us are incompetent." He rejected that assumption and argued that the two major obstacles to improving student achievement were that "teachers have too little authority over academic standards and too great a workload for effective instruction." He argued that administrators "have far too much power over the educational process" and urged that teachers be given "the real authority over their classrooms" (Mooney, 1983).

Mooney carefully built a CFT campaign called "Bargaining for Better Schools," which was designed to garner public support for teachers' assuming new powers in public education. Using an extensive survey of CFT members' views, he sought to identify issues "that would respond well with members and play well with the public." Although he recognized the limits of conventional bargaining, Mooney thought that contract demands were the only way to get the board's attention and the community's support. Given the past history of labor strife, he believed that "the board wouldn't relent without a strike and the teachers wouldn't strike again. Therefore, we needed a better strategy."

That strategy was to reframe the issues, emphasizing the teachers' pursuit of better education and downplaying teachers' demands for better working conditions. Albert Shanker, president of the American Federation of Teachers, had encouraged local unions to address matters of professionalism, lending further legitimacy to the CFT's approach. As Mooney explained, "The AFT gave us the sanction internally. That makes the stuff easier to sell." The list of teachers' priorities derived from the 1983 survey was not so different from what one might expect of teachers anywhere:

1. Class size limits/reduced workload
2. Expanded health benefits
3. Across-the-board raise
4. Improving salary schedule
5. Greater authority over academic standards

However, in taking its case to the public, the CFT leadership emphasized the professional side of members' demands and sought to convince those outside the schools that they had a stake in the outcomes of negotiations. The press took up the union's case and frequently published articles and editorials explicating and advocating the teachers' positions. Over time, the CFT came to be represented as a responsible and authoritative advocate of better schools. The *Cincinnati Enquirer,* known to be a conservative newspaper, praised their priorities: "Cincinnati teachers have shown that need not greed motivates their current negotiations with the Cincinnati Board of Education . . . " ("Teachers: Reaction to Passage of School Levies . . . ," 1984).

In December 1983, the CFT and board met at the table for what was to have been an economic reopener, focusing solely on salary. However, the union put nonwage demands on the table as well, and the board's representatives walked out in response. Mooney's persistent public campaign continued throughout the following year, and when the school board returned to bargaining a year later, it was with some resentment. One board member reflected on the union's success with a mixture of admiration and annoyance: "The union decided to go public on educational issues. They did a marvelous job of boxing us in. . . . The Board felt beleaguered by the onslaught."

The Issues and the Process

Of the many issues on the table, four proved to be central:

1. *Class size.*   The CFT sought class size limits of twenty-five and overload payment for teachers whose classes were larger. Management agreed that smaller classes might be better but was not convinced that this was the best way to spend limited funds. Further, it regarded class size as a right of management that should not be bargained away.

2. *Peer assistance.*   Believing that teacher appraisal practices were "aggressive and abusive" and forced the union and management to spend too much time in court, the CFT had proposed that the Cincinnati Schools institute a peer appraisal program like the one in Toledo. Management generally supported this proposal, although some principals and central office administrators contended that the plan would seriously compromise their authority and that money would be better spent on hiring more supervisors.

3. *Committee appointment.*   The CFT sought the authority
to make all appointments of teachers to citywide committees,
arguing that when administrators had selected teacher representatives, their choices had limited the success of the committees.
The Board regarded this proposal as an abridgment of
managerial rights.

4. *Grading.*   The CFT proposed higher standards for
students' promotion and demanded that principals be prohibited
from changing teachers' grades. The board regarded this as a
nonnegotiable issue.

5. *Salary and benefits.*   The CFT sought to significantly
increase senior teachers' pay by changing the salary index of
the pay scale. In addition, it sought a 12 percent across the board
raise in each of two years. The board offered a three-year salary
settlement of 3 percent, 3 percent, and 4 percent that was coupled
with a proposal to add ten work days over the course of three
years.

The board, represented by a labor lawyer who had
negotiated on their behalf since the inception of collective
bargaining, proceeded in a conventional fashion, responding
negatively to proposals set forth by the CFT. They did not formulate their own position, seeking instead to protect the rights
of management and determine the best use of available funds.
In retrospect, some members of the management team regard
that reactive stance as a mistake. One central office administrator
said that management's greatest "blunder" was that "we didn't
have our own agenda." Another recalled that all negotiated
changes were "teacher initiated with board acceptance." A
union negotiator observed that during the first three months
of bargaining, the board repeatedly opposed change by responding, "We can't afford it" or "It's not a proper subject for
bargaining." One administrator recalled that because the progress of negotiations was so well publicized, management took
stands that permitted little retreat or compromise: "We dug
ourselves in. We said that we would never give in on class size."
Eventually, they did.

There were some on the board who would have prefer-
red bargaining that was more cooperative and more focused on

problem solving. However, there was no leadership or clear authority to proceed in this way, the former superintendent having "avoided negotiations totally." There were few models available to board members who wanted to move beyond conventional tactics. The accounts of those interviewed coincided with that of one administrator who reported, "Bargaining was adversarial to the end."

Over time, the press focused on the broad issues of educational policy as Mooney had hoped. An editorial writer in the *Cincinnati Post* observed: "The Cincinnati Board of Education is trying to negotiate a labor contract with the teachers' union. The Cincinnati Federation of Teachers is trying to negotiate a new way of making policy for public schools" ("Spelling It Out," 1984). From the public's perspective, negotiations centered less on demands and concessions than on improving the standards of the schools.

As initial agreements were reached on the teacher appraisal plan and teachers were assured greater authority in grading, the *Cincinnati Post* criticized the board for its slow response: "It is tempting to wonder why the board of education dragged its feet so long, only to adopt the union's proposals in the end. When the CFT came forward with constructive initiatives a year ago, why wasn't the board responsive? The very policies now being announced could have been launched as cooperative ventures, instead of coming as concessions extracted from a halfhearted school board by CFT pressure and publicity in the midst of labor negotiations" ("Education Quiz," 1984).

Although agreements were reached early about the peer assistance program and grading standards, most issues were not settled until February 1985, when the CFT threatened a one-day strike and prompted round-the-clock bargaining. Differences were ultimately resolved by Mooney and Lynn Goodwin of the Central Office, who had earned each other's respect over time and were committed to reaching a settlement. Goodwin reflected that "the relationship that Tom and I had developed personally over time helped us get some problem solving done directly. Even though our bargaining was positional and very, very difficult, there could come a time when we could isolate ourselves

very much outside the process . . . and really resolve some of
the issues in a problem-solving forum.'' After four days of in-
tense deliberations, during which, as one participant said, ''Man-
hood was at stake on both sides,'' an agreement was reached,
a strike averted, and a settlement was unanimously ratified by
the CFT membership.

The Settlement

The contract settlement was widely viewed as a victory for the
union. Noteworthy agreements included:

1. A three-year salary agreement that granted teachers raises
    of 8 percent, 4 percent, and 5 percent across the board.
    In 1987, the final year of the contract, salaries would range
    from $16,864 to $38,383.
2. Class size limits in academic classes of twenty-eight in the
    primary grades and thirty in grades 4 through 12. An ad-
    ditional reserve pool of thirty teachers would be assigned
    to alleviate overcrowding, and overload payments would
    be made to teachers whose classes continued to exceed the
    negotiated maxima. A joint CFT/Board Allocation Com-
    mittee was established to review initial staff allocations, to
    assign surplus teachers, and to distribute overload funds
    where necessary.
3. The board agreed to new grading and promotion standards,
    and included in the contract a procedure by which teachers
    might dispute grade changes.
4. The district agreed to pilot test for two years a peer ap-
    praisal plan, in which ten consulting teachers representing
    the major academic areas and selected jointly by the CFT
    and the administration would assist and evaluate first-year
    teachers.
5. The CFT won the right to make all appointments of teachers
    to joint committees in the school district.

    In addition, much that the CFT accomplished during
negotiations was not codified in contract language. The school

board agreed to deal afterward with issues that were not negotiated directly. Joint committees were formed to review and
recommend policy. Mooney saw great advantage in having
established this "skeleton for participation": "If we just had
the language without the joint committees, we'd only have lots
of grievances and no interpretive ability. Joint committees are
flexible and faster than the grievance procedures. You can get
things in the guidelines of joint committees that you could never
get past the board's attorney."

The Aftermath

Although teachers were reportedly pleased with the contract settlement and with Mooney's leadership in achieving it, the schools'
administrative staff were generally discouraged or angry, ex-
pressing particular concern about the Peer Appraisal Plan. As
one central administrator explained, "The process set up the
administrative staff to feel like losers. The principals and line
staff felt that the board had given away all their authority."

Despite this resentment, there was a commitment on the
part of the union, some central administrators, and board members to make the contract work. Much of the implementation
of contract language depended on the work of joint committees, such as the Peer Review Panel, which would select consulting teachers, and the Teacher Allocation Committee, which
would assign additional teachers and disburse additional funds.
As one administrator explained, "We had a lot of structure set
up in that contract that we could fall on our face on. So we made
a commitment to assign some decent people. We both thought
through who the collaborators of these initial efforts ought to
be and worked hard to get that done, and I think with fair success. We had good results, but that was with those people who
were problem solvers. They were just good people."

The Allocation Committee, composed of three union members and three administrators from the Department of Curriculum and Instruction, was reportedly more effective than
anyone had expected. Members suggested new organizational
arrangements to schools that reported being understaffed. When

those recommendations did not alleviate the problem, committee members assigned additional teachers or aides from a reserve pool. Where conditions still violated the negotiated guidelines, the committee spent $85,000 to compensate teachers for overload. As one administrator explained, "They were to use thirty teachers, thirty-seven aides, and $85,000 as best they could to solve the problem." Reportedly, there were few complaints, even though the board's lawyer had predicted 100 grievances during the first year. One administrator judged the Allocation Committee to be "the best joint committee." Another said, "I had some reservations about the infighting that might occur, but I saw that attitudes were flexible. They did a whole lot of work . . . Everyone was about the effort to achieve the best possible balance."

Similarly, the Peer Assistance Plan achieved early success. The ten consulting teachers selected by the Peer Review Panel, a joint committee administering the program, were widely regarded as skilled and well intentioned. Each worked with approximately sixteen beginning teachers in ten schools, providing assistance and assessing their progress. The consulting teachers' assessments of beginning teachers' performance were reviewed by the Peer Review Panel.

During the first year, the consulting teachers recommended that 5 percent of the contracts of beginning teachers not be renewed. This was twice the percentage that administrators had turned down in the subject areas that they still reviewed. Although some teachers had expressed initial concern that the union was abandoning its members, and although some principals were angry at first that their right to appraise new teachers had been eroded, support for the program grew steadily. Teachers widely agreed that the consulting teachers were providing valuable remedial assistance and that if teachers failed to improve under this program, they should probably not be teaching. As one active union member explained, "It's fantastic. It's time we cleared up our own ranks. The principals have ignored these teachers because they didn't want to deal with Downtown. This has encouraged the principals to review these people. If the problems can't be corrected, then they should seek a new profession."

Meanwhile, principals found the consulting teachers' work to be a valuable supplement to their own efforts. As one consulting teacher observed: "It's the kind of job a lot of people don't want to do anyway." A year-end survey of teachers' and administrators' responses to the program revealed widespread satisfaction. During the second year, consulting teachers extended their assistance to more experienced staff who were initially identified by their principals as requiring intervention.

During 1985–86, the CFT moved well beyond the task of implementing their contract. Members were active politically in the successful campaign of school board candidate, Virginia Rhodes, a former teacher and union activist. Campaigning for strong neighborhood schools and improved academic standards, Rhodes received more votes than any incumbent. As a member of the board, she pursued some of the issues that had been raised by the CFT in its public relations campaign of 1983–85.

Union members joined with Rhodes in drawing attention to what they regarded as inequities in the instructional programs. A preliminary analysis by the CFT of school system data revealed that curricula varied greatly from school to school, with college-oriented instruction being concentrated in the magnet schools. They found that schools with few advanced courses experienced higher transfer rates, larger percentages of students reading below national norms, and higher failure rates. Their analysis further concluded that course offerings were driven by student enrollments rather than by a fixed-core curriculum. If too few students enrolled for an advanced course, such as calculus, that course would likely be canceled for the year, diminishing student interest and expectations in subsequent years.

This analysis of course offerings prompted a School Board motion in October 1986, directing Superintendent Powell to recommend a core curriculum for all high schools in the district. Again, a joint committee including ten CFT members was formed to address the issue. Initially, there were disputes between administrators and teachers about the task and procedures of the committee. Eventually, however, the committee issued a report analyzing the current course offerings and setting forth recommendations for change. Subsequently, the board voted to provide a core curriculum in all schools, and the Superintendent wrote to thank CFT participants for their efforts.

In addition to bringing the board's attention to the core curriculum, the CFT sought to raise concerns about the continued failure of certain neighborhood schools. Although central office administrators regard neighborhood schools as an option for parents who prefer that their children be educated within their communities, the public perception is that students in these schools tend to be less successful academically than those who attend magnet schools. This perception has not been borne out by central office studies of student performance on standardized tests. Still, in a rank order list of schools in the district, the lowest-performing schools are neighborhood schools, although not every neighborhood school falls into this category.

Some critics attribute this lack of success to inadequate resources or unfocused programs. Others contend that although much money and many new programs have been directed at these schools, teachers have been excluded from the process of designing reforms and that, consequently, the programs have not been well conceived and executed. A teacher in one of these neighborhood schools explained that several years ago, the seven lowest-performing schools in the district received $100,000 a year under the Bronson desegregation agreement. She and her colleagues wanted to spend that money to reduce class size, to purchase more hands-on materials, and to hire a full-time visiting teacher. Although teachers initially believed that they would have discretion over these funds, in the end, they did not. The central office spent $30,000 for a new reading program and $30,000 for a curriculum leader, and eventually "the staff got nothing that they'd said they wanted."

In June 1986, the CFT sought to increase teachers' say in school improvement. Publicizing their concern about these at-risk students, the CFT set forth a ten-point proposal that included recommendations for all-day kindergarten, preschool programs, reductions in class size, expansion of visiting teacher services, training in social skills, the appointment of counselors in the elementary schools, more parent involvement, the maintenance of k-6 or k-8 elementary schools, in-school disciplinary measures, and clerical assistance for teachers. In presenting these proposals, Mooney urged that if the full reform program could not be funded, the school board should designate two pilot schools where they might be instituted.

In addressing the needs of at-risk students, the board voted to spend $516,000 to track low-achieving students on a computerized system that had been recommended by Acting Superintendent Raymond J. Brokamp. Further, the board authorized that two pilot programs such as those proposed by the CFT be funded at $50,000 each. CFT members publicly challenged the worth of the computerized tracking system and contended that the funds would have been better spent on the pilot projects. One union member was quoted as saying: "I think it's time that we stop spinning our wheels and continually doing the same things we're doing and use some creative ideas and let the teachers in the schools develop their own programs."

With the appointment of Superintendent Powell in the fall of 1986, support for the pilot schools grew. She recommended that the school board fund all-day kindergartens at these schools and provide them with mini-grants of $100,000 each to address their problems.

A joint planning committee composed of teachers and administrators was formed to oversee the program. At first, the committee generated its own proposals for reform in the demonstration schools, but stopped when members realized that the purpose of the project was to encourage teachers to plan for their own schools. Instead, the committee confined itself to identifying eligible schools and conducting a selection process.

Ten elementary schools were deemed eligible on the basis of high poverty and low achievement. In their applications to the planning committee, the six schools that chose to apply attested to their enthusiasm, a willingness to try new things, and community and parental involvement. The Taft Elementary School, serving poor black students, and the McKinley Elementary School, serving poor white Appalachian students, were selected to be pilot schools. They would be free from the constraints of the union contract and school system regulations in designing their programs. Each would be provided with $50,000 to cover training in participative management and time to plan their programs. The faculties could spend their allotted funds as they saw fit.

There was some dispute on the planning committee about whether teachers should be required to compete for the right to teach at the demonstration schools. Initially, most committee members thought that all staff should be removed from the pilot schools and interested teachers be required to reapply. However, the superintendent rejected this plan because the model could not be replicated at other schools. If these were to be demonstration schools, then they must succeed with the staff at hand. Of twenty-six teachers at Taft Elementary School, three chose to transfer to other schools, although one teacher leader said that at least four more appeared to have little interest in the program. Although principals were removed and required to reapply, the selection process was reportedly not very exacting, and the same principals were reappointed without competition. Those who believe that the principal is central to school improvement regret that this process was not more selective.

Despite initial enthusiasm for the project, the first months of planning in the schools were trying. Teachers are said to have been ambivalent about the project and to have spoken frequently about their "fear of the unknown." They are reportedly uncertain about how to devise new programs that will achieve the success that has been so elusive. A teacher who is active in the project said that she had recently had "real doubts about whether it's going to work in this building. . . . They're afraid to have all this decision-making process on their shoulders."

Teachers also express dismay at the time required beyond the school day to make routine decisions. One teacher said, "It's been meeting after meeting. The staff just can't come up with anything. It takes a four-hour meeting just to get one answer for one really small thing. It's been a very difficult process all year." The principal of one school is said to be reluctant to assume leadership in the project, leaving all decisions to the staff. Sometimes they find themselves "paralyzed by the smallest decisions." Teachers are hopeful that the upcoming training in participative management will enable them to move ahead more confidently and efficiently.

Teachers in the pilot schools talked about using the discretionary funds to provide more time for teacher collaboration, buy better student support services, involve parents in the schools, and develop programs that would improve students' social skills. Although the staff at these schools presumably were to act without the constraints of district policies and contract language, participants did not expect that such discretion would be readily available. A central office administrator said that her colleagues' initial responses to suggestions for change were likely to be, "Oh, but you can't do that." Such cautious attitudes, she said, "have got to change." One member of the planning committee anticipated that the group would continue to oversee the demonstration schools "to see that this program is going to move and that they get what they were promised."

The CFT representative in one building expressed her hopes for the program: "I think that there will be a real upgrade in the professionalism in the building and a teaming approach. There will be more grouping and more decision making by groups, maybe by teams. I tend to think that there will be a lot more community participation in the classrooms." In her view, the worst outcome would be that "it doesn't work, that it's just the same old thing—lots of meetings, lots of long meetings where nothing gets accomplished . . . a lot of interruption to the instructional time."

Moving Ahead

In many ways, the time was right for greater collaboration in Cincinnati as the union and school board entered the final year of their contract in 1987. Support for Superintendent Powell was strong, with teachers generally believing that she didn't "carry an administrator's perspective." She had demonstrated her ability to confront a regimented and inbred administrative staff and had made it clear that principals must be prepared to promote leadership among teachers in their schools. Key school board members and central administrators also advocated more cooperative relationships with teachers, hoping to promote further joint endeavors and to expand teachers' professional roles. As one board member said, "It's been our experience that the leadership of the union is serious about school improvement.'' Mooney was widely recognized for his integrity, good intentions, and problem-solving skills. He was credited with having successfully led his teachers from conflict to cooperation and was expected to persist in his efforts to professionalize teaching.

There remained, however, some questions and challenges that deserved close attention. First, would there be sufficient interest and energy among teachers in Cincinnati, or in any comparable district, to sustain extensive professional involvement outside the classroom? Those teachers involved in the first two years of collaboration exhibited remarkable initiative and commitment. They worked long hours and achieved much, but participation was not widespread and some of the teachers involved worked on several committees. As one remarked, ''It's the same people over and over again.''

There was evidence that interest in new roles was growing—seventy teachers applied to become consulting teachers in the second cycle of the Peer Assistance Program—but it might be unrealistic to expect large numbers of teachers to devote many hours to nonteaching responsibilities. If the district seriously intended to support teachers' involvement in decision making, it might have to provide release time for participating staff in other ventures as it had for the consulting teachers. Moreover, many teachers in Cincinnati and elsewhere might have little interest in policymaking, preferring instead to concentrate on their teaching. If the district were to introduce a career ladder, it seemed important to define roles that fit the strengths of their best teachers, both those choosing to teach full time and those choosing to assume broader leadership roles.

Second, those in Cincinnati had to consider whether teachers could be expected to have the answers to complicated, seemingly intractable problems. There is an important difference between being responsive to teachers in decisions that affect their teaching and assigning them full responsibility for solving the district's instructional problems. Early experience with the pilot schools suggested that the difficulties would not be automatically eliminated with more money or more discretion. The necessary changes were likely to be complex and long-term, and all the answers might not emerge from the schools. As one teacher said of the pilot schools, "People have no idea what's supposed to happen. What if it fails? You have to leave room for failure. We're pioneers."

Third, teachers and school officials in Cincinnati had to anticipate what the eventual balance of administrative authority and teacher power would be. Would there be limits to teachers' involvement in policymaking? Would teachers ultimately run the schools, or would they cross some yet unspecified boundary of acceptable influence or authority? Mooney suggested that there were "no limits" to where his union might take this initiative, largely because "the credibility of the existing structure is very low." But what happens when that existing structure changes? There are great expectations among those who favor teacher empowerment that the new superintendent will successfully reorganize the central administration, redefine priorities there, and ensure bureaucratic support for experimental, collaborative projects. Respondents recognized that it is a formidable task to undo organizational procedures, to reassign authority from the center to the periphery, to transfer power from Downtown to the schools. However, if decentralization works and teachers assume far-reaching responsibility for their schools, will the need for administrative leadership and oversight disappear?

Fourth, it was important to follow how principals would adapt to the changes occurring around them. Until recently, Cincinnati principals relied largely on their formal authority in managing their schools. They had long been expected to quash teachers' initiatives and reward compliant behavior. Superintendent Powell had made it clear that she expected principals to be strong leaders in their own right and to promote influential roles for teachers: "If your principals become leaders, they can let their teachers be leaders." If and when the role of principal is redefined and reinforced, Cincinnati principals might well seek to reclaim lost authority. It is not clear what the relationship between teachers and administrators would then be.

Finally, with the current contract soon to expire, both sides wondered how the 1987 negotiations would affect long-term collaboration between teachers and administrators in Cincinnati.

By all accounts, the next round of collective bargaining would be a major challenge. Funding was uncertain. Teachers' expectations had been raised. Some central administrators and principals were wary. Although the parties had successfully collaborated since signing the last agreement, their bargaining history had been decidedly combative.

Under Mooney's leadership, the CFT again surveyed its membership in early 1987 and publicized the findings in what one administrator called a "carbon copy process" of that used to garner public support for the 1985 negotiations. This administrator further observed that "a lot of media positioning tends to solidify positions" and that pursuing collaborative relations through oppositional tactics is "a conflict of message." However, Mooney anticipated that this time "the public outreach [would] be more positive," and he predicted that the CFT would "sit down in a less publicly confrontational way and see what we can get done." However, teachers readily recalled being treated as functionaries, and school board members had not forgotten the embarrassment of the last negotiations. Both parties were likely to pursue collaboration with caution.

Management wondered whether the CFT would be as responsible about program costs as they were about program design. The recent survey of CFT members indicated that teachers continue to seek improvements in their schools, to pursue improved working conditions, and to expect more professionalized roles for themselves. But the proposals for reducing student transience, improving high school curricula, and supporting more pilot schools were costly. One board member who respected these CFT initiatives worried about the costs: "I have yet to see the union take a good look at how we're going to fund this." In response, CFT leaders pointed to their past efforts to win public support and legislative approval for school funding. If teachers in Cincinnati or elsewhere assume roles in policymaking and program administration, must they also accept the burden of finding funds for such efforts and bearing responsibility for the outcomes? Is this where collaboration and participative management ultimately lead?

Negotiating the 1988 Agreement

Cincinnati negotiators had long prepared for contract talks in separate camps, withholding data from their adversaries, devising competitive strategies, and concealing their actual preferences and priorities. Preparation during the fall of 1987 was different, however, as negotiators spent several days together learning how to substitute cooperative problem solving for combative bartering. Working with trainers from Conflict Management Incorporated, whose professionals were formerly associated with the Harvard Negotiations Project, they practiced new approaches to negotiation that encouraged them to be candid about their interests, to share data openly, to jointly explore alternative solutions, and ultimately to arrive at "principled" settlements. (This approach to negotiation is described in Fisher and Ury, 1981.)

Initially, some of the teacher negotiators were skeptical about the trainers and the process they advocated, but gradually all participants came to value them both. During the first phase of bargaining, there were brainstorming sessions when negotiators explored alternative solutions together without making offers or demands. They formed joint task forces that focused on specific issues and recommended changes to the full group of negotiators. During the second phase of bargaining, a drafting committee, including members from both sides, prepared contract language that codified those changes. In the final days of bargaining, Mooney and Goodwin again met to resolve the "sticking points" of the talks, this time with the assistance of a facilitator from Conflict Management Incorporated.

The outcomes of their first venture at cooperative bargaining were impressive. Whereas salary settlements are the centerpiece of most labor agreements, the wage increase of 16.8 percent over three years for Cincinnati teachers was but one issue of concern to these negotiators. More notable were changes in "professional teaching and learning conditions" that reorganized many features of teachers' work.

The parties agreed to simultaneously decrease high school teachers' work load from six to five courses and increase the average amount of instructional time for high school students by reconfiguring the daily schedule. Class periods in most high schools would be increased from forty-five to fifty minutes and teachers would be assigned to two nonteaching periods each day—one for preparation and one for tutoring or student activities. Teachers in middle schools that featured interdisciplinary team teaching were expected to teach five rather than six courses and were guaranteed one daily period for team planning in addition to their preparation and conference period. At the elementary level, teachers were guaranteed an average of fifty minutes of preparation time each day.

In another major initiative, the parties established a Career in Teaching Program that will include four promotional steps leading to the position of lead teacher and begin in 1990. During the next two years, a joint committee will develop an implementation plan for the program that defines criteria for eligibility, proposes assessment procedures, and develops role definitions. The final plan must be ratified by both the union and the board.

In other provisions, the union and school board agreed to amend their transfer policies so that school officials could identify vacancies early and hire staff when the best candidates are still in the job market. They established a Professional Development Fund and a joint committee to oversee its use for conferences, in-service training, and sabbatical leaves. They increased the number of consulting teachers in the Peer Assistance and Appraisal Plan, reduced their caseload, and stipulated that participants could not be appointed to administrative positions for one year after serving as consulting teachers.

In addition to these legally binding provisions, Cincinnati negotiators crafted a Trust Agreement pledging "mutual faith and commitment to implement" initiatives for the recruitment and training of minority teachers, development of professional practice schools, and training programs for first-year teachers. (Such trust agreements were initially proposed by Kerchner and Mitchell, 1986.) They agreed to seek funding for preschool education, smaller classes in the elementary grades, and all-day kindergarten. They urged that a communitywide task force be formed to review and recommend improvements in the district's art, music, and physical education programs. They proposed that the district move toward implementing a middle schools model and consider sponsoring a high school pilot program with the Coalition of Essential Schools. They urged that school sites maintain better contact with parents. They agreed to develop a plan to assist teachers in copying and duplicating instructional materials.

Ultimately, the impact of this latest bargaining agreement will depend more on the understandings and commitment of its signers than on the literal interpretation of its language. For although the agreement's provisions are carefully drawn and specifically worded, they address complex issues and initiate programs that cannot yet be prescribed in detail. Implementation must be left to the well-intentioned efforts of those determined to make this contract work for all parties.

The negotiators envision that their new relationship and problem-solving skills can serve the school district well beyond formal bargaining. In the Preface to their formal agreement, they commend the "structured collaborative decision-making process" to others in the district and offer to train interested teachers and administrators, particularly those working in the pilot schools. They avow that the process can "make a significant change in the climate of our system and in the education for children in our city." By the end of these negotiations, the participants had fashioned a new working relationship that bore little resemblance to the adversarial standoff of several years before. As they explain in their Preface, "we have become a team of fellow professionals." Those in Cincinnati are exploring new and promising territory for which there is no map as yet. However, the accomplishments of the past three years suggest that if any urban school district can successfully find its way, this one will.

10

School-Based Management and Shared-Decision Making in the Dade County Public Schools

by Eugene F. Provenzo, Jr.

Miami and Dade County, Florida, bring many images to mind: the cool pastels of the Art Deco District on Miami Beach, the waves of immigrants from Cuba and other Caribbean, Central, and South American countries, and the glamour and violence of the drug wars portrayed on "Miami Vice." The power of these images tends to obscure many other aspects of the city: its role as the cultural and financial capital for Central America and the Caribbean, its startling architecture and lush physical environment, and its complex and extremely interesting public school system.

The Dade County Public School System is the fourth largest school district in the United States. During the 1987–88 school year it served 254,235 students. It employs over 23,000 full-time staff, of which just over 14,000 are teachers. Its budget is nearly $1.5 billion a year (Dade County Public Schools, 1987).

The school system has a highly diverse population and spans an enormous geographical area. In the southern part of the county, which is the winter vegetable production center for the East Coast and Midwest, the school system serves a largely rural population, including not only permanent residents but thousands of migrants who come to work in the area on a seasonal basis. To the north of Hialeah and "Little Havana" there are the recently arrived Cuban and Nicaraguan families; the Haitian boat people live mostly in Little River and the Russian immigrants in Miami Beach. There are middle class black neighborhoods in Richmond Heights; and desperately poor and neglected black neighborhoods in Overtown, Liberty City, and Opa-Locka; and affluent white suburban neighborhoods in Kendall. There is also Coral Gables, with its Anglo and Hispanic populations and its slightly stuffy Mediterranean elegance.

All of these neighborhoods, with their diverse populations and different needs, place enormous demands on the school system. Yet despite these demands and often insufficient resources, the school system has managed over the past couple of years to be on the cutting edge of a number of important innovations in education. Through its program in School-Based Management/Shared-Decision Making, as well as experiments as varied as satellite schools, Saturday morning schools, and academics for the professional growth and development of teachers, the Dade County Public School System is redefining many of the traditional ways in which schools operate and function. In doing so, it is creating new professional roles for teachers, support staff, and administrators.

The Origins of the School-Based Management/Shared-Decision Making Program

The cornerstone of the recent innovations in the Dade County Public Schools has been the concept of School-Based Management/Shared-Decision Making. The purpose of this program has been to professionalize teaching and to decentralize the schools, placing them more under the control of building administrators and teachers and parents from the communities they serve. School-Based Management/Shared-Decision Making has origins that date back to 1971 and the Citizen's Committee on Education. This group, which had been appointed by Governor Reuben Askew to make recommendations concerning the improvement of Florida's public schools, concluded that educational reform and the "complexity" faced by the educational system "is best handled *where* and *when* instruction occurs" (Office of

the Deputy Superintendent, 1986, p. 3). As part of its recommendations, the citizen's committee specifically suggested
that (1) funds be awarded to the schools based on the needs
of students; (2) the educational objectives for a school be set
by the individuals most immediately connected with the school;
(3) the decision of how funds are to be spent be made in each
school rather than in the central office; (4) the organization of
instruction be made at the school level; and (5) parents become
involved in decisions involving the school (Office of the Deputy Superintendent, 1986, p. 3). The recommendations of the
Committee were acted on by the legislature and eventually
became the core of what is now known as School-Based Manage-
ment/Shared-Decision Making.

The report by the Citizen's Committee on Education,
while not necessarily having an immediate impact, set an important precedent. In 1973, the school system negotiated its first
contract with the local teachers' union—the United Teachers
of Dade. At that time, the union set up task forces with members
of the union and the school administration that would meet during the year in order to try to reconcile differences that could
not be worked out at the bargaining table. According to Pat
Tornillo, the head of the union both then and now, it was in
these joint task force meetings that the beginnings of the development of the School-Based Management/Shared-Decision Making model could be found. As Tornillo explained in an interview
in February 1988, the model that evolved "didn't happen overnight." He said that "each contract moved us along, including
that first contract, when we agreed to form joint task forces,
and in the next contract, when we established faculty councils
in every school. And then when we expanded the collaborative
model to include other joint task forces and we began working
collaboratively on little pieces and found success in that." What
was at work was a new type of cooperation and collaboration
between the teachers' union and the school system's administration.

On a national level, the evolution of this model is of particular interest, since it suggests the movement of teachers' unions
such as the United Teachers of Dade away from traditional

confrontational relationships with management toward models based on more cooperation and joint planning. It is also a relationship that has led critics to declare that the union is in collusion with the school system. To these types of comments the Superintendent of Schools, Joseph Fernandez, has responded: " 'The administration is in bed with the union, and vice-versa.' You hear it second- and third-hand. The interesting thing is that the union gets the same kinds of comments from its membership. . . . We're not forgetting our roles. My role is to provide the best education I can to the children of the district. If one way to do that is through a better working relationship with the union, then I'm all for it" (Olson, 1987b, p. 19). In fact, the close relationship between the school system and the United Teachers of Dade has taken many years to achieve, and in large part has been a result of the efforts of Pat Tornillo to work in careful collaboration with various administrators in the school system. Without this relationship—one based on mutual trust, personl respect, and joint interest—it would probably have been impossible to undertake many of the reforms and experiments that have been attempted recently in the Dade County Public Schools.

The Role of the United Teachers of Dade in the Development of School-Based Management/Shared-Decision Making

Pat Tornillo has headed the United Teachers of Dade for the past twenty-five years and the main statewide teachers' union, the Florida Education Association-United, for the past nine years. Tornillo, who is in his sixties, is among the most effective educational leaders in Dade County and Florida. He also serves nationally as a vice-president of the American Federation of Teachers.

Tornillo's relationship with the local school system has gone through a remarkable transformation during his tenure as head of the union. Twenty years ago teachers struck throughout the state for increased salaries and collective bargaining rights. Early in 1968 Tornillo headed a three-week strike in Dade County that was responsible for 210 schools being closed and 5,000 teachers walking off their jobs. As a direct outcome of the strike, the Florida Supreme Court ruled that teachers had the right to bargain collectively with management over wages, hours, and working conditions. Together with Bob Martinez, head of the teachers union in Tampa (and now the governor of Florida), Tornillo helped draft a collective bargaining bill for teachers that was finally enacted into law by the state legislature on January 1, 1975 (Malafronte, 1974; "Union Chief Remains . . . ," 1986; Berger, 1988).

Since the teachers' strike in 1968, the United Teachers of Dade and Tornillo have moved away from confrontation and more toward cooperation with the school system. Tornillo has emerged as an elder educational statesman in the community. The keynote today seems to be one of collaboration rather than confrontation. Relations between Tornillo and the former superintendent, Leonard Britton (since July of 1987 the superintendent of the Los Angeles school system), were so good that the local media referred to them as "The Leonard and Pat Show" ("Union Chief Remains . . . ," 1986). Tornillo seems to be enjoying the same type of relationship with the new superintendent, Joseph Fernandez. In the corridors of the school system's central office and at the headquarters of the teachers' union, there are frequent positive references to the new "The Joe and Pat Show."

The impetus for collaboration was encouraged by recent educational reforms at the national level. Tornillo recalled in an interview in 1988 that after the federal report *A Nation at Risk* was released in 1983, he began to meet regularly with Leonard Britton: "We had breakfast or we had lunch periodically where we would talk. I would raise some things I was concerned about and he would raise some things, but we would also begin talking about what we could do together. . . . I remember at one breakfast we talked about the whole professionalization movement that came out in Carnegie—'Do you agree that what we're doing is not what we should be doing?' And I remember we agreed to come back and at dinner, maybe a week later . . . both decide whether or not we wanted to make a commitment to move in that direction. . . . After discussion we said let's do it and that was how the 'Pat and Leonard Show' was formed. And from that point on we went out and sold it, I, as the leader of the union, he as the leader of the school system. . . ." According to Tornillo: "What gave it continuity was that Leonard and I agreed that we were going to put into the collective bargaining contract the professionalization of the teaching task force and the (necessary) flexibility that was going to give us, in terms of exploring a whole variety of different avenues. . . . Once that was done, it became part of the contract and we began to get legitimacy, in terms of what was happening, and it didn't matter that Leonard left and Joe came in because Joe was part of that whole movement, in terms of the professionalization, and he embraced it totally."

Fernandez was, in fact, the individual on the administrative side most responsible for the school system's pursuing the professionalization program and what eventually became School-Based Management/Shared-Decision Making. Fernandez had become interested in the professionalization movement as a direct outgrowth of his work as a school principal at Miami's Central High School. During the 1970s, he had been involved at Central with an experimental budgeting system known as CASAS (Computer Assisted School Allocation System) that gave principals at the building level much more control over the financial resources of their schools. The program continues to be in operation today. Many years later, in 1985, when he was deputy superintendent under Leonard Britton, Fernandez got in touch with Gerald Dreyfuss who had been involved with managing the CASAS program, and talked to him about the possibility of expanding parts of the older program.

With the support of Britton, Fernandez as deputy superintendent called together a committee of principals and other administrators to develop a program that could be presented to the school board. In an interview in February 1988, Fernandez recalled that in 1985 the business community was very interested in what was going on in the schools. The Holmes and Carnegie reports proposed many of the ideas that he wanted to pursue as part of the professionalization movement—ideas being advocated by the business community as well. As he recalls the situation: "There was a lot of screaming out there in the business community that the schools had to do something different, (that) they weren't producing the kind of students, supposedly that they wanted and everything just kind of coalesced together. At the same time we had our research report, in terms of our high priority locations, and it spoke to the workplace."

In preliminary discussions, it was decided that it was crucial to maintain the stability of the faculties in the inner cities. A key part of this was to maintain good relations between principals and their staffs, as well as to improve the conditions of the workplace. According to Fernandez, things seemed to logically come together. In the same interview, Fernandez said that Tornillo "was interested in it, for his own reasons, and we got together and decided that we were going to do this. So we put a very innocuous statement in the contract. . . . I don't think people realized what they were signing when they agreed to it. We basically said that we wanted to establish a professionalization task force to look at issues dealing with professionalization. If they had questioned it they would have probably gotten cold feet . . . but they didn't question it, they signed on board. . . ."

In fact, a careful examination of the bargaining agreement put together by Tornillo and Fernandez reveals a number of crucial sections that laid the foundations for the innovations currently underway in Dade. Section 2 of the "Tentative Agreement," for example, states that "no one is more knowledgeable than teachers about the educational programs and other aspects of the teaching/learning process. The teacher's view in these matters is therefore critical. Shared-decision making at the school site, including such models as Quality Circles, with an expanded role for Faculty Councils, can significantly improve the quality of education and morale of teachers" (Office of School-Based Management, 1987, p. 29). Under Section 7, a "School-Based Management Pilot Program" was agreed to. According to its conditions: "The parties agree that professionalization of teaching can be significantly enhanced through implementation of learning-centered school models which promote shared-decision making and the utilization of collaborative problem-solving strategies. Accordingly, the school-based management pilot program is being established to initiate and implement new models for staffing, planning, and decision-making at the school level'' (Office of School-Based Management, 1987, p. 29). Elsewhere in the same document reference is made to other innovations that were eventually implemented, including the Dade Academy of the Teaching Arts (Office of School-Based Management, 1987, p. 32).

In July 1986, the School Board unanimously voted to support the development of a pilot program involving School-Based Management/Shared-Decision Making (Office of School-Based Management, 1987, p. iii). The program was revised to include thirty-two schools (elementary through high school) of the approximately 250 in the system. During the 1986–87 school year, the Professionalization of Teaching Task Force was set up to review and make recommendations concerning the School-Based Management/Shared-Decision Making Pilot. Members of the Task Force were selected by both the school system and the union. It was cochaired by Fernandez and Tornillo (Office of School-Based Management, 1987, p. iii).

On January 13, 1987, a memorandum from Fernandez and Tornillo (as cochairs of the Professionalization of Teaching Task Force) was sent to all of the principals and union stewards in the school district. The memorandum asked interested principals and faculties to submit proposals for participation in the School-Based Management/Shared-Decision Making Pilot Program. Basically, schools were asked to generate plans for undertaking innovative programs that focused on shared decision making among administration, faculty, staff, and parents; the development of structures for greater collegiality; increased community involvement; and so on. Applications and program proposals paralleled the format of the Quality Incentive Merit Pay Program (a school-based merit pay program) that was then operating throughout the county.

Fifty-three proposals were eventually received, and a total of thirty-two schools were selected for participation in the program. This number included seventeen elementary schools, ten junior high schools, four senior high schools, and one vocational technical center. The executive summaries of the proposed

programs for the schools give an idea of the types of innovations that were being proposed under the program. At Olympia
Heights Elementary School, for example, the use of Quality
Circles was proposed, together with the development of a special
bilingual and basic skills curriculum. Nontraditional staffing
techniques were to be implemented, and an energy conserva-
tion program and a "wellness" program for the staff would be
established. At Lindsey Hopkins Technical Education Center,
a schoolwide committee was established to implement changes
in curriculum and instructional techniques. At Nautilus Middle
School a shared-decision-making model involving the administration, the faculty council, and student teacher teams was set
up to focus on problems related to student attendance, motivation, and achievement. At South Miami Senior High School
a shared-decision-making model was established within the
school's departments that empowered committees to recruit and
hire new teachers. In addition, new scheduling procedures were
proposed for implementation throughout the school (Office of
the Deputy Superintendent, 1987).

It is interesting to note that in the case of nearly every
program proposed, waivers to the existing union contract had
to be made on a school by school basis. In addition, the new
programs were designed not only to include teachers and principals, but parents and students as well. Just how much the
individual character of a school and its administration could be
changed is indicated by looking at what has occurred during
the 1987–88 school year at a single site, Olympia Heights Elementary School.

Olympia Heights Elementary School has the reputation
of being an extremely well run and innovative school. Its principal, Clifford Herman, is a dynamic and at times "slightly off
the wall" educator. Several years ago, he agreed to serve barbe-
cued hamburgers to students from the roof of the school, if attendance rates went up to a certain level. On another occasion,
he agreed to let students in the school shave off his beard if daily
attendance increased. Yet in between these cases of showman-
ship, Herman is a thoughtful and innovative administrator—
one who fits the descriptions provided by the research literature
concerning the "effective" principal.

Under the School-Based Management/Shared-Decision Making program, Herman expanded an already existing Quality Circle Program he had implemented on an experimental basis several years before. Now with official sanction from the school system for his program, he expanded it. Speakers were brought in to discuss the use of Quality Circle techniques, and further training was given to teachers and members of the staff. A series of quality circles were set up, including ones for teachers dealing with the area of curriculum as well as one for members of the office staff and cafeteria. An attempt was made to integrate individuals into the decision-making process, from the janitors to the principal.

Out of these groups came decisions to develop new programs, as well as to implement many of the plans proposed as part of the original School-Based Management/Shared-Decision Making plan. An innovative science/reading program, using the *World Book Encyclopedia,* was developed by the staff; a wellness program, involving the establishment of a training and exercise room, was undertaken, with supervision being provided by a research physiologist at the University of Miami; a plan for reducing absenteeism among teachers was developed—the financial savings being put into special school projects; faculty committees were established to hire new teachers; social problems, such as gang infiltration and recruitment from the local neighborhood into the school, were addressed.

In observing Quality Circles meetings and talking to members of the staff, one gets the sense of a school that is not only well run, but one in which people, from the janitorial and cafeteria level to the teachers and principal, are involved and excited about what they are doing. In an interview, Ynes Cruz—a third grade teacher and a team leader of the Primary and Intermediate Quality Circle—described her feelings as follows: "My experience is that it is working very well for us because we have a principal who is very supportive and we have a group of teachers who are willing to work very hard towards the same goal. It is not an easy job. It takes a lot of planning. You really have to be dedicated, but it is the only chance we have ever really had to have input into the decision-making process—before then, all of the decisions were made downtown. Now we have the opportunity to work on different problems that really affect us; scheduling [and] spending the school's budget according to the priorities that we have are just [two] examples.'' Whether the school is achieving increased academic gains for its students is something that will have to be determined by further research, but from interviews and observation, it is clear that the school has managed to foster a superior working environment for both staff and children.

Greater Teacher and Community Involvement as the Key to the School-Based Management/ Shared-Decision Making Experiment

Greater teacher and community involvement have been the key to the School-Based Management/Shared-Decision Making program. In a large centralized school system such as Dade County, the attempt to place greater control of individual school sites into the hands of teachers, the principal, and the local community is of particular interest. The School-Based Management/ Shared-Decision Making program recognizes that individual schools and their staffs have highly specific needs that cannot necessarily be effectively addressed by directives from a central office administrator. Ruby Johnson, the principal of Bunche Park Elementary School, stated the problem quite clearly: ''Right now the district kind of dictates. The state and federal government tell us what to do. This program gives us an opportunity to make decisions about what we do best.'' A social studies teacher at Filer Junior High School, Ignacie Ortega, explained that ''the way I look at it, it's like a candy store and they say go ahead and pick what you want. . . . There's no reason to complain anymore if we let this opportunity pass.''

There is no doubt that there is a good deal of rhetoric and grandstanding going on as part of the innovative programs that are being set up in Dade County. The superintendent has a great deal to gain if these programs are perceived in a positive light by the community, as does the teachers' union. Despite all the hoopla and statements about ''innovation'' and ''improvement,'' one does get the sense that a number of very important changes are taking place—ones that have the potential to be not only long lasting but of national importance. In the context of School-Based Management/Shared-Decision Making, many of these changes are at a very basic level and involve things as simple as differentiated staffing or alternative scheduling techniques. At Palmetto Elementary School, for example, funds normally used for hiring a teacher to teach students Spanish were used instead to pay the Berlitz School of Language to provide instruction to students. The feeling on the part of the teachers and the principal was that better instruction might be possible using Berlitz than more traditional methods. If the experiment does not work, then the school can try a more traditional approach to Spanish instruction or experiment with a different type of innovation that can address the same problem. Also at Palmetto Elementary School, teachers have given up their planning time in order to reduce class size during basic-skills instruction.

Beyond innovations at the school level, a number of special programs are going on in the district that are of particular interest. These are loosely included as part of the School-Based Management/Shared-Decision Making program, but are in fact usually operating independently of it. These innovations, which include Satellite Schools, Saturday Morning Schools, the Dade Academy of the Teaching Arts (DATA), the Partners in Education Program (PIE), and the Teacher Recruitment Internship Program (TRIP), are among just a few of the interesting experiments that deserve careful attention for possible implementation in other school sites across the country.

Satellite Learning Centers

In June 1987, at a Chamber of Commerce meeting, Superintendent Fernandez introduced the possibility of setting up a network of satellite early learning centers in conjunction with local businesses. These would be classrooms set up to operate and function at actual business sites. Parents working for a corporation or business would be able to have their children attend the school. The building's maintenance and insurance would be paid for

by the corporate or business sponsor. The school would be run
by the school system as a regular public classroom.

The project is currently being tried on a pilot basis at the
International Headquarters of American Bankers Insurance
Groups. American Bankers has approximately 1,000 employees
and is among the largest businesses in the southern part of the
county. Since 1984, it has been running a highly successful
preschool program for its employees and expanded it recently
to accommodate ninety children from six weeks to six years
of age.

American Bankers had become convinced through its
preschool program that setting up schools for the children of
employees made sense not only for morale, but from a financial point of view. In an interview, in March 1988, Philip
Sharkey—senior vice-president for human resources—stated
that the overall annual employee turnover rate is 17.6 percent
and is only 4.2 percent for those with children attending the
company's preschool center. Absenteeism has been reduced 30
percent.

For the 1987–88 school year, American Bankers agreed
with the school system to set up a kindergarten class for the
children of their employees. Housed in a portable school building
on adjacent public high school property, the experiment has been
well received by employees, who talk about having more time
to spend with their children, better relationships with the teacher,
and fewer worries should there be an emergency and they need
to leave work.

A building that will house kindergarten and first and second grade classrooms is currently being constructed by American
Bankers on its grounds. Sharkey says that from a corporate point
of view the investment in the building makes a great deal of
sense, since it cuts down on the need for American Bankers to
have to recruit and train as many new workers as they had to
in the past. The availability of day care, as well as the continuation of classes into the early elementary school years, represents
an important recruiting tool.

When asked if there is a potential for the American Bankers management to impose itself on what takes place in the

school, Sharkey explained that the school runs entirely separately from the business. In fact, when a request was made by the author to visit the school, it was explained that it would be necessary to contact the school system for permission to visit rather than American Bankers. According to Superintendent Fernandez, the pilot kindergarten class is among the most racially and ethnically mixed populations to be found in the county.

It is interesting to note that the teacher assigned to the project, Roberta Kaiser, will be given a special title as lead teacher when the program starts in its new school building this fall. While record keeping and other types of administrative tasks for the school will be done through a local elementary school, the day-to-day operation of the school will be under the supervision of the lead teacher. This new model was jointly developed by the union and the school system and will be extremely interesting to observe as it develops.

In a school system that is short on space, wanting to meet the needs of the business community, and concerned about greater interaction and contact between teachers and parents, the satellite school program is clearly a promising innovation. At present, the school system has contacted the chief executive officers of 150 corporations about the program and 11 of them have indicated an interest in setting up satellite programs—including Barnett Bank, Mount Sinai Hospital, and the Miami International Airport—(O'Hara, 1988, p. 48).

Saturday Schools

An interesting example of a single-school innovation that has spread to other schools in the district is Charles Drew Elementary School's Saturday morning tutorial program. Drew, which is a predominantly black inner-city school, established tutoring sessions for grades 1–6 every Saturday morning from 9:00 to 12:00. The program is strictly voluntary and is intended to provide children with additional help in basic skills such as mathematics, reading, and writing. Regular teachers are used in the program and paid for their extra work.

Initially, 200 of the school's 550 students participated in the program. Its success led other inner-city schools to adopt the same program. Taking advantage of a federally funded program to prevent dropouts, a total of sixty-seven schools throughout the county followed Drew's example and set up Saturday programs or supplemental after-school programs. Schools were selected for the federal funding program on the basis of having the highest proportion of students on free or reduced lunches—free and reduced lunch being an indication of the socioeconomic level of families. A total of about $20,000 was made available for each of the schools in the program, to cover the hiring of janitorial assistance, teachers, and teacher aides. Each school could select up to 60 students who had scored low on standardized tests such as the Stanford Achievement to participate in the program (Fernandez, 1987).

Dade Academy of the Teaching Arts

Another interesting innovation to come out of the School-Based Management/Shared-Decision Making program in Dade County has been the Dade Academy of the Teaching Arts (DATA). DATA is a nine-week program involving teachers in a series of seminars and clinics in which they are assigned as part of a "mini-sabbatical" to Miami Beach Senior High School. In the fall of 1987, eight specially selected teachers—experts in high school English, mathematics, social studies, and science—were brought to Miami Beach Senior High School to work as mentors with other teachers. Each of these eight mentor teachers had two teachers assigned to work with them during each of the four nine-week grading periods. While teaching a reduced load of regular classes, each mentor and his or her "externs" have the opportunity to develop a special research project, develop innovative methods of teaching, and trade ideas and techniques. DATA is run collaboratively by the school system and the teachers' union with the participation of consultants from local colleges and universities. A teacher/director, Eileen Campbell, heads up the day-to-day operation of the program.

The DATA program was based on a similar model used in the Pittsburgh school system. It has been adapted to the particular needs and programs of the Dade County system and fits into the union and school system's desire to expand the professional opportunities open to classroom teachers. At present, the program is limited to a relatively small group of specially selected teachers. In order to have a significant impact on the school system, the program will have to be expanded considerably.

Partners in Education (PIE)

In an attempt to address some of the serious problems confronting inner-city schools in the district, Superintendent Fernandez established the Partners in Education (PIE). Modeled after the School-Based Management and Shared-Decision Making program, the PIE program is a joint program of the school system and the Urban League of Greater Miami, the United Teachers of Dade, Miami Dade Community College, and the Mitchell Wolfson Senior Foundation. Eleven inner-city schools were chosen for the program.

In each school participating in the program, a five-member committee, consisting of a principal, an assistant principal, a union representative, and two teachers elected by the school faculty developed programs for their schools. Limited grant support was provided to implement the programs in each of the schools. At Olinda Elementary School, parent clubs were organized. At Orchard Villa Elementary School, a parent choir and a dial-a-ride service in order to help get parents out to school events were established. At Miami Northwestern High School, a dollars-for-grades scholarship program was established, in which sophomores who achieve certain levels of academic performance are given money to put into a college scholarship fund.

Other Innovations in the Dade County Public Schools

Other innovations being implemented in the Dade County Public Schools include the Teacher Recruitment Internship Program (TRIP), a collaborative program between the University of Miami and the school system. In this program, individuals with a four-year degree in a field outside of education may begin to teach with a reduced work load under the supervision of a master teacher while continuing to take course work toward a master's degree in education at the university. The project, which is part of a national program sponsored by the American Federation of Teachers, has the potential to contribute significantly to an expanded role for master or lead teachers in the training of beginning teachers. A total of approximately thirty students are enrolled in this program on a pilot basis. Funds have been approved for its continuation and expansion in the coming year.

As part of the superintendent's attempt to recruit the best teachers possible for Miami's inner-city schools, an agreement has been drawn up between the University of Miami and the school district that will provide teachers with free tuition to work on both a master's and a doctoral degree provided they agree to continue to work at their assigned inner-city school for at least five years.

Conclusion

Superintendent Fernandez, representing the school system, and Pat Tornillo, as head of the teachers' union, have invested not only a great deal of energy but their reputations on the success of School-Based Management/Shared-Decision Making in Dade County. In fact, what they are pursuing is a greatly expanded role for parents, administrators, and specific teachers in their schools. Their efforts have the conscious purpose of expanding the professional role and status of teachers. In this sense, they are redefining many of the traditional structures found within most schools. The experiment has been given a three-year trial period. Fernandez believes that the program is almost certainly here to stay. As of February 1989, fifty additional schools have participated in the program. As to expanding the program to the entire system, Fernandez maintains that the program will need to be piloted for a much longer time and evaluation results reviewed before it is adopted on a larger basis. With slightly over 30 percent of the schools in the district participating, there are sufficient numbers to determine the effectiveness of the program. This will only be possible, however, as the pilot program advances into its third year and possibly beyond.

Even if the Dade County Public Schools' current experiments prove less successful than is hoped, the diversity of highly original programs bears careful watching. While some will undoubtedly fail, others should succeed. Those that do will provide models for innovation and reform for other school districts throughout the country. Finally, it should be noted that in the Dade County Public Schools the possibility for innovation and reform exists because of the cooperation and joint planning between the school system and the teachers' union. This type of joint effort—one involving labor leadership and school management working together—is a new phenomenon and of tremendous importance to the future of American education.

11

Improving Quality of Work Life to Achieve Excellence in Education: The Duluth, Minnesota, School System

by David C. Helms

In recent years, American industry has been borrowing strategies from its foreign competitors to improve its work effectiveness. Concepts of participative management, which encourage worker participation in decision making, and quality of work life circles, which provide workers with a decision-influencing role, are cases in point. Now, some public school districts have begun to borrow these same strategies from American industry to help teachers and management work together in their effort to improve education.

The general purpose of this chapter is to describe the experience of the Duluth public school system with participative management and quality of work life circles (PM/QWL), which are being employed by the district to renew and reform the working relationship of teachers and management and their joint conduct of the educational process. More specifically, the objectives of this chapter are to (1) describe the origin and nature of PM/QWL in Duluth and the methods that have been employed to involve teachers in decision-making processes, (2) explain the roles and responsibilities of a variety of individuals and groups involved in the use of these methods, and (3) provide information on the effects of and prospects for PM/QWL in the Duluth school system

Trauma, Renewal and Research, and Reform

The current collaborative effort to improve education and the work life of educators in the Duluth public schools began as a reaction to a period of confrontation between teachers and management. The collaboration found life in the resolve of the antagonists to rise above their adversarial struggle and to find better ways and means of working together toward their common purpose, providing education for the children of Duluth.

The Teachers' Strike of 1983.   Most teachers, administrators and supervisors, and board members agree today on three points: (1) the strike of 1983 was a bitter, unhappy affair that no one wants to repeat; (2) the dissatisfaction teachers felt about their poorly respected professional status, according to their own perceptions, was the real cause of the strike and not the money issues reported at the time; and (3) the remedy for low staff morale had to include a new way for teachers and management to work together to improve the quality of work life for all.

Renewal and Research.   Pursuant to their contractual commitment, management and union, together, established a labor-management committee to find a new working relationship. The committee consisted of two school board members, the superintendent, the assistant superintendent for instruction, the assistant superintendent for buisness affairs, the director of personnel, two building principals, the executive board of the Duluth Federation of Teachers (DFT), and the district's communications facilitator (who is also a teacher).

Hoping for an early implementation of their new process, whatever it might be, the committee sought help outside the district. There was no point to reinventing the proverbial wheel, and other districts that had already traveled this path could save them much start-up pain. The search put them in touch with many educators in many parts of the country to little avail. The concept of collaboration among colleagues was certainly not new, but few districts or schools had made much progress with a sustained districtwide process that matched the committee's aspirations. Eventually, the committee resorted to developing its own model of a collaborative process. The committee acknowledges that significant guidance was obtained from the Duluth Labor-Management Council. The council is funded by local employers and unions and is dedicated to the improvement of labor-management relations in the Duluth area. The Duluth school system is one of the important public agencies that participates in the council. Strategies and techniques of collaborative action were also borrowed from a variety of other sources, especially from the Minnesota Educational Effectiveness Program (MEEP), a state program that provides training to school districts. Some Duluth educators stress the importance to PM/QWL of staff training in the team-building and problem-solving processes that MEEP provided to the district. According to Janet Olson, a principal at Woodland Junior High School, "MEEP stresses grassroot decision making and process training, which enable us to work together to make decisions."

Reform. Gradually, as its efforts went forward, the district's labor-management committee was converted to the Quality of Work Life Steering Committee. Based on the concepts, strategies, and techniques assembled through its search and development efforts, the committee was able to compose (1) a philosophy, and (2) a set of rules, procedures, and guidelines to guide and facilitate a Participative Management/Quality of Work Life process. The school board adopted the philosophy as revised policy in September 1984 and the rules, procedures, and guidelines as regulation in November 1984.

Philosophy. Forms of participative management, common to many districts, existed in the Duluth system for several years prior to the emergence of PM/QWL. According to a paper prepared by the superintendent and the district communications facilitator (Moeser and Golen, 1987, p. 2), "Efforts had been made to involve staff in the budgeting process on the district level; individual schools had formed senates and elected staff for the purpose of determining building-level objectives and budgets; and a variety of advisory committees had been established." There was not, however, a systematic process operating on a continuing basis that opened the broad spectrum of district operations to review and recommendations by staff on their own initiative and assured staff of due process attention to their recommendations.

The 1984 revision of board philosophy signaled the board's intention to work for a correction of these deficiencies by stating its conviction that the only way the goal of excellence "may be achieved is through pooling the talent and wisdom of all the employees of the district." Then the board went on to make it the "policy of the district that programs of employee involvement and participation in problem solving and decision making processes shall be encouraged." The board seemed to recognize that this might not be an easy task, and went on to make explicit its understanding that "excellence in management shall be understood to be that management which: encourages participation and creativity among staff, builds commitment to shared goals, structures employee involvement so employees are routinely involved in decisions which affect them, sets a high priority on advocating for ideas generated by subordinates, develops a strong sense of trust and collegiality among all staff members in pursuit of the goal of excellence" (Golen, 1987, p. 20).

Rules, Procedures, and Guidelines. But, a philosophy without—or with only rudimentary—rules, procedures, and guidelines to aid its implementation in practice is apt to be regarded by those it's meant to guide as little more than a ceremonial gesture. To assure that PM/QWL would be an appropriate implementation of the collaborative decision-making process that everyone wanted, the board-adopted regulations on rules, procedures, and guidelines provided specific directions for (1) the establishment of a districtwide steering committee and building-level problem-solving groups, (2) the organization and standards of problem-solving groups, and (3) methodology/ techniques to be employed by the problem-solving groups. In brief, the regulation calls for the districtwide steering committee to (1) nurture the growth and development of participative management at the school level, (2) assist school building groups by providing guidance, direction, and training in group problem-solving techniques, and (3) engage in identifying and solving problems that are of concern to employees on a districtwide basis. With respect to the school groups, in brief again, each is to establish a problem-solving group that includes the principal, the union steward or stewards, and volunteers selected by employees of the building. The principal and the union steward or stewards are not permitted to serve as chair for the group. Neither do they need to serve on all subcommittees that may be established. The membership, other than the principal and steward or stewards, is to rotate periodically. The groups will work on objective problems only, never on problem personalities. Matters that have been settled by contract or grievance process or are in negotiation are not appropriate topics for discussion. School building groups will submit reports and recommendations to the districtwide steering committee as well as to administration and staff in their own buildings. Decisions will be announced by someone other than the principal or steward, and all decisions will be accompanied by a full explanation.

The regulation also sets out the steps of the problem-solving method to be used by the groups: (1) identify the problem, (2) gather information on the problem, (3) generate solutions, (4) evaluate solutions, (5) reach consensus on the best solution, and (6) implement the decision when this is the prerogative of the group, or make a recommendation or report to the appropriate decision maker or to the districtwide steering committee (Golen, 1987, pp. 21–24).

The Duluth Education System and PM/QWL

Although PM/QWL is changing the Duluth Public Schools, it must be recognized that PM/QWL is only one element, albeit a key element, among a complex set of influences that shape the way education is conducted in Duluth. Sometimes these influences seem to be mutually supporting; at other times they appear to be in conflict. Almost always, they interact. Doubtless, there are lessons from the Duluth PM/QWL experience that can profitably enlighten other districts and schools in search of their own way to empower teachers. But, to be genuinely useful, these lessons need to carefully note the interactions between QWL and the context in which it is being implemented.

The City of Duluth.   The larger contexts for Duluth educators and students are the school district and the city. Duluth is the third largest city in Minnesota, with a population of over 84,000, as well as a regional cultural, educational, banking, retail, medical, and entertainment center serving some 750,000 people in northern Minnesota, northern Wisconsin, northern Michigan, and Ontario, Canada.

Economically, Duluth benefits from several significant new manufacturing and retail investments in the area. However, recent economic history here has been mostly a tale of struggle against the effects of low-priced imports of foreign iron ore, the downsizing of the steel industry, the recession in agriculture, and the collapse of land values.

Education ranks high in Duluth and the greater Duluth-Superior, Wisconsin, area. Important branches of the state universities of Minnesota and Wisconsin as well as other institutions of higher education are located here. The citizens of Duluth take special pride in claiming that more local college scholarships are available here per high school graduate than in any other community in the United States.

The School System.   Independent School District No. 709, the official designation of the Duluth public school system, serves approximately 15,000 students in its eighteen elementary schools, four junior high schools, three senior high schools, vocational institute, secondary vocational center, and a variety of alternative programs for special needs students. The $80,000,000 budget in 1987–88 is supporting over 2,000 employees, of which 1,015 are teachers. The teachers are represented by a strong union, the Duluth Federation of Teachers (DFT), which actively works to improve instruction as well as to improve working conditions for the teachers.

To the extent that standardized test scores are indicative of the quality of education, it is significant that the children of the district regularly score above the national average on such tests. More important, over 60 percent of Duluth students go on to college, and many of these go on to graduate schools. Twenty percent of high school graduates actually receive scholarship awards.

To an outsider, it appears that educators and students in the schools are representative of the community from which they come. They are predominantly white and from a working class constituency of mostly moderate means, which has a strong belief in the need of every citizen for a good education. District staff also seem much like members of an extended family in that they sometimes have fierce, if not terminal, disagreements, but always there is the hope for healing that is rooted in their common base values. In such family-like tiffs, the most pressing need may be for an equitable means of bringing disputants together. Such is the nature and promise of PM/QWL.

Glimpses of the Circles

In-depth discussions with participants have provided some insights into the understandings, assessments, and hopes of those involved with the PM/QWL process. Some impressions gathered from observations and discussions are reported below.

Districtwide Steering Committee. In Duluth, district decison making is not beyond the reach of teachers who are effectively represented at the district level. They have this representation through the district quality circle known as the districtwide steering committee.

The districtwide steering committee has eighteen members. Unlike the school and program circles, which are made up of popularly chosen representatives from work groups or caucuses, the membership of the steering committee is determined by position and appointment. Two members of the board are on the committee, including the board chair and the chair of the board's personnel committee. The administration contingent includes the superintendent and his appointees: the two assistant superintendents for business and instruction, the director of personnel, the two directors of secondary and elementary education, a high school principal, and an elementary school principal. Six people make up the teachers' contingent: the president of the DFT and five teachers appointed by the president and approved by the local's executive committee.

Issues that are consistent across schools or programs in the district are legitimate grist for the steering committee agenda, with the exception of those that are settled by contract or that are in negotiation. This provision has, no doubt, helped to get the circles started without opening old wounds or threatening the official bargaining process, but the provision also has removed many substantive issues from consideration. The superintendent knows this and hopes that the exclusionary provision will one day be withdrawn. The union knows this, too, and also hopes that one day all matters will be open for discussion in all quality circles. But this is not likely to happen until an orderly way can be found to do so without confounding PM/QWL discussions, negotiations, and the contract.

In one example of a districtwide steering committee meeting, discussion focused on a detailed report on The Duluth Plan (Teacher Development Committee, 1987). The plan, which was developed by the teacher development committee (TDC) in collaboration with the curriculum director and her staff, sets out a full program and process of staff development for teachers based on the latest research findings and local evaluations of instruction. Additionally, the plan assigns responsibilities for its implementation to the district, the TDC, and the union. Despite the care and thoroughness with which the plan was developed, some steering committee members questioned the relationship of the plan to current district policy and practice and agreed to send the plan and the minutes of that day's meeting to the TDC with instructions that the TDC clarify its own intentions.

The meeting could not have been very satisfying to impatient reformers on the steering committee. The extended consideration of The Duluth Plan consumed almost all the meeting time, and the steering committee was obliged to roll over a number of agenda items to its next meeting. Moreover, this seems to be a common occurrence in steering committee meetings, judging from the comments of some members. It was also

evident that certain gaps exist in the processes both for communicating PM/QWL recommendations and for moving them
into practice. Similarly, it seems that a number of overlaps exist between the domain being staked out for PM/QWL and a
variety of structures and operations in the current domain of
management. Finally, it was difficult not to notice the tenseness
of a number of participants as the ebb and flow of discussion
touched the special interests of first one and then another of the
committee members. Still, one had to be impressed with the
fact that this group of teachers, administrators, and board
members was working intently and together, as professionals,
on issues of major concern to all educators and the community:
instruction, teacher evaluation, staff development, and educational improvement (Teacher Development Committee, 1987).
The Duluth school community is also exploring ways to develop
a more participative budget process in the district. A recently
appointed committee, including district, union, and school representatives, and parents, is studying initiatives for increasing
school-level control over financial resources.

At the School Level.   People in a position to know how
things are going in the district mostly share the opinion that
PM/QWL is having greater success in the schools than at the
district level. But, they hasten to add, success isn't uniform across
schools. It is their opinion that the principal's commitment to
the participative process appears to be the variable that most
affects the degree of success. Administrators who find PM/QWL
a bit strange and, for them, uncomfortable, tend not to be proactive supporters of participative decision making. Administrators who have found PM/QWL an excellent way to enlist
teachers in the solution of problems that slow their school's improvement tend to emphasize implementation of the process—
and infuse it with their own enthusiasm.

Woodland Junior High School.   After only a short con-
versation with Janet Olson, principal of the Woodland Junior
High School, one has a strong impression that this person likes
the decision-making role, is good at it, and is, at the same

time, a key reason why Woodland is considered an outstanding PM/QWL success story. Olson described how "QWWL" (Quality of Woodland Work Life) made her job easier by providing her with a method for delegating some of her responsibilities to willing colleagues. According to her, the game has changed; now it is wise for principals to be more subtle leaders. Effective tools of the principal in the new game are more likely to be anticipation, enthusiasm, affiliation, suggestion, and conflict resolution rather than out-in-front, directive leadership.

It is evident that this principal has studied PM/QWL well and is confident that, with appropriate support from her, the process can be a surer, more pleasant means of achieving important, common goals. Five major goals or priorities the QWWL group agreed on during the 1987–88 school year are to: (1) train new QWWL members and staff members new to Woodland in brainstorming, consensus building, and the fifteen Characteristics of School Effectiveness, (2) provide staff in-service and follow-up to improve efficiency, (3) increase time for professional involvement, (4) emphasize cooperatively established educational goals (written by staff, students, and parents) based on Woodland's mission statements, and (5) create more flexibility in programming to meet the needs of junior high students. According to Olson, PM/QWL is designed to promote sharing in decision making and implementation, and the circles will take pride in their participation in the outcomes of their work. She explains that success for the principal in the new process varies directly with the degree of teacher participation and, inversely, with the directiveness of the principal's leadership.

Karen Alfonsi, teacher at Woodland and past chair of its PM/QWL circle, appears to be a friend and strong supporter of the principal, a fellow booster of the participative process, and another reason why PM/QWL has been so successful at their school. While Olson and Alfonsi agree that the teachers like the principles of PM/QWL and are pleased with its implementation so far, Olson points out that at Woodland the agreement did not come easily: "We fought over processes and issues until the conflicts were resolved in a mutually satisfactory manner. This took considerable tolerance for conflict and considerable skill in conflict resolution from all those involved. Through the process we maintained respect and our good fights changed the way we work together.'' According to the two women, 80 percent of the staff participate in the process and a realistic estimate of potential participation is 100 percent. Participation, in their opinion, has made the staff believe that they really do influence decisions that vitally affect their life and work. As a consequence, the two leaders believe that teachers are more enthusiastic about their work and students benefit from the more positive climate that has resulted.

"The process we have developed is one that can change and evolve to deal with new problems," Olson stresses. "We keep the process going by in-servicing new staff and practicing the skills in our biweekly QWL meetings."

Both women are also convinced that the teachers believe, as they do, that staff has used the PM/QWL process to attack and resolve significant problems. One of the most pressing concerns, according to members of the school's QWWL group, is the need for increased time for collaborative planning and for developing collegial relationships among staff and administration. The group has implemented, on a limited basis, a "professional activity assignment" (PAA) as a replacement for the traditional sixth-period assignment, such as study hall or cafeteria supervision. The QWWL group will review the use of the PAA to see what modifications may be needed and will report back to the districtwide QWL Steering Committee regarding results and/or recommendations.

With district permission, Janet Olson and Karen Alfonsi both believe that their school could take on more significant budgeting and instruction problems. Indeed, both believe that through PM/QWL, staff could virtually run the school, although they admit that there would be a time problem if they had to implement all their own recommendations. Even if they could use the time now spent on nonteaching assignments there might not be sufficient time to accomplish all the work. They do not perceive, however, that staff running their own school would ultimately render the principalship obsolete, only different. The principal would need to be an excellent facilitator and an economizer of time. Janet Olson, in fact, would regard the opportunity for staff to run the school as further empowerment of the principal.

Views from Management

The Superintendent. District Superintendent Elliott Moeser is quick to respond, when asked, that the role of PM/QWL is "to eliminate the 'them versus us' attitude" in this district, especially with respect to administrators and teachers. It is the superintendent's view that administrators have been trained to be decision makers, that they like this role and try to be good at it. But, he explains with some firmness, times have changed and teachers have changed. "Increasingly, teachers see themselves as professionals, and they want a piece of the action. QWL is an attempt to bring administrators and teachers together, to end a terrible grievance history."

Elliott Moeser knows very well that much work needs to be done before the board will have the district it envisions in its philosophy. His comments indicate that he knows much remains to be done just to get PM/QWL implemented. Still, he is pleased with what has been accomplished, and he believes that teachers are feeling better about their role and the efforts that are being made to include them in the district's decision making. He is especially proud to point to the precipitous decline in grievances from 152 in 1984 to only 15 in 1986.

Although relations between the board and the teachers are much better now, Moeser is concerned that relations between middle management and the teachers are not as good as he would like. Principals are the main group at the middle-management level, and he finds the principals skeptical about the need and the promise of PM/QWL. Since teachers and principals are on the instructional front line together, there is reason for Elliott Moeser's concern.

Since the board considers participative management essential for the success of PM/QWL, the district is looking for management employees who will improve the climate for participation in the district. One way to do this is to hire administrators who are already favorably disposed to a participative style. It has been suggested that Elliott Moeser's apparent commitment to participative management was the board's principal reason for signing him as superintendent.

From his own perspective, the superintendent observes that management retirements presently provide excellent opportunities to bring in people with the commitment and talent for participative management. It has also been suggested that some administrators who found participative decision making unacceptable were encouraged in their decisions to resign.

The question of the importance of PM/QWL impact on district and school operations seems more difficult for Moeser. He's quick to say that bringing teachers into the decision-making process and reducing divisiveness has been a very significant accomplishment. He is less clear about significant decision outcomes for the district as a consequence of this accomplishment. He asserts that the districtwide steering committee has provided an important forum for discussions of vital issues such as the leadership role of principals and the participation of teachers in curriculum decisions. And he feels sure that the quality circles at the school and program levels have made progress in dealing with problems that are important to their colleagues.

As yet, however, QWL deliberations have not been an important influence on the two issues he believes are most important to teachers: a role in curriculum development and representation in the superintendent's cabinet. These kinds of concerns will receive important treatment in the QWL process in the future, he believes, and he is of the opinion that all topics should be eligible for PM/QWL consideration, including provisions of the teachers' contract and issues in negotiation.

The superintendent also concedes that teachers have not been, until now, an important factor in the implementation of decisions which their quality circles have recommended. Making it possible for teachers to take an implementation role is a difficult challenge, but not insoluble. Overall, the superintendent seems to believe that PM/QWL is the most important game in town, that it has made substantial progress, and that it will be crucially important to the future of the Duluth public schools.

The School Board. Susan Banovetz, board chair, makes clear that "the board is very supportive of PM/QWL," and so is Banovetz, who explains that four years ago she ran for election on a PM/QWL platform. She "felt the void between teachers and administrators led to the bitter strike, and, somehow, the two sides needed to be brought together." According to Banovetz, Marvin Swanson, the former director of personnel, first had the idea for a QWL process in Duluth. After discussing it with the union, he brought the idea to her attention, and she liked it. She thought it might be the way to get the teachers and the management to work together.

The chair believes, like others, that money was not the crucial issue that separated teachers and management in 1983. Rather, the state's rescinding of $6 million of budgeted district funds precipitated the crisis that split teachers and management, she explains. In the face of the district's shortfall, district leadership decided that personnel layoffs were necessary. The dissatisfaction teachers were feeling about their very limited role in district decision making was exacerbated by the new expectation that they would cooperate with the leadership's layoff solution. The stress was too much, and the bitter strike ensued.

The board chair does not claim that PM/QWL has yet had a marked influence on the major issues before the district as she sees them: stability of state funding, working conditions in the schools, and district organization. She believes it is too early to expect a lot because they are still learning to use the process. She is convinced that "QWL has done much to alleviate stress and that it has created a sense of ownership among teachers. It does work.

"Nevertheless, there are problems that need attention," according to the chair. The QWL process "seems cumbersome, and there is some danger that the steering committee will be perceived as a power center—above the building committees." Additionally, she recognizes "some difficulty with the line between QWL issues and negotiations." There are also costs associated with QWL, many of which she believes are not charged as such. As a budget item, she guesses that QWL costs about $20,000.

From Banovetz's perspective, QWL is a strategy and process to facilitate teacher participation in district and school decision making. But success of the process, in her view, is dependent in large measure on a management that is disposed toward, and nurturing of, participatory decision making.

Jean Olson is a former chair of the school board, and she has a special interest in PM/QWL, which reflects her training in psychotherapy. She firmly believes that people are more effective when they are given the opportunity and the training to solve their own problems.

Asked how QWL got started in the district and how she sees it performing, Olson states that PM/QWL was a union proposal, and "the board accepted the idea because it matched what they saw as their need." Her further comments make it clear that, in her opinion, bringing teachers into the decision-making process was necessary to heal the breach between the teachers and the district. She goes further, saying, "One of the real contributions of QWL is the identification of issues that need attention," indicating, perhaps, that she feels the teachers are more likely to identify the district's real needs.

One of the most pressing needs of PM/QWL is more training for administrators, says Olson. "People who are already disposed to participatory management make it easier, but principals who do best are the ones who received the effective schools training (team building and problem solving). Administrators can be changed by clear expectations from the board and training." She is firm on the point.

Speculating on the ultimate possibilities of PM/QWL, Jean Olson says, "I don't believe a fully implemented QWL necessarily means a greater management role for the board." She further explains that she doesn't think the board and the teachers could or should run the district without help from administrators. She adds that administrators are held accountable under law for some of their responsibilities, and the proper "role of the board is to oversee the process, to be the guardian for the district," not its administrative arm. But, she does feel strongly that "a great many more school operations could be managed more effectively through the QWL process."

The Union.   Frank Wanner is the president of the Duluth Federation of Teachers, and he, like the superintendent and the board members, believes that the most important objective of PM/QWL is to "get rid of the us/them feeling." Although it is his opinion that the union suggested the PM/QWL idea, he concedes that it is not working perfectly. Nevertheless, he says that "we'll stick with it," and says it in the manner of one who has a significant stake in the game.

According to Wanner, the process is working better in the schools than at the district level. But later he states that middle management (mostly building principals) is attempting to subvert the process. Until this point, he has stated his case with some emotion, and has made little effort to differentiate among schools or principals. But, as he goes on, he acknowledges that some schools are doing well and some principals are supportive of PM/QWL. Eventually he observes that "teachers do like the idea of QWL; they see it as part of work life, part of their expectations." In the QWL setting, he says, "principals should be facilitators, not leaders."

He turns his thoughts to the future, and his comments appear to echo his column in the DFT's newsletter (Wanner, 1987). They suggest that he sees PM/QWL as part of a much larger union plan for the future, one shaped by these DFT long-term goals: (1) raise salaries, (2) improve levels of benefits, (3) enfranchise teachers in decision making, (4) improve opportunities for professional growth and exploration.

The column recognizes that "the first two goals are really one and the same," and "designed to make the system competitive in attracting and retaining top notch persons." The last two goals represent opportunities for teachers "to be masters of their own destiny." According to the president, "teachers and administrators need to be partners in the educational process, in making decisions." Teachers also want "the chance to work on curriculum, to help new or troubled teachers, to do research, to work with universities, and to have these opportunities without completely leaving the classroom."

Further into his column, Frank Wanner explains that the DFT proposal to eliminate sixth-period nonteaching assignments (to free school time for participation in decision making and implementation) is in keeping with their long-term goals. "So is our work on the 'Duluth Plan,' which deals with internship, mentoring, and peer assistance and evaluation, and our ongoing development of QWL. Both of these came about as the result of previous negotiations. Part of our present proposal is to incorporate both into contract language." Negotiations clearly are a critical function of the union, in Wanner's opinion. The union president regards PM/QWL as an important part, but only a part, of a larger improvement process—a belief that is also held by the school board chair.

In the perspective of the school board chair, as noted earlier, PM/QWL needs a participative management environment in which to operate. In the perspective of the union president, PM/QWL needs the back-up support of negotiations and contract language to be effective. Indeed, Frank Wanner says it is his vision that one day quality circles will surface, discuss, and resolve most issues. At that time, negotiations will be necessary only as a device of last resort, something to turn to when PM/QWL recommendations have been rejected.

Gerald Brown is the current executive secretary of DFT and its past president, and, when asked about the most pressing concerns of teachers, he doesn't hesitate to day "QWL." He goes on to explain that one concern of teachers and their union is for PM/QWL to receive the acceptance of administration; another concern is for everyone to participate in the process and learn how to make it effective.

Of course, Brown goes on, there must be time for the circles to meet and discuss problems and to develop their recommendations. Under agreement with the administration, members of quality circles are freed, at least once a month, from sixth-period nonteaching assignments to participate in circle meetings. When these meetings run over the allotted hour and past the end of the teachers' school day, the agreement permits the PM/QWL participants to accumulate equivalent compensatory time.

Teachers are using the PM/QWL process to discuss a range of day-to-day concerns in their lives, and, as a result, many concerns have been disposed of, according to the executive secretary. Mostly, these concerns involve nonteaching activities, such as assignments before and after school hours, bus duty, lunch duty, and parent conferences. Now the teachers are getting into professional development areas, as well, including what is taught and how. The secretary observes, however, that deliberations of the quality circles do occasionally overlap with those of other committees of the district when professional development is the topic. Presently, this is the case with the teacher development committee (TDC), which the district established pursuant to its contract with DFT. Gerald Brown says the union is giving thought to merging TDC and PM/QWL.

The union secretary is well aware that one implication of QWL is a new role for administrators, but he isn't sure what the role should ultimately be. Certainly, he feels there is a pressing need now for administrators to facilitate implementation of decisions made in the PM/QWL process. And much time beyond what is provided for meetings would be required if teachers were to take the major responsibility for implementation. He realizes that freeing all teachers from all nonteaching assignments could be interpreted as a start toward a totally PM/QWL operated school. Although he admits to some passing speculation on this possibility, he and the union are much more concerned, for now, with the more mundane tasks of getting PM/QWL well implemented and institutionalized. Indeed, he is not sure teachers could be freed sufficiently to run a school without radical changes in school organization and staffing and the assistance of new technologies.

Communications Facilitator. Leonard Golen is the district communications facilitator. He is also the district's PM/QWL facilitator. To an outsider, he seems to function as a true administrator. He and Mary Greene, his secretary (more an editor/production manager), have an office in the central office building on the same floor and only a few steps from the superintendent's office. Both Golen and Greene appear to have excellent relations with all the administrators, and Golen actually reports to the superintendent. But Golen, in truth, is a teacher in good standing with the teachers' bargaining unit, the DFT. This information might only have curiosity value if it were not for the fact that, on closer examination, both the position of facilitator and Golen's unique presence in the position appear to be significant factors in the success of PM/QWL in Duluth.

As communications facilitator for the district, Golen is continually involved with a wide range of activities, such as regular and irregular publications to the community, press announcements, awards ceremonies, and television productions. As PM/QWL facilitator he is the listening post for the district, always alert to developments in the schools, to the concerns of the board and the management, and to the steering committee (the district's quality circle). But he isn't just listening; frequently he must move the information on, sometimes directly, sometimes subtly, to those who need to know.

Golen must often respond in person in a variety of roles: host to curious visitors, sympathetic listener, investigator, emissary, and PM/QWL trainer. In the latter role, he is responsible for helping to maintain a consistent process districtwide by providing training for school and program groups, based on the "Rules, Procedures and Guidelines" approved by the school board. An observer of PM/QWL in Duluth comes quickly to the conclusion that implementing the process districtwide requires a lot of facilitation. Moreover, the job needs to be done by someone who has the trust and respect of all interest groups, knows the district and his or her job thoroughly, is committed to the process, is sensitive and adroit in dealing with people, is a tireless worker, is cool in a crisis, and has strong back-up assistance in his or her own office.

Progress and Promise

For all practical purposes PM/QWL has been successfully installed in the Duluth school system, and the district is deep into learning how to implement it and adapt it to meet its own special needs more effectively. PM/QWL has affected for the better the quality of work life of teachers and management, and children, together with these groups, are the likely beneficiaries of the more positive climate. Specific tactics Duluth has used to enlist involvement of teachers in decision making are numerous. The more significant tactics include

1. The district's joining with the union in collaborative development of PM/QWL
2. Adoption by the school board of policy and regulations to signal its own commitment
3. Recruitment of a superintendent favorably disposed to participative processes
4. Provision of time and resources to support the training of staff and their sustained use of the process
5. Appointment of an effective PM/QWL facilitator who has the trust of management and the union
6. Willingness to implement promptly appropriate recommendations of the quality circles
7. Willingness to consider changes in district structures and procedures to render PM/QWL more effective

At this time, the major promises of PM/QWL in Duluth are (1) that the district and the union will stick with it and gradually eliminate the glitches that render the process cumbersome on occasion, and (2) that improvements will be made in the process and in district operations that will make PM/QWL more proactive, as well as reactive, in more substantive areas of teacher concern.

12

Expanding the Teacher's Role: School Improvement in the Hammond, Indiana, School District

by Jill Casner-Lotto

An unusual and, in some ways, unique experiment is under way in the Hammond, Indiana, public schools. The Hammond School Improvement Process (SIP), which draws on the collective energy and expertise of teachers, administrators, students, parents, and other community members, is fundamentally changing the way some schools operate and enhancing the opportunities for learning. For the first time in the Hammond School District, the teachers have a major say in decision making and in shaping the educational programs they believe are best suited to the students in their particular schools. Decisions in a wide range of areas that traditionally were under the sole jurisdiction of school principals and central administrators—curriculum planning and development, instructional strategies, staffing needs and hiring, professional development, disciplinary procedures, and scheduling, to name a few—are now being made jointly by teachers and administrators, working together with parents and students on school-based improvement teams.

What further distinguishes this school improvement effort is the active involvement of the teachers' union, Hammond Teachers' Federation, Local 394 of the American Federation of Teachers. The union, besides being philosophically committed to the school improvement process, has developed some innovative language in the master contract, which union leaders believe increases the decision-making authority of individual teachers while protecting the interests of the union as an institution. On a school-by-school basis, the teachers may set aside elements of the contract in order to pursue their improvement plan.

Another outstanding—and perhaps the most crucial—feature of the School Improvement Process is the nature and quality of support that emanates from the central administration. The district superintendent has demonstrated his commitment to SIP through both words and action, such as by providing resources so SIP teams can function properly, honoring decisons reached by SIP teams, and actively challenging state-legislated regulations and other external mandates that limit the effectiveness of SIP.

Though the improvement process is still in the early stages of development—it was piloted in one school in 1982 and then implemented districtwide in 1984—a number of schools can point to significant programs or projects created as a result of SIP:

- A transitional first-grade/kindergarten program was created for youngsters who experienced difficulty in kindergarten and needed more preparation before entering first grade. The program, which was researched, reviewed, and designed by teachers and administrators working closely with parents, represents a major departure from the established curriculum.
- At another middle school, teaching techniques and instruction have been enriched through adoption of state-of-the-art methods that address the individualized learning styles of students. The SIP committee at this school also implemented a special rotating schedule that adapts to the unique characteristics of middle school learners.
- Last year, at Hammond High School, the pilot school, the SIP team screened and interviewed candidates for the principal's position and made recommendations to the district superintendent and board. This year, four other schools followed suit, with teams of teachers, administrators, stu-

dents, and parents interviewing and ranking candidates. In all five cases, the final choices of the SIP teams were approved by the central administration.

- The teachers and administrators at one elementary school informally agreed on a peer evaluation program. Pending further research and examination, the model could be adapted at other schools.
- At another school, a coaching mentor program, which requires cooperation between the central administration, local school administrators, and the affected teachers, represents a constructive approach toward helping new teachers who are experiencing difficulties by having seasoned career teachers work with them.

Another indication that the process is working is the change in roles and attitudes evident among the various SIP participants. Both the union president and the district superintendent remark that each side is moving from an "us versus them" stance that characterizes the traditional labor-management relationship to a more cooperative approach that better serves the interests of both sides. A principal at one school notes that his autocratic management style is becoming more and more participative so that the improvement process can function effectively at his school. Another principal observes that her role is enhanced since she has more time to concentrate on and assure the delivery of high-quality instruction at her school. Parents point to SIP as providing a new channel of communication for them and a way to get actively and meaningfully involved in their schools, while students who have acquired new leadership skills through the improvement process are able to assume greater responsibilities for their own learning and for the programs established in their schools.

More and more teachers—though there are still a significant number who remain cynical toward SIP—point not only to their decision-making authority, but also to the means for carrying it out (for example, the provision of release time by the central administration so that SIP teams can meet, plan agendas, and develop in-service educational programs). "To take a half day to plan such activities would have been unheard of before the school improvement process was in place," observes one elementary school teacher who is also a SIP chairperson. While it is too early to tell just how much overall influence teachers have gained through the improvement process, two key sources—Pat O'Rourke, the local union president, and Wayne Pecher, a teacher who was recently appointed as the SIP coordinator of training—say that certain schools are developing programs that signal a "gradual yet fundamental shift in the decision-making authority."

What Is SIP?

Participants in Hammond's School Improvement Process define it as a building-based process of managing schools that, if properly applied, can lead to significant gains in the quality of education. When asked to describe the nature of the process and what they have learned about it so far, participants point to the following features:

- Significant change through SIP will come about at the school, not the district, level. Though the process has been implemented throughout the district, teachers and administrators stress it is school-based decision making, the theory being that those most closely affected by the decisions should have a major role in making those decisions and that the most effective reforms are carried out by people who feel a sense of ownership of the process and programs established in their schools.
- School improvement is an ongoing process rather than a finite program and should be under constant review. It is a long-term, evolutionary process of change, not a "quick fix" to remedy the schools' problems.
- SIP is totally compatible with the collective bargaining process and, in fact, strengthens it, since it involves teachers in policy decision making, which is a natural extension of the bargaining process.
- Certain key ingredients are required if SIP is to thrive: ongoing district support, access to current or state-of-the-art information on which to base decisions, training, time, and money.

- It is impossible to completely divorce the process from the personalities involved. In fact, at Hammond, certain individuals have emerged as key figures or "champions" of reform, whose energy, intelligence, and willingness to assume increased responsibility have helped promote the process toward improvement.
- SIP has not undermined the authority of administrators nor lessened their power; instead, by involving teachers and others in decision making, it has enlarged the "pool of power" in which everyone can share.

Background

The city of Hammond, with a population of about 100,000, is in the northern tip of Indiana, sandwiched between Gary, Indiana, and the Chicago metropolitan area. Located in the middle of the steel belt—more accurately referred to as the "rust belt"—the Hammond community has felt the trauma of plant closings and job layoffs. The Hammond school district, formally called the School City of Hammond, is the eighth largest school system in the state. It has a work force of over 1,600; of that total, about 900 are teachers and 70 are administrators. There are 25 schools in the district: 4 high schools, 2 middle schools, and 19 elementary schools. Student enrollment—which declined by 3 percent from 1983 to 1984—is now over 13,000. Achievement scores have shown steady improvement in the district since 1984. Overall results of the spring 1986 testing program showed that student scores in 11 of the 12 grade levels averaged at or above national norms.

When David O. Dickson became superintendent in 1985, the district faced a $2 million deficit, with a projected increase to $7 million. In two and a half years, the deficit was reduced to half a million dollars—a feat accomplished, he says, through the combined forces of the school board, administration, teachers, parents, and patrons. A team representing these groups met with the State Tax Control Board to discuss solutions to the district's financial problems. As a result of that meeting, the state board approved the transfer of certain funds and the payment of a $4.3

million delinquent utility bill with a general obligation bond issue. In addition, administrative and teaching staff reductions through attrition resulted in savings of $1 million. ''We reduced the deficit without closing one neighborhood school and without emasculating any educational programs, and we still managed to award competitive salary raises,'' Dickson boasts.

In several ways, the Hammond school district is typical of urban school districts across the nation. Yet, in spite of its size and urban nature, there is a sense of camaraderie and informality among the teaching and administrative staff that seems to distinctly reflect its ''small-town'' Midwestern character. Several teachers and administrators grew up in Hammond and have known each other since their school days—in fact, some have attended the same schools in which they are now employed.

That camaraderie was certainly evident at a group interview, which was conducted to find out how the school improvement process was affecting the various parties. The setting was a local restaurant and the district superintendent, two principals, two board members, the local union president, and a teacher were having lunch and talking about school improvement and sharing their experiences in a totally candid, uninhibited manner. Several persons at that meeting felt that the mutual trust and camaraderie that have evolved—while not a prerequisite— have helped facilitate the school improvement process. It is not unusual for Pat O'Rourke, the union president, to drop in at Dickson's office for an impromptu meeting about SIP-related business or problems at some schools. ''I think that, in one sense, SIP lends authority and structure to what we've been doing informally, away from the bargaining table,'' notes Dickson.

The spirit of togetherness, however, was not always present in the district. In 1981, the problems at Hammond High School were mounting, and administrators and teachers had run out of solutions. The school, formerly top ranked in the state, had experienced continuous decline since the early 1970s. Academic achievement had slipped dramatically, while absences and dropouts were on the rise. Racial tension, roving youth gangs, vandalism, drug abuse, graffiti, and fighting in the halls were rampant. Teacher morale was at an all-time low, while the level of hostility and distrust between teachers and administrators was mounting. By early 1980, observed Wayne Pecher, a Hammond High teacher, "we had hit close to rock bottom."

Elizabeth Ennis, then the assistant principal at Hammond High, and Raymond J. Golarz, the former assistant superintendent, had heard of the school improvement efforts initiated by the Institute for the Development of Educational Activities (IDEAS), which was part of the Charles Kettering Foundation, and the Eli Lilly Endowment. In December 1981, a group of teachers, parents, school administrators, and board members met with representatives of these organizations to discuss their research and its possible applications at Hammond High. Though several teachers remained doubtful about the school improvement process and its relevance to their situation, the group reached a decision to give it a try. In March 1982 the school board selected Hammond High to pilot the school improvement process. Initial costs for this pilot project were underwritten by the Eli Lilly endowment, the Kettering Foundation, the School City of Hammond, and the Indiana Criminal Justice Institute. Gary Phillips, the consultant who has worked closely with the district and who, at the time, was with the Kettering Foundation, states that the major form of support came through technical assistance, mainly training in the skills judged necessary to carry out the improvement process, while the amount of money—a few thousand dollars—was not that great. "The Kettering Foundation had always stressed that first it was important for the schools to have a process in place and for ownership of the process to develop in order to assure that something substantive would happen. Providing money before that occurs can almost act as a deterrent to the process," says Phillips.

A small group representing teachers, administrative staff, students, parents, and community members received initial training from Phillips in such skills as creative problem solving, reaching consensus with diverse points of view, leadership, group dynamics, brainstorming, conflict resolution, and forecasting. Because the ultimate aim is to become self-directed rather than rely on outside assistance, this group of trained individuals, in turn, trained others in the school until there were enough reasonably expert people to form a school improvement committee. That committee, says Pecher, included about twenty individuals: "students (not all A students), teachers (not all cooperative teachers), administrators, parents, representatives from Inland Steel and Northern Indiana Public Utilities, and a minister from a local church. The purpose was to get as many varied opinions and viewpoints as possible."

Through the combined efforts of teachers, administrators, parents, students, and community members working on this committee and successfully extending their reach to their peers in the school and community, Hammond High achieved a remarkable turnaround in a two-year period. Several measures taken led to both visible and documented successes: less vandalism and graffiti, cleaner halls, fewer fights, increased attendance, higher levels of student achievement, and a dramatic reduction in academic failures. And, for the first time, parents became actively involved in the school's activities, as did the students. A student offshoot of the SIP committee, called Student Leaders in Progress, or SLIP, was formed. SLIP was an instrumental force in mobilizing student support and involvement in the improvement process—and continues to be so today by sponsoring such activities as schoolwide academic competitions, peer counseling, leadership training, and drug awareness programs.

During the summer of 1983, two additional schools— Eggers Elementary/Middle School and Spohn Elementary/Middle School, the so-called "feeder schools" into Hammond High— became involved in the school improvement process. Though the Hammond Teachers' Federation was not directly or formally involved in the process, several individual members and union leaders—including O'Rourke, who was a faculty member of the Hammond High SIP committee—were active participants. "While there was some initial concern that SIP could conflict with the collective bargaining process," O'Rourke notes, "our feeling was that with only three schools involved as pilots, we could monitor the development of SIP and intervene as an institution at the proper time should we feel threatened."

Impressed with the achievements made thus far at the three pilot schools, the school board appointed a citywide task force during the 1983–84 school year to investigate the possibility of extending SIP to the remaining twenty-two schools. The task force, made up of parents, teachers, and administrators, recommended districtwide implementation. In order to ensure that the schools were not being forced to participate, the board of trustees and superintendent sponsored a one-day "School Improvement Project Awareness Workshop." The session was attended by at least one teacher, one parent, and one administrator from each school. Sixty-six of the sixty-seven attendees gave their support to involvement in the school improvement process. As a result of that support, the task force's recommendations, and the successful experiences of the three pilot schools, especially Hammond High, the board approved the implementation of the school improvement process in the remaining twenty-two schools.

How SIP Operates Today

Understandably, implementation of SIP has been uneven throughout the district. As O'Rourke observes, depending on its particular culture, each school is changing and adapting the process at its own pace. While some schools are developing programs "that have great potential for setting educational policy, others have simply put in place the mechanisms for change and conducted the initial training," he adds. The mechanisms for change at each school include an improvement committee of about fifteen to twenty members, representing teachers, administrators, parents, students, and, when possible, community members. There is also a smaller core team, which determines the agenda and usually consists of the principal, one or two teachers from the larger SIP team, and a parent. The principal may also serve on the larger SIP team or occasionally attend SIP meetings, when budgetary or other types of information could affect the committee's work. Though Hammond school representatives have made it a point not to set any rigid rules concerning SIP committee membership or meeting times and procedures, there is one rule to which all teams are expected to adhere—that a principal should never serve as the SIP committee chairperson, as this would merely perpetuate the traditional top-down management approach.

While the consultant Gary Phillips continues to provide some technical assistance to the schools, the major responsibility for initial and ongoing training and for overseeing other SIP-related activities has been assumed by Assistant Superintendent Thomas C. Knarr, who in 1986 was appointed by the district superintendent as coordinator for the school improvement process. Pecher conducts the initial training workshop when a school first becomes involved; then, in the traditional "train the trainer" approach, the individuals who have gone through the workshops train others in the school community. Initial training consists of skills in consensus building, brainstorming, creative problem solving, and group dynamics. In addition, Pecher and Jane Kendrick, a principal at one of the elementary/middle schools, and a leading advocate of SIP, have conducted ongoing workshops in leadership skills for SIP chairpersons and for principals. "Several principals are still uncomfortable in their new roles because they perceive it as a loss of power. What we've tried to do is convince them that their power is strengthened since the policies implemented have the full support of the faculty," says Pecher.

In general, Pecher describes his role as that of "a troubleshooter, prodder, and coach. Basically, I'm there to lend support, whether in training activities or in facilitating meetings where there may be tensions between the administration and the faculty." For example, at one elementary school, struggling to improve itself but thwarted in its attempts due to the mistrust and hostility between the faculty and principal, Pecher helped to facilitate a faculty meeting. Through the application of such SIP methods as consensus building within small groups and brainstorming techniques, what would have most likely turned into just another gripe session instead became a productive meeting at which teachers and the principal at least agreed on some of the barriers to change and possible ways to overcome them.

Pecher, chairman of the math department and teacher at Hammond High School, is able to continue in his regular job duties at full salary because he has been granted "half-time release" by the central administration to carry out his SIP-related responsibilities. He also receives a small stipend for his SIP work.

After the initial training is completed, the SIP team's first task is to develop a "vision of excellence"—where they want the school to be or what they want to achieve in five or ten years. Specific long- and short-range goals and priorities are determined, and then a strategic improvement plan, consisting of viable ways to reach those goals, is developed. Often, the teams go on weekend retreats—preferably in a peaceful setting away from the school environment—to develop their vision and start work on an improvement plan.

A key component of the school improvement process is the concept of "pyramid structuring" or "pyramiding," which, when done properly, maximizes decision making and involvement and thus assures greater acceptance of any programs or policies implemented. Basically, pyramiding requires that each of the SIP team members interrelates on a regular basis with five to seven of his or her peers. The purpose is both to communicate information concerning the team's work or program proposals and to get responses and feedback from others outside the team. The initial five to seven individuals contacted are then expected to reach additional people, who, in turn, contact others, until a significant portion of the school population has been reached. The extent of pyramiding in the schools varies, depending on the degree of organization and the level of commitment to the improvement process.

In addition to receiving money and support from the Eli Lilly Endowment and the Kettering Foundation, in 1986 the Hammond School District, through the efforts of principal Jane Kendrick, received a $50,000 grant from the Indiana State Department of Education to provide incentives for teachers to participate in the school improvement process. The grant money, which has been allocated among the various schools, can be used for whatever purpose the SIP committee chooses, such as travel expenses for weekend retreats, attending special training sessions or conferences, or visits to other schools experimenting with new ideas or implementing progressive programs and to universities where applicable research is being conducted. Some SIP teams have used the money to pay for substitute teachers so that the teachers on the SIP team can take more time to participate in school improvement activities.

In 1987 the Hammond School District was awarded a $66,000 grant from the Federal Mediation and Conciliation Service. The money will be used for additional personnel to help coordinate SIP activities and train participants and for sponsoring other events, including two labor-management conferences for principals and teachers during the school year.

Another precious resource—time—has been provided through the central administrative office. SIP teams can request release time in order to meet during the school day. It is up to each SIP team to decide when and how often it needs to meet. Depending on the work load, some may meet monthly or weekly—either on their own time or, if their request for release time has been approved, during school hours. If a major block of time is required, some teams have worked out arrangements whereby they combine the release time granted with the members' own time.

Inside the Schools

The best way to understand how the improvement process works is to examine how individual schools are applying it to their particular situations. Described here are the experiences of two schools that have made significant gains in their effort to improve: Lafayette Elementary School and Eggers Elementary/ Middle School.

Lafayette Elementary School. Lafayette Elementary School is considered one of the finer schools in the district, with a committed and highly competent faculty, particularly in working with students coming from disadvantaged, low socioeconomic backgrounds. About 53 percent of the student body are minorities; of that proportion, 35 percent are Hispanic and about 15 percent are black. At Lafayette, the SIP committee has broken up into three design teams, organized around the current needs of the school as determined by faculty members, administrators, and parents. These include teams for the kindergarten program, staff development, and student recognition.

The most important project initiated thus far through the school improvement process has been the new transitional kindergarten program. Kindergarten teachers at Lafayette have been particularly concerned about the high percentage of children experiencing learning difficulties in their classes. Many students, considered to be unprepared for first grade, were repeating kindergarten. In February of the 1985–86 school year, the SIP kindergarten team began to research alternative programs. "We all agreed that the problem required a major adjustment in the curriculum," notes principal Donald Sohacki. "It was the committee's job to come up with some concrete suggestions."

As part of the team's investigation, all of the teachers at Lafayette were asked to supply information on student achievement in order to detect learning trends. A group of kindergarten teachers visited other school systems to observe a method of instruction known as the Gesell Developmental Kindergarten Class. Intensive efforts to involve parents also took place. Translators were hired so the research material could be presented in Spanish in order to be fully understandable to some of the parents. Parents, teachers, and administrators were asked to review the material and give feedback—which they did. In addition, the affected kindergarten teachers attended a special "kindergarten roundtable" at Indiana University. Based on the information gathered and an analysis of additional diagnostic screening profiles, the SIP committee recommended the creation of a transitional kindergarten program, focusing on skills that first-grade teachers have identified as most crucial for a smooth entry and success in first grade. The program was approved and implemented through the pyramid structure.

For both teachers and administrators, the new kindergarten program represented a fundamental departure from the established kindergarten curriculum, which has been in place for several years. And, interestingly, it was not the type of program that the principal would have decided on had he been making the decision on his own. "I was definitely leaning toward a full-day kindergarten," he notes. Today, however, he is pleased with the results so far and hopeful about the program's future.

Donald Sohacki's role as principal has changed significantly since his involvement in the school improvement process. By his own account and that of others, his management style is considered to be autocratic. He claims, however, that he is becoming less autocratic and points out some of the incentives for making that change: "Teachers are now involved in decisions where before the burden of decision making was entirely mine. They are looking at the possible avenues to a solution and figuring out the available resources, so that it's not necessarily the administration coming up with all the answers." What initially attracted him to the school improvement process was the "terminology—the notion that there was room for improvement, even at a school considered to be good, like Lafayette. I think, in that sense, SIP has lent additional spark to what we've already been doing. . . . And, in my own case, though I believe I'm a fairly decent principal, I'd like to be a better one."

Apparently, there are teachers who agree with Sohacki when he says he is adjusting his style of management. According to an informal random sampling of faculty responses concerning areas of decision making, teachers say they are involved in the selection of textbooks and other instructional materials, curriculum development and evaluation, disciplinary procedures, student placement, determination of personnel needs, scheduling, setting policy goals, and complying with external mandates. Professional development is another important area in which the school improvement process has made a difference. At Lafayette, it has meant that teachers are now determining their own workshops for in-service education.

Another major change at Lafayette since the implementation of SIP has been the involvement of community members who, though they have no direct ties to the school through children, have demonstrated an interest in the school's activities. The school has a partnership with a nearby retirement community in which senior citizens come into the school on a regular basis to serve as classroom aides, provide tutoring assistance, or take part in student recognition activities, such as presentation of special T-shirts to reward good attendance or high grades.

Eggers Elementary/Middle School.   The Eggers school has made significant progress in its self-improvement efforts because it has several supportive components in place: an existing organizational structure that promotes the concepts of teacher involvement and ownership; the school improvement process that complements and is enhanced by the school's organizational design; a principal who is a strong leader, yet who is also committed to shared decision making; an energetic, dedicated faculty who welcome increased responsibility and control; and a high level of parental and community involvement.

Current enrollment at the school is over 900, with students representing a wide variety of socioeconomic groups. As one school counselor put it: "Our kids range from those whose parents are lawyers with Inland Steel to those whose folks move every month to avoid paying rent." Seventy-five percent of the student body is enrolled in the middle school (grades 6–8), while the remaining 25 percent attend the elementary school.

Since 1976 the faculty and student body at the middle school have been organized into small groups, known as "learning communities." Each learning community consists of 125 students and an interdisciplinary team of five teachers, each of whom is responsible for one of the following areas: language arts, social studies, math, science, and special education. Rather than moving about the building from one class to the next, the same group of students remains within their "communities." Teachers at Eggers say the learning community structure has created a sense of belonging for students, since teachers are able to establish more meaningful, longer-term relationships with them. And it has also reduced the sense of isolation among the teachers by promoting increased communication and sharing of problems.

While the use of interdisciplinary teaching teams has long been recommended by the National Middle School Association, the teaching teams at Eggers have evolved into something that goes well beyond the association's recommendations. Today they are cohesive, collegial teams actively involved in staff development, curriculum planning, scheduling, disciplinary procedures, and program development. The teams are provided with back-to-back community planning and individual planning periods each day, so there is ample time for group problem solving and decision making. In addition, the leaders of each learning community meet once a week with the principal, Jane Kendrick.

Both Kendrick and teachers say the learning communities are vital to the continued success of the school and to teacher participation and control.

The broader school improvement process has been strengthened by the learning community structure since both emphasize shared decision making and ownership. SIP has also acted as a unifying force for the entire school, bringing together faculty and student members of the learning communities, administrators, and parents. Representatives from each of these groups serve on the SIP planning committee. In addition, there is the core committee made up of the principal, a parent, and a teacher. One project recently implemented through the school improvement process was adoption of the 4-Mat Model, considered to be a state-of-the-art technique that enables teachers to address the various learning styles, weaknesses, and strengths of individual students. The planning committee researched various alternative models and a small group, including a counselor, administrator, and three teachers met with a professor at Western Kentucky University. Before the 4-Mat model was actually adopted, committee members utilized the pyramid structure to get as much feedback as possible and reach a final consensus.

Other SIP-related accomplishments include the adoption of a course schedule in which the time slots for various subjects are rotated every twelve weeks, thus responding to the needs of both morning learners and afternoon learners; development of a reading center for teaching across all grade levels; and receipt of a $20,000 middle school recognition award from the Eli Lilly Endowment to plan and pursue further school improvement activities.

Jane Kendrick believes her role as principal has been enhanced through the school improvement and learning community structures. "I'm no longer just a manager, but also a facilitator and a leader of instructors. I believe that principals who feel threatened by increased teacher participation in decision making have never truly understood their role. I find that it has freed me to concentrate on the quality of instruction versus being a firefighter. Also, I'm more aware of what's happening in this school—even if it means knowing more kids by their first name, which is important to me."

Kendrick finds that both the quality of decisions made and their acceptance can increase when working through the improvement process. "I'm finding that through my work on the SIP core team, three heads are better than one. And because the teachers and parents are involved in the decision making, there is more ownership and greater acceptance than with the typical top-down approach."

Yet, even at a school that has so fully embraced the concepts behind school improvement, the process—if not applied properly—can occasionally backfire. When first introducing the 4-Mat Model, the SIP committee members did not properly take it through the pyramid structure, so many teachers felt they were being coerced. "It did create serious problems at first, but once we were able to pinpoint what went wrong, we eventually straightened it out by involving many more teachers in the decision making," notes a teacher who serves on the SIP committee. "In general," he adds, "SIP has brought about good ideas and kept our school on focus."

Over the past six years, Eggers school has shown steady and significant improvements in standardized test scores and in attendance rates. In addition, besides being awarded the Eli Lilly grant, Eggers has been chosen as one of only twenty-five schools across the nation to serve as a member of the Middle Schools Future Consortium. This means that during the next two years Eggers faculty and administrative representatives will attend national meetings with other middle school representatives to plan and develop future goals and programs for middle school education. These achievements are due to a combination of factors, Kendrick emphasizes, including the learning communities, school improvement process, quality of leadership, and parent involvement.

Union Involvement

As noted earlier, during the initial stages of SIP, the union was not formally or directly involved. That changed, however, in 1985 when it was becoming increasingly obvious to union leaders, building representatives, and rank-and-file members that shared decision making in the local schools could potentially conflict with the collective bargaining process. More and more schools were considering programs, such as peer evaluation, that clearly deviated from contractual procedures.

As O'Rourke notes, SIP represented both a threat and an opportunity. On the one hand, the prospect of teachers, parents, administrators, and students working together to implement programs at the individual school sites "seemed to threaten the very institutional balance of power that existed within the district," according to O'Rourke. On the other hand, the union viewed this new model of shared governance as giving teachers the opportunity to develop programs and policies that had previously been off limits, thus broadening their scope as professionals. "We concluded it was possible to move in this direction by working within the traditional collective bargaining process, while simultaneously developing new relationships with management that go beyond bargaining."

In September 1985 the union negotiated a three-year contract with the school board that endorses the school improvement process and includes lanugage permitting local schools to deviate from the master contract in order to pursue their improvement plans—providing a specific procedure is followed. O'Rourke believes the language frees the individual teachers at each school to make decisions without union interference or without weakening the contract.

The procedure is fairly complex and will only be summarized here. Briefly, the procedure requires that all the faculty members at a school reach a consensus on the proposed program, discussing its pros and cons. The faculty then determines a time period—not to exceed one school year—for a trial test of the program. Criteria are established by the faculty to evaluate the program at the end of the trial period. The faculty then votes on the proposed change on a scale of 5 to 0, with a 5 indicating enthusiastic endorsement of the limited trial test and 0 indicating that the teacher is strongly opposed to even a limited trial test and would exercise a veto if it were within his or her power to do so. If the procedure is followed correctly, the union then no longer has the right to file a grievance alleging that a school improvement project violates the contract provision; however, an individual teacher may still file a grievance, providing it bears his or her signature.

At one elementary school where an innovative, cross-grade-level reading program created through SIP has dramatically improved student reading levels and eased teachers' work loads, the faculty members went through this procedure since the program required teaching arrangements that violated certain work rules in the contract. "The procedure allowed us to meet our individual needs at this school," says a teacher, "without making a blanket statement for all the schools."

In general, union involvement in the school improvement process has boosted teacher support, says Wayne Pecher. "I think that by getting the language in the contract, it convinced many teachers, who had been skeptical toward SIP or who had a 'wait-and-see' attitude, that the school improvement process was not just another fad or new program, but instead was something that was here to stay." O'Rourke, who has used general union membership meetings as a vehicle for "selling" SIP and informing members of its progress, estimates that today about one-third of the teachers are actively participating in the school improvement process, while the remaining two-thirds are equally divided among the skeptics and those with a "wait-and-see" attitude.

Support from the Top

David Dickson, Hammond's district superintendent, says his job has become easier as a result of the school improvement process. "Because teachers, parents, and principals have ownership in the decision-making process, we don't have the traditional negative feelings toward the central administration. People are working together, there's better communication, and the pool of expertise has been broadened," says Dickson. "I've become an adherent to the politics of involvement rather than the politics of confrontation," he adds. A strong believer in the "professional integrity of the classroom teacher," Dickson believes that teachers should have decision-making authority in many areas, such as curriculum development, instructional strategies, and disciplinary policies. Though he has been in his present position only since 1985, he is viewed—by both teachers and principals—as an instrumental force in mobilizing the support of school board members behind SIP.

"We have five people on the school board this year who bought into SIP because the district superintendent urged them to get behind it," observes Pat O'Rourke. Today, three school board members are active members of SIP teams. Jane Kendrick, the principal at Eggers, says Dickson's most valuable contribution has been in "letting the principal and the faculty run their school without interfering. His leadership sets a tone and allows building-based management a chance to operate."

Perhaps the most tangible demonstration of district support has been the provision of release time so SIP teams can meet. Recently, however, some SIP teams have had their requests for release time turned down by the central administration because of certain state rules mandating the number of days students must be in the schools and the number of hours and minutes in the classroom. Dickson is committed to challenging such rules—"many of which are educationally unsound," he says. Together with union president O'Rourke, he is currently working toward the development of various measures and alternatives permitting SIP teams to adjust the school schedule in order to have adequate time to meet and plan their activities. "It's not fair to ask SIP team members to formulate a 'vision of excellence' at 3:45 on a Tuesday afternoon," he remarks. "If it means sending kids home for the afternoon, they should be able to do that. Any loss of school days," he concludes, "is far outweighed by the advantages of SIP: improved curriculum, more creative instructional strategies, and a positive educational climate."

Conclusion

Because the school improvement process has been in place only since 1984 on a districtwide basis, Hammond school representatives say it is premature to evaluate its impact on districtwide trends in student achievement scores, attendance rates, and other indicators of student performance. But, based on the programs developed thus far, the impact on attitudes, and the changes in teacher/administrative roles and relationships, the school improvement process has clearly made a difference in the Hammond school district—and will continue to do so in the future, say SIP participants. "We have a process in place that will enable change to occur. And all things are possible," O'Rourke states. "Decentralized authority is no longer theory nor is the concept experimental, but rather it is a process that has proved to be workable in the private sector, and given the sophistication of today's work force it is certainly applicable to any public institution that seeks better productivity through management/employee harmony," notes Knarr.

That optimism shared by O'Rourke and others, however, is tempered by the awareness of some of the forces that can act as constraints to school improvement. The existence of federal and state laws that limit the effectiveness of SIP is one obvious factor, and teacher cynicism is another. Less obvious, however, is the departure of key leaders who have been strong advocates of shared decision making and school improvement. And in school districts—where changes in leadership occur regularly— this becomes an especially important factor.

At Hammond High School, the school improvement process has lost some of its momentum since its early days, and while various factors probably account for this, several members of the school community say the departure of the principal, Elizabeth Ennis, who "brought" SIP to Hammond, was a major one. Nonetheless, even the loss of a strong leader like Ennis is viewed as a temporary setback.

Today, there are signs that the School Improvement Process at Hammond High is being revived. An alternative mathematics program, conceived and designed by teachers, was recently introduced. The program relies on such nontraditional methods as small-group instruction, peer tutoring, and team teaching. Students advance according to their mastery of the subject matter rather than according to time spent. Said Wayne Pecher, "We got lazy. But now we're ready to get the engines started once again."

"The School Improvement Process is based on the conviction that there are extraordinary possibilities in ordinary people who forgo an immediate personal gain or advantage for the good of the youngsters they serve. The future of the School Improvement Process in Hammond is not in doubt, but just how far it will permeate the system has not yet been determined. Furthermore, there should be no artificial restrictions or restraints put in its path or placed on it," concludes Knarr.

13

Restructuring a School System:
The Jefferson County Public Schools

by Wendy Kohli

In Jefferson County, Kentucky, a host of education and civic leaders committed to educational reform and improvement are engaged in the "restructuring" of the school system. Changing large bureaucratic structures and their concomitant policies and practices is no small task, as Max Weber and other sociologists have reminded us. Nor is it easy to change the values, beliefs, and actions that are a prerequisite to sustaining significant, systemic change. Yet, in Jefferson County, the schools are trying to accomplish no less than educational change on a grand scale. They are doing so, over time, and through many "little tries." ("Little tries" is an expression coined by Philip Schlecty, director of the Gheens Center. It was used frequently by school district people interviewed for this chapter to describe the process of change in the Jefferson County Schools.)

Unlike many of the reform efforts occurring nationwide since the publication in 1983 of *A Nation at Risk* and other reports on education, the Jefferson County efforts focus on systemwide practices, not just individual school-based reform or teaching effectiveness. This is not to say that school-based change is irrelevant. On the contrary. In Jefferson County, there is a concerted effort to relate the guiding systemwide vision for change to the individual needs of each building and staff. "Let 1,000 flowers bloom" was a common refrain among the many educators interviewed for this study. This bouquet of changes will come about through the invention of a means "of restructuring schools, restructuring the teaching occupation, and redefining the role of teacher education in relation to schools" (Schlecty, 1987, p. 6). As an active, intentional process, "invention" serves as a means of empowerment for teachers and principals in the system. This kind of empowerment is essential to the quality of the cultural change occurring in the Jefferson County Public School System today.

When Jefferson County people speak of restructuring the system and transforming the professional culture, they do not use these terms lightly. For them, the change they envision embodies fresh conceptions of what it means to be a teacher and what it means to be a principal. They speak of "reconfiguring teacher roles and responsibilities." Although that concept has yet to be translated into concrete policies and practices on a districtwide basis, there is momentum building to transform the traditional hierarchies and top-down directions of decision making. In several schools, there is already a precedent for this.

The concept of the "lead teacher" as defined by the Carnegie Forum Task Force (1986) has considerable support in Jefferson County, particularly in the middle schools, where "teaming" and "team leaders" have worked successfully for nearly a decade. The team leaders in these schools have grown to expect primary responsibility and decision-making authority for key curricular and teaching matters. By several accounts, the structures are in place and the leadership skills developed in at least seven middle schools for teachers to assume "Lead Teacher" roles. As one experienced teacher exclaimed, "I love the concept of Lead Teacher—of differentiated staffing where I get to do different things *as a teacher* without having to leave teaching and go into administration." She echoed common research findings that suggest that the teaching profession does not provide very many opportunities for growth and change *within the role as it is now defined.* Suggesting that this static concept of the role is inhibiting, she declared that "the only thing I've stayed with for more than ten years is my husband! Why can't we have more variation in our lives as teachers?"

One thing that is clear in Louisville is the commitment to sustain a sound infrastructure to support reform efforts. It is not enough for certain district or union leaders to *declare* that schools will ''restructure'' or have ''lead teachers.'' There must be fertile soil in which to grow these experimental seeds. Jefferson County is rich in the experience of a decade of teaming, leading to considerable changes in building-level governance in many schools. As one team leader described it, ''It's like being a mini-principal where you get your fingers on discipline, budget planning, scheduling and counseling. I feel that's what's changed the attitude of many people in the middle schools.'' This is not to say that all of the nearly 160 schools in the district have the same degree of teacher participation. Clearly they do not. However, since change is viewed from a developmental perspective, all schools *are not expected* to be working on the same things at the same time, in a standardized manner. Just as children start at different places and move at different speeds, so too do faculty— individually and collectively—go through different stages of growth and change. Those schools that have been moving in the direction of redefining decision-making roles can become models of change from which others can learn. The developmental perspective on change and invention is testimony that Jefferson County is in this ''for the long haul.'' There is a genuine commitment to continued growth and reevaluation.

A Center of and for Change

The Gheens Professional Development Academy serves as a pivotal factor in the districtwide restructuring effort. The Academy resulted from a collaborative effort between the school district and the community, particularly the Gheens Foundation, a local foundation committed to public education and community development.

Five years ago, the trustees of the Gheens Foundation approached the school superintendent, Donald Ingwerson, to see how they might get involved in educational reform in the Louisville area. Impressed by Ingwerson and all he had accomplished since coming to Kentucky in 1981 from the Orange County

(California) School District, the Foundation agreed to underwrite the "Center," as it is referred to locally, as a place that would "enhance the human resource development capacity for the district, serve as a focal point for moving the Jefferson County Public Schools into the forefront of the national reform movement, and to provide leadership and direction in the restructuring of schools and the restructuring of the teaching occupation" (Schlecty, 1987, p. 4). The Gheens Foundation pledged over $600,000 in start-up operational money, contingent on the school district's finding and appropriately renovating a good building to house the center. Included in the operational expenses was the salary of the director, who, from the inception, was to be someone nationally known for his or her commitment to restructuring schools and the teaching profession. Such a person was found in Philip Schlecty, who was brought on as a full-time director in the fall of 1985.

The restructuring effort in Jefferson County has several components that are inspired, coordinated, and implemented through the Gheens Academy. Professional Development Schools (PDS), the brainchild of Phil Schlecty, is developing a prominent role in efforts to redefine the professional roles and culture of JCPS. The PDS initiative is complemented by participation in the Coalition of Essential Schools, a group of schools across the country that are trying to reform secondary education with the assistance of Theodore Sizer and his staff at Brown University.

Jefferson County has five high schools involved in the Coalition, all moving in the direction of rethinking and reorganizing how things are done in secondary education. The Gheens Center also houses a federally funded collaboration with the University of Louisville that is redefining the induction process for the teaching profession and experimenting with new roles for student interns and teacher-supervisors. A recent federal grant to support "Learning Choice Schools" provides additional opportunities to develop more participatory structures for teachers, children, and parents and for conceptualizing the role of the principal. The Middle Grades Assessment Program (MGAP), coordinated by the Gheens staff, provides the documentation for, and insight into, decision-making processes at the middle school level that have supported fundamental changes in management and leadership in the district. All of these components are different spokes on the wheel known as "restructuring" in Jefferson County. These exciting changes and the hope permeating the district since 1984 are a far cry from the pain and turmoil in the community a decade earlier.

A Turbulent History

All had not been well for some time in the Louisville-area schools. Nineteen seventy-five was a watershed year for this former frontier county situated near the Ohio River. In that year, a U.S. District Court had ordered that the Louisville City Schools and the surrounding suburban schools in Jefferson County had to desegregate. By September 1975, all 160 schools in the new county district of 92,000 students had to be racially balanced, based on a 70 percent white to 30 percent black ratio. All school administrations and teaching staffs had to be racially balanced as well, so this entailed the transfer of students, principals, and teachers to fulfill the court order. Massive busing occurred, and upheaval was the norm. Many parents abandoned public schools. The black community suffered blame and harassment, even though it was as opposed to busing as the white community. Blacks did hope, however, that the change would mean better schools for their children. Commitment to public education dropped so low during this period that the Chamber of Commerce portrayed the educational system of Louisville as a barrier to economic development.

With the formation of the new district, the Jefferson County Teachers Association became a more powerful body. To register their dissatisfaction with what they felt were arbitrary transfers and changes, the teachers organized several "incidents," including a "sick-out" in 1975 and a strike in 1976. The teachers walked out for eleven days and schools were closed for the duration. Several weeks prior to the strike, as many as 1,000 to 1,200 teachers showed up at every school board meeting to register their feelings on the master contract, which was up for renewal. In the 1970s, both the American Federation of Teachers (AFT) and the National Education Association (NEA) had strong support in the county. The AFT has virtually no presence now, a unique factor in that most of the nationally recognized districts in the school reform movement are represented by AFT affiliates.

The Jefferson County Teachers Association, with its new-found power, could and did influence the election of school board members. This made for interesting (and often conflicting) relationships between the board and the administration. The county superintendent became the superintendent for the merged district and the city superintendent left the area.

In the 1979–80 school year, the board decided it was time for "visionary leadership" to turn the situation around. As one central office administrator put it, "They were hungry for it. They saw the potential of the district because, even with the conflict and abandonment in the system, Jefferson County had many programs that were gaining national attention." One of those was its Middle Schools Program, which has become the bedrock on which much of the current restructuring is built.

A Time for New Leadership

The school board hired Donald Ingwerson as the new superintendent. Here was someone who had a vision for making things different. He knew he was being called on to "clean up a real mess." Immediately, he began to cultivate the support of the business community. Prior to his arrival, the contributions from corporations to public education were virtually nil. He has increased that to nearly $15 million through the actions of 500 school-business partnerships. One could argue that conditions were ripe for these changes, regardless of who the superintendent was, but as one person put it, "It takes leadership and vision to make the conditions come together." The trustees of the Gheens Foundation were watching him. Convinced that he was on the right track and impressed with his low-key style and commitment, the trustees began laying the groundwork for what now has become the Gheens Academy for Professional Development. By most accounts, Donald Ingwerson's leadership and vision created the environment for change and renewal that has put Jefferson County on the "cutting edge" of school reform in this country, along with such districts as Rochester, New York, and Miami–Dade County in Florida.

Two other significant actors have helped bring national recognition to Jefferson County: Philip Schlecty and Terry Brooks. When the Gheens Foundation committed the money for the Academy, they knew that it was necessary to hire a director who was a leader in educational reform and teacher education if they were to propel the Gheens Academy into national prominence. The Foundation and the superintendent were wise enough to bring on board Regina Kyle, a unique consultant who acted as philosopher, planner, and evaluator to help shape the direction of reform in Jefferson County. Kyle worked with them to conduct a national search, which ended with Schlecty. According to many who work with him, Schlecty is the person in the district who conceptualizes the grand scheme and infuses others with the language, vision, and inspiration to "think big" and "try a little—a lot." He has widespread support in the district and is affiliated with the University of Louisville as well. Terry Brooks is the local "insider," who has worked in the system for most of his professional life. A former teacher and middle school principal, Brooks has helped to systematically build the structural base at the middle school level that supports much of the teacher empowerment initiative. But his influence is really grounded in his personal power, resulting from years of association with the best teachers and principals in the district. Teachers testify repeatedly to their loyalty to Brooks and insist that if it were not for his talent, commitment, and knowledge of school-based participatory governance and leadership, the changes in Jefferson County would be empty rhetoric, just as they are in many other highly publicized school districts. He has been a mentor to many of the teachers and principals responsible for key changes in the district. Thus it is not entirely accurate to suggest that Schlecty is the "idea person" and Brooks is the "operational person" at the center. Their success at cooperating and building on complementary strengths has allowed the Gheens Academy to become a model of reform.

The relationship of the three major figures in the district is worth noting. Schlecty reports to Ingwerson in the official organizational chart. Yet it is clear that Ingwerson allows Schlecty to think and act independently because he knows that it would not work any other way. The superintendent's legitimate authority in the district and the mutual respect for that role by Schlecty and Brooks is clear. In some respects, the relationship between the Gheens Center administrators and middle management in the district office is more problematic. When Gheens was organized, Ingwerson was clear that many of the traditional staff development activities being conducted by the district should be moved to Gheens under one umbrella organization. This meant that some personnel would be moved to carry out an integrated district in-service program. By all appearances and by most accounts, that transition was carried out with minimal jealousy or resistance.

The Role of the Teachers' Union

The Jefferson County Teachers Association has been involved in the restructuring effort from the beginning, starting with the early conversations with the Gheens Foundation. The current president, June Lee, says that the JCTA "is very interested in the concept of participatory management" and has supported it at many levels. She cautions, however, that it must be "*real* participation." In a state that ranks forty-eighth or forty-ninth in teacher salaries, it would be irresponsible for teachers' associations to ignore fundamental "bread-and-butter" issues while pursuing what might appear to be more lofty reforms. Certainly, the two goals are not mutually exclusive, but Lee warns that basic needs of teachers must be met before expanded participation in decision making has any real meaning.

Relations between the union and the district management are positive and productive. The same could be said for relations with the school board. (As noted earlier, the JCTA wields powerful influence in electing school board members.) All parties generally reach negotiated contracts amicably and cooperate to achieve other objectives that will benefit the Jefferson County schools.

For example, in mid-1988, all involved parties came together strongly to protest massive, brutal budget cuts proposed by the governor at the state level. A demonstration at the State House in Frankfort brought out teachers, principals, board members, and district management in an effort to block the cuts. Everyone knew that any attempts at districtwide reform and restructuring would be hampered by the proposed state budget cuts to elementary and secondary education.

It is here that "the new professionalism" movement and the traditional "bread-and-butter" union issues come together. Without money and other resources to support changes in role definition and functions, teachers and principals alike will tire of "going the extra mile." Several teachers active in both the restructuring movement and the union don't see any incompatibility between the interests of the union and the interests of the new "professional culture." However, they did note that they cannot go on doing many of the things they are doing to implement new approaches without being compensated for the time it requires. Unlike Rochester, New York, for example, where a ground-breaking contract was recently negotiated creating salary steps commensurate with different types of teacher functions and levels, Jefferson County is still far away from institutionalizing such differentiation.

Restructuring—Kentucky Style

With this background established, we can begin to describe the components of the school restructuring effort in Jefferson County that are inspired, coordinated, and implemented through the Gheens Academy. As mentioned earlier, the center has several functions as it carries out its role as the pivotal point for change. From a corporate perspective, Gheens is the nerve center for all of the systemic changes in the district, including the Middle Grades Assessment Program (MGAP), a collaborative program with the University of Louisville, funded by the U.S. Office of Educational Research and Improvement; the Coalition of Essential Schools; Learning Choice Schools; and Professional Development Schools. It is also the place in the district where personal and professional development, or traditional "in-service," programs are conducted.

The attractiveness of the center is worth nothing. The building is a renovated elementary school that immediately conveys to the teachers and principals who enter it a feeling of professionalism. It is important to note that principals see the building as a place for them as well as for teachers. It is not a Teacher Center in the common understanding of that term, but teachers, in particular, feel that it is their building. As one teacher puts it, "The environment Gheens is trying to create is one where you feel like a professional. It really works!"

The rooms are bright, clean, and plentiful. There is always a fresh supply of coffee, tea, soft drinks, and other refreshments available for teachers who are attending meetings or workshops. There is a media center and a curriculum resource center as well as a professional library that is available to all district teachers. Over and over teachers attested to the respect and dignity with which they are treated when they come to Gheens. They have a high regard for the staff at the center and feel that they exhibit a form of professionalism and collegiality that is genuine and innovative. Principals and teachers alike remark about the first-rate talent and intelligence of the center's staff.

When district personnel come to Gheens, they invariably go away renewed and satisfied. But not too satisfied. If anything, the Gheens Center is about raising expectations—and teachers are encouraged and supported to raise their expectations for themselves, their peers, and the children in their classes. The bottom line for reform in Jefferson County is the children. All of the innovation and invention is to make sure that each child can learn.

One common thread that runs through all the programs at Gheens, whether aimed at structural or individual change, is collegiality. According to Schlecty, "The Academy promotes success (for teachers and principals) by designing programs and activities that encourage collegial interaction and support, by providing meaningful recognition for success, and by creating opportunities for intellectual and job variety" (Schlecty, 1987, p. 8). The thinking behind this is that if governance is to be shared, teachers must perceive themselves as colleagues. Furthermore, the traditional boundaries between principals and teachers must be dissolved if true collegiality and sharing are to occur within buildings and across the district.

The Gheens Center supports the formation of colleague support groups for the professional staff in the district, modeled after I/D/E/A groups. (I/D/E/A stands for the Institute for Development of Educational Activities in Dayton, Ohio. Affiliated with the Kettering Foundation, this consulting firm has developed models for school improvement and collegial support groups that have been replicated in dozens of school districts around the country.) Principals come together in these groups to share their ideas and concerns; teachers come together to do the same; and now there is even a cross-role support group that brings together people with a variety of staff roles. One principal said: "Our IDEA group meeting is a sharing session, where twelve principals talk about specific topics and ideas, read books, and do a lot of problem solving. It's very professional and meets once a month, all day. We are in our third year."

Intellectual, emotional, and other professional needs are met through this regular sharing with colleagues. As one teacher summed it up, "The Gheens Center is wonderful. It provides a variety of activities, and the quality of in-service education is much better than it was before. The support groups help us take risks. Leaders need to know that we can try."

Professional Development Schools

To some extent, the reform effort in Jefferson County is conceptual in nature—changing the professional culture in which educators work. As Schlecty puts it, "We are saying that what is needed is a new paradigm, a new way of thinking about how to involve the system." Consequently it is a bit difficult to convey the subtle changes that have occurred in the past few years as the restructuring effort has taken hold. One component of the effort that can be described is the Professional Development School. Conceived along the medical model, these schools are "real" schools in the district that volunteer to become part of a program "to serve the school system in much the same way that teaching hospitals serve the medical profession" (Schlecty,

1987, p. 11). By "real," they mean that these schools are not exceptional or unique in any way. The notion behind the "real school approach" is aptly stated by Regina Kyle: "If you can do it with these schools, you can do it *anywhere*. We are not *creaming*."

A school can become a PDS if a majority of its faculty chooses to do so, knowing that they must have some commitment to a "shared vision." The PDSs are the brainchild of Philip Schlecty, and he has written extensively on the subject. One reason Schlecty came to Louisville was his hope that this district would support the concept of PDS and help nurture it as the keystone of the effort to restructure the teaching profession. In the spring of 1986, this "shared vision" was hammered out over months of meetings, reflection, and writing. The "guiding images" or principles of this vision are best put by Schlecty:

1. The purpose of schools is to get students to do those forms of school work which produce the performance results suggested by schools system goals and priorities.
    a. Students are successful when they complete the school tasks they are assigned.
    b. Teachers are successful when they get students to do what they want them to do with a minimum amount of coercion and a maximum amount of good will.
    c. Schools are successful when students are motivated to complete forms of school work which produce maximum personal and academic achievement.
    d. School systems are successful when the level of personal and academic achievement of students is sufficiently high to satisfy parents and members of the community.
2. Given the assumption that the purpose of schools is to get students to do school work, the JCPS/Gheens Professional Development Academy views students as workers. However, students are viewed as special kinds of workers, specifically, "knowledge workers." About knowledge workers, Peter Drucker writes, "knowledge workers are persons who put to work what they have learned in systematic education, that is, concepts, ideas and theories rather than putting to work manual skill or muscle." Thus, students are not perceived as factory workers; rather, they are perceived as workers in organizations which require one to work on knowledge, to manipulate symbols, and to organize ideas and facts.
3. Given the assumption that students are workers, then teachers become "executives" who manage and lead knowledge workers. As executives, teachers must be empowered to make decisions regarding the best way to get the job done, and they must be provided

with the resources and autonomy to act on these decisions. In return, and again as executives, teachers must accept the responsibility for being accountable for the results of their decisions and actions.

Both teachers and administrators must understand that there is no one best way to teach. Results, goal achievement and student success are the primary concern of the teacher/executive, just as is the case for executives elsewhere. And not unlike other effective leaders, the teacher/executive understands that the key to excellence is the nurturance and development of those with whom they work (colleagues and peers) and those whom they must inspire and lead to work (students).

4.   If teachers are to be perceived as executives—and therefore as instructional leaders—then the traditional conceptions of principals as instructional leaders must change. Principals are, therefore, perceived as leaders of instructors and managers of managers. The skills, attitudes, and orientation that principals need in order to lead and inspire teachers who are perceived as instructional leaders differ substantially from the skills, attitudes, and orientations required if teachers are perceived to be production-line workers and students are perceived to be products. And in the new relationship, the effectiveness of the principal depends upon mutual respect, shared values, and shared decision making. In other words, leadership is not so much a position filled by one individual as it is the function of one's ability to develop relationships and inspire others to lead.

5.   The curriculum is the raw material with which students work. The job of the students is to transform the knowledge embedded in the curriculum into knowledge they can use, skills they can apply, and attitudes and understandings they can rely upon to direct action. Thus, the richness of the curriculum becomes a critical determinant of what students produce, since inferior raw materials (i.e., a weak curriculum) will produce inferior products.

6.   The products of schooling are the knowledge, skills, and attitudes which students use and take with them. Students are *not* the products of schooling; students are the products of their total life experiences; however, students are the carriers of the products of school. Students carry from school what they have learned. What students learn depends upon two things: (a) the extent to which students are successfully engaged in doing school work, and (b) the kind of school work students are expected to do [Schlecty, 1987, pp. 12–13].

The concept paper from which these six guiding visions was extracted has become the operating educational philosophy of the district. The paper was distributed to all 153 schools and an "invitation to invention" was issued to all teachers and principals (Schlecty, 1987, p. 14). By November 1986, twenty-four schools had elected to become PDSs: eight at the elementary level, eight at the middle school level, and eight at the high school level. In order to become a PDS, 51 percent of the faculty and the principal had to agree to the "guiding vision." The initial twenty-four schools are a diverse lot in terms of their need for improvement. According to Brooks, "None were in crisis, several were already far along in their process of change, and some were schools that *wanted* to do wonderful things but weren't." Although the guiding principles are sustained as a central vision, each school tailors its changes to meet its individual needs: invention occurs in lots of ways. Schlecty and Ingwerson stress that the restructuring process in Jefferson County must be, using Theodore Sizer's concept, "personalized" in each building. Although many of the guiding principles are similar to those articulated by such national groups as the Carnegie Task Force and the Holmes Group, "what is occurring in JCPS is a home-grown, local initiative that takes guidance and substance from the national reform agenda" (Schlecty, 1987, preface).

What does it mean if you are a PDS? Depending on the school, it means different things. For example, several of the middle schools are far along in participatory governance structures, so what they do in their next steps would be very different from an elementary school that has yet to do much "teaming" or interdisciplinary curriculum planning. Once a school elects to become a PDS, it selects two teacher representatives who go to monthly meetings at the Gheens Center. These representatives share information and experiences with each other and communicate back to their buildings. Each faculty must devise a plan, tailored to meet their own needs. It sets goals and works to meet those goals, at the individual and school level. Being a PDS also provides a school with access to some "Gheens money" and resources. For example, at one elementary PDS, the faculty got Gheens money to implement "something we've wanted for a long time—a science lab and a general store." For another school, "it has meant more resources—people and material, a chance to be more professional and a chance for more input at the district level."

Before one middle school became a PDS, its principal had systematically built a teaming structure among the faculty, which created "schools within a school" for each team. In the past four years, the school has benefited from flexible scheduling and interdisciplinary teaching. Both teachers and students have met with success. There has been a dramatic rise in test scores, student attendance, and student achievement as well as a decrease in teacher transfers. The Interdisciplinary Team concept helps empower people to make decisions on how learning is going to occur, on who will teach what, on who will teach when and who will teach whom. The PDS Program legitimizes this endeavor and helps to sustain it through new forms of support. A teacher from this school commented: "To me this is the way. Teachers have all the power they could possibly want. We have lots of meetings, but we make all the decisions. For example, lunch hours, students' schedules—the team does it. We do have to work around a skeletal Master Schedule, but we make the bulk of the decisions. There is a wonderful interdependence in teaching in our team. Most teams try to do at least two interdisciplinary units per year. It keeps getting better. Team teaching— teaching with others—is almost like a marriage. There are Team Leader meetings regularly as well; there is open communication. In lots of schools, teachers are saying, 'I'm getting tired.' With the Gheens Center, there is a whole new resource for us: consultants, materials, financing of projects. We are getting key people in the right places to spread the word. Jefferson County is definitely growing in a positive way. There is anticipation, excitement. Overall, we are trying things and are committed to kids."

The positive response to PDS and Gheens was echoed by a principal of an elementary PDS who indicated that "instruction is our major focus. Teachers do not feel confident to share their skills so we are trying to provide them with a feeling of basic confidence and competency. Our PDS Plan is to have substitute teachers come in so that teachers can observe other teachers in the building and other buildings. Then, the next step will be team teaching. Teachers want change. Once they see things happening, it's contagious! It's the exposure, a chain reaction. . . . More and more, I see this unfolding in the first year. PDS was a shot in the arm. Because the teachers were part of the plan from the beginning, they were ready to accept new ideas. Each teacher initially developed a goal statement. We initially had 60 percent support to go PDS, now we have 90 percent.''

Since it is only the first year of the PDS process, it is difficult to capture the quality and extent of the changes in any given school. And to focus on any one innovation in Jefferson County would not do justice to the overall effort that has begun to permeate the system. Each and any of the individual components of restructuring are but the means by which this new vision of professionalism can be accomplished.

Other Programs in the Restructuring Effort

Professional Development Schools are but one spoke in the wheel of change in Jefferson County. As mentioned earlier, several other initiatives will have as profound an effect on the restructuring effort as PDS. Briefly, these efforts include the MGAP (Middle Grades Assessment Program), which has given the middle school teachers considerable opportunity for input into planning and decision making. In most MGAP schools, the principal and teachers use the data they have gathered to set goals, plan programs, and develop appropriate professional development opportunities through the Gheens Center. The MGAP Process (designed by the Center on Adolescence at Chapel Hill, North Carolina) is one of the foundation blocks of the infrastructure that has supported the successful restructuring of several middle schools. The district is so pleased with MGAP that it is currently seeking ways to adapt the process for elementary and high schools.

Another component of the change effort is the collaborative program with the University of Louisville. This partnership is focusing on the reconceptualization of the student teacher role, the teacher role, and the university supervisor. As part of the plan, two classroom teachers were selected to become Clinical Instructors at the University, serving in an adjunct capacity as supervisors of interns and teaching faculty for methods courses in the teacher education program. Several university faculty have become involved in the schools as part of the exchange. Among the many things the faculty are doing with classroom teachers is conducting "action research groups," which focus on the needs of real schools and teachers. One group studied in-school suspension policies and made recommendations to the district. As a result of their thorough work, their recommendations were taken seriously by the district and implemented. Another group is busy studying shared decision making. Redefining the process of induction into the teaching profession is a major subtext of this collaborative endeavor.

Other changes involve the Coalition of Essential Schools, which has named five Jefferson County Schools a part of its group. The Gheens Center helps to bring together the principals and teachers from these five schools. They are beginning to look at teachers' job descriptions to see what they do all day, all week, all year. The Coalition is trying to break down some of the isolation high school teachers feel. They have begun a Middle School–High School Exchange, focusing on the ninth grade to begin with in an effort to make the transition from middle to high school less difficult for the students and more collegial for the teachers.

The Learning Choice Schools are another component of the exciting changes taking place in Jefferson County. The district was awarded $2.4 million from the federal government in the form of a Magnet Assistance Program Grant. The grant is to support the concept of "choice for parents and children" in the district. Indirectly, it will serve to maintain the level of compliance with the desegregation order of 1975. Currently, Louisville and the other Jefferson County schools are, arguably, the most substantially integrated schools in the nation. Eleven schools are involved in the Choice initiative. Some of them are PDSs, but most are not. The district is in the planning phase for this grant. One "Choice" teacher stressed that she was involved from the beginning through "summer workshops that were organized to meet and discuss what kind of programs they were going to develop with the grant money. Each teacher received $800 for reading materials alone, for each classroom." Fundamental to this project is the notion of significant teacher involvement in decision making.

With this all-too-brief account of other change efforts in the district, one needs to be reminded that the Gheens Center serves as the coordinator and catalyst for all of them. The "shared vision" of the Professional Development Schools is present in all of these inventions as well. It is also important to remember that the current climate of support for change in Jefferson County had its roots in actions taken over the past decade. The Gheens Center and its visionary leadership capitalized on the good work already done in the district, legitimized it, and provided the support and encouragement for even more change. However, significant, sustainable change doesn't happen overnight.

Reflections

So far Jefferson County has proceeded with a minimal amount of conflict—between union and management or between levels within management. However, it is still unclear just how far the issue of "power" has been stressed as they move toward empowerment. For example, what happens when the district rhetoric and the teachers' expectations are compatible, but the building principal is resistant to change? Who decides what degree of participation teachers should have? Or, is peer evaluation a next step in redefining the role of the teacher? This has not yet been addressed in Jefferson County. Ingwerson's strength as a leader is to create a positive environment that reinforces behaviors and attitudes for others to emulate, if they so choose. He succeeds by persuasion and patience rather than by mandates or coercion. There are many principals and teachers in the district who are not yet convinced that their roles should be redefined. Furthermore, what happens if and when the union takes up the issue of "working to the contract" and demands compensation for all the time teachers spend in planning and implementing changes? Will the Board be ready to make that investment? Another crucial variable that makes change possible in Jefferson County but that may affect the quality of replication around the county is the unique role of the Gheens Foundation and other sources of outside funding. It is clear that the annual investment of nearly a quarter of a million dollars from the Gheens Foundation has allowed for a level of professional development and reform in the district that wouldn't be possible in other places. Even though the district must wean itself from the Foundation within the next three years by picking up the salary of the Center Director and other programmatic expenses, the effects of the investment are significant.

There are many unanswered questions and uncharted paths in Jefferson County. At this time, however, much of what is occurring there has been positive and is contributing to a new vision of what it means to be a professional educator for the twenty-first century.

14

Encouraging Teacher Professionalism and Autonomy: Central Park East Secondary School

By Melanie Barron

This case study of Central Park East Secondary School (CPESS) examines the role of teachers in making the school work. The question of how to encourage teacher autonomy is complex, and yet simple. The history of the four schools in District 4 in East Harlem collectively known as the Central Park East network has been written by the teachers who started, administer, and teach in the schools. They share a vision of what quality education is, and how it can be delivered to students in the New York City Public Schools. The schools are deliberately kept small; teachers work together as a team; they are given support, respect, leadership; and they are treated as professionals.

Deborah Meier, the principal of the school, recently received the full status of principal after creating and running the schools for almost fourteen years. The words *boldness* and *patience* are her description of what is needed to sustain reform in education. Nationally recognized as an educational leader, she is an outspoken defender of excellence and success for children in urban schools. But a principal alone cannot run an effective school. Central Park East Secondary School is being defined and created by the teamwork of teachers, within an unusual constellation of support, including the United Federation of Teachers; the District 4 Office; the Division of High Schools of the New

225

York City Board of Education; the Coalition of Essential Schools of Brown University, a group of public and private schools that is seeking to reform secondary schools in the United States; and a MacArthur Foundation Fellowship.

This chapter summarizes the history of the Central Park East network in District 4, states the principles of the Coalition of Essential Schools that set the philosophical framework for the school, and outlines the school's program and structure. Teachers' perceptions of their roles and power are discussed, and the issue of leadership is examined.

First Encounter with Central
Park East Secondary School

Where is the door? One of the first items of business in visiting any school is finding the unlocked door, a particularly challenging task in a New York City school. Central Park East Secondary School is located on the upper floors of Jackie Robinson Junior High School, JHS 113, in School District 4 of Manhattan, on the northeast corner of 106th Street and Madison Avenue. Both are wide, heavily trafficked avenues on which many teachers need to doublepark their cars during the school day. The school is in a low orange/red brick building, close to another elementary school on 108th Street and Madison, two blocks from the Museum of the City of New York, and one block from Fifth Avenue and Central Park. Elevated trains screech and whistle past the east side of the school.

A cracked flagstone sidewalk and graffiti-marked walls lead to the entrance in an inner court of the school, one of several steel-barred doors. As I walk in, uniformed school guards sign me in and wave me toward the staircase. Because in District 4 for the last fourteen years it has been customary for different schools to share one building, I was not surprised to be passed on the stairs by a group of seven-year-olds purposefully carrying their violins to class. There was still no evidence that this was the location of one of the most publicized alternative high schools in New York City, except for the long list of visitors' names in the school log.

However, when I entered the library on the second floor, it quickly became clear that I had found the Central Park East Secondary School. Three students were working on an Apple computer, and several other groups of students were working alone, without a teacher in sight. Students were helping one another gather information about various countries, using both packaged computer programs and library resource materials, such as almanacs and encyclopedias. It was obvious that they were working against a deadline and were concerned with the difference between "cheating" and getting information from resources. About twelve students were checking other students' work, teaching one another how to use computer software, and actively controlling their behavior so that the group could concentrate on the task at hand. These ninth-grade students were working on projects in their own way—noisy and yet intent on their projects, respectful of, and helpful to, one another. Teachers were in the back reference area of the library, but their active presence was not needed for the students to continue their work. This encounter was a powerful example of one of the main principles of the Coalition of Essential Schools: students as workers.

Central Park East Network

Why is there a high school physically in the middle of a junior high school building, sharing space with an elementary school? To understand the strength of Central Park East Secondary School, we need to examine briefly the history of both an idea and its implementation.

Central Park East Secondary School is one of two alternative high schools in District 4 of the New York City Public Schools. The New York City School System was decentralized in 1969, with the creation of thirty-two separate school districts run by locally elected school boards and administered by community superintendents hired by the school boards. The more than ninety high schools are administered by the Division of High Schools of the central administration, while elementary and junior high schools are controlled at the local district level by the community school boards and their superintendents. The central administration of the New York City schools is always struggling to find ways to control and improve education at the elementary and junior high level and finds itself blocked by the local decentralized structures; at the same time, local districts struggle with the central board to improve high schools in their neighborhoods. The decentralized organization of the New York City schools is repeatedly identified as one of the major structural barriers to school reform, particularly as it defines what the chancellor can and cannot control.

An exception to the usual despair generated by educational programs created at the district level is Community School District 4, East Harlem. The district is on the east side of Manhattan, beginning at 96th Street and extending north to 125th Street, stretching from Central Park to the East River. Currently, there are about thirty alternative schools within the district, including two high schools that are cooperatively run by District 4 and the central Division of High Schools. One of the first two alternative schools in the district was Central Park East Elementary School, established in the fall of 1974 by Deborah Meier at the invitation of Anthony Alvarado, then District 4 superintendent. Alvarado was encouraged by his school board in 1973 to make radical changes to improve student achievement (the district had the lowest standardized reading scores in the city at the time) and lower the dropout rate. The district was also facing declining enrollment and, consequently, school closings. Since 1973 academic achievement in the district, which is one of the city's financially poorest, has improved significantly. It ranked in the middle among all city schools in reading scores in June 1987, and ranked twenty-first out of the thirty-two districts in math scores.

The new partnership between a teacher with a vision of what teaching could be like if only teachers had control, and an administration that was willing to break and bend rules and make new ones to support innovative programs and people, has helped to create a district with many alternative schools, including the four schools that make up the Central Park East (CPE) network. Deborah Meier is the principal of Central Park East, a network of four schools in District 4: Central Park East

I (1974), Central Park East II (1980), and River East (1982) elementary schools, which feed into Central Park East Secondary School (1985). Previous to the opening of CPE, Meier had taught at the Workshop Center for Open Education at City College, directed by Lillian Weber, which trained teachers in the management of open classrooms. The initial CPE staff was drawn from teachers who were at the center; both Meier and her staff were inspired by the center's principles and philosophy of open education.

The first school began in shared space in P.S. 171, on 103rd Street and Madison Avenue, with approximately 100 children from kindergarten and first and second grades. All children from the district were welcomed, including a large number of children with special needs. Parents were involved in the educational process through conferences and extensive written and personal communication with teachers. The school differed radically from traditional modes of learning: it didn't look, sound, or operate like a standard elementary school. Children learned actively by moving around in what appeared to some to be chaos; teachers worked together in teams, using not only textbooks but all kinds of learning materials; and there was no principal, but a director who taught full time. Curriculum responded to the needs and interests of the students rather than to standardized, required syllabi from the central board. Curriculum was in the hands of teachers, who were encouraged and supported in the design and implementation of their own ideas.

In addition to control over the curriculum, teachers were committed to working together democratically to administer the school. Teachers had shared responsibility for the school, while Meier shouldered the double role of teacher and head administrator, without clear definition of roles and responsibilities. In the third year, she became a full-time administrator, supporting her belief that "a good staff needs someone to play an advisory role, to provide both stretch and support. Such a role is as important for competent and experienced teachers as it is for inexperienced ones" (Bensman, 1987, p. 20).

A pattern of teacher collaboration and interaction evolved in the school both on the development of curriculum and pedagogy and on the teachers' own professional development. Freed from sharing the administrative burdens of running the school, teachers could spend more time and energy on creating an effective and enriched education program. This shift in teacher emphasis took about three years. It was an important lesson for the faculty of Central Park East Secondary School on what kinds of roles and responsibilities are appropriate or functional in a school that demands a great deal of energy and commitment.

Central Park East II began in 1980 in another school building, P.S. 109, because of the increasing number of applications to Central Park East from parents all over New York City. The small, initial student population at this school grew in three years to 190 children, with classes from prekindergarten through sixth grade. Initially, Meier was director of both CPE I and II, and also taught, but with the continued growth of CPE II, a separate director was appointed. Both schools, however, shared applicant pools of students and teachers, and many administrative support systems. Sy Fliegel, who directed the growing alternative junior high school network for the district, and Meier chose the director for CPE II—a teacher trainer with experience in the City College Workshop on Open Education. Thus, the educational philosophy of the teachers who started the first CPE school was continued at CPE II.

Carlos Medina, who succeeded Alvarado as District 4 superintendent after Alvarado became chancellor of the New York City schools, supported the opening of a third open classroom elementary school, River East, in 1982. This school became part of the new k–12 education complex, Manhattan Center for Science and Mathematics, which replaced the Benjamin Franklin High School at the East River and 116th Street. The director of this school also was trained in open education and continued the District 4 tradition of a teacher-run alternative school. These three elementary schools continue to be the only schools in the district at this level where parents can choose to send children, even though they do not live in the immediate neighborhood.

Several issues identified with the survival of this complex of schools have a bearing on the role of teachers in the Central Park East Secondary School. The schools each started with a small dedicated group of teachers who shared an educational philosophy and worked as a democratic community. "We saw it as equally important that the school life of adults be made more democratic . . . [although] remaining committed to staff decision making was not easy" (Meier, 1987, p. 755). The small staff and school size helped retain flexibility for problem solving. Crucial to survival and continuing implementation has been the creative and active guardianship of the District 4 office. Anthony Alvarado, Sy Fliegel, who directed the district's growing alternative junior high school network, Carlos Medina, who succeeded Alvarado as District Superintendent, and Deborah Meier have, together, been responsible for providing the administrative security that is essential to protect the risk taking that created and sustains this network of schools. Parent and teacher ownership of the schools kept them involved and determined to ensure survival. "Most of all, the directors have allowed teachers to exercise their own judgment in developing their curricula and techniques. In short, teachers are treated as professionals" (Bensman, 1987, p. 46).

The leadership of Deborah Meier is unquestionably the linchpin of this whole process, for she had a vision of what education could be and the intellectual capacity to transform the vision into reality. In spring 1987, she was awarded a MacArthur Foundation Fellowship for educational leadership, focusing national attention on the schools in District 4, particularly on Central Park East Secondary School. She has been named a member of the National Board for Professional Teaching Standards set up by the Carnegie Forum on Education and the Economy to examine the establishment of voluntary national teacher certification. And she was considered a finalist for the position of chancellor for the New York City schools late in 1987. Her role of leader/principal is pivotal in understanding the capacity of teachers to assume autonomy and their freedom to be professionals in Central Park East.

Central Park East Secondary School

History and Educational Philosophy. In 1984, at the tenth anniversary of Central Park East, as a response both to the educational needs of the graduates of CPE schools and to the verbal challenge of Theodore Sizer (chairman of Brown University's Education Department and director of the Coalition of Essential Schools), planning began for a secondary school at Central Park East. The success of Manhattan Center for Science and Mathematics in District 4, the first high school ever cooperatively run by a district and the central board, encouraged the district to establish a second district high school, Central Park East Secondary School (CPESS). The conversations, negotiations, meetings, and memorandums that preceded the opening of the school doors in 1985 would astound and deter most educators of average will and energy, as would the vast number of creative interpretations of rules, agreements, and waivers of required high school courses and standardized examinations that were discussed and agreed to by all parties.

Close cooperation between the United Federation of Teachers (UFT), the largest local union (75,000 members) in the United States, and Central Park East Secondary School permitted this experiment in secondary education to proceed. Sandra Feldman, president of the UFT, met with Meier and administrators from District 4 and developed a close, cooperative working relationship with them. The UFT provided both encouragement and support for CPESS, reflective of its recently negotiated contract with New York City, which explicitly advocates increasing flexible and innovative educational approaches to expand professional opportunities for teachers. During the discussions, the union provided input to program design; it is considered an ally by teachers in this effort at CPESS.

The negotiations between District 4 and the Division of High Schools succeeded for a variety of reasons: ten years of district experience with Central Park East's flourishing open-education elementary schools; almost thirty alternative schools and programs in the district; an increase in student achievement; a growing national reputation for innovation in urban education; consistent, skillful leadership; active teacher-union cooperation and support; and the involvement of a national school reform project.

Central Park East Secondary School is now a cooperative project of Community School District 4, the New York City

Board of Education, and the Coalition of Essential Schools. Theodore Sizer's Coalition of Essential Schools consists of twelve public and private schools, and forty associate schools throughout the country, which are attempting to reform the structure and content of secondary education. Of the nine general principles that are the essence of the Coalition's plan, four are highlighted in Central Park East's current program description:

1. *Less is more.* It is more important to know some things well than to know more things superficially.
2. *Personalization.* Although the course of study is unified and universal, teaching and learning are personalized. No teacher is responsible for teaching more than 80 students, or for advising more than 15.
3. *Goal setting.* High standards are set for all students. Students must clearly exhibit mastery of their school work.
4. *Student-as-worker.* Teachers at CPESS "coach" students, encouraging students to find answers and, in effect, to teach themselves. Thus, students discover answers and solutions and learn by doing rather than simply memorizing what others have discovered [Central Park East Secondary School, 1986, p. 3].

These and additional principles of the Coalition were used as the organizing principles behind the structure of Central Park East Secondary School. Five imperatives for better schools were identified in *Horace's Compromise: The Dilemma of the American High School,* one of three volumes resulting from "A Study of High Schools" (Sizer, 1984, p. 214). These imperatives, which preceded the establishment of the Coalition, further define commitments made by CPESS. These are:

- Give room to teachers and students to work and learn in their own, appropriate ways.
- Insist that students clearly exhibit mastery of school work.
- Get the incentives right, for students and for teachers.
- Focus the students' work on the use of their minds.
- Keep the structure simple and flexible.

These charges are echoed in the statement of purpose for CPESS written for prospective parents and students: "The fundamental aim of CPESS is to teach students to use their minds well, to prepare them for a well-lived life that is productive, socially useful and personally satisfying. The school offers an academic program that stresses intellectual achievement. Mastery of a limited number of centrally important subjects is emphasized. This goes hand-in-hand with an approach that emphasizes learning how to learn, how to reason, and how to investigate complex issues that require collaboration and personal responsibility'' (Central Park East Secondary School, 1986a, p. 2).

Structure and Program.   Central Park East enrolled 240 students in grades 7–9 during the 1987–88 school year. A new class will join each year until 1990–91, when the school will reach a total of 500 students in grades 7–12. The first class will graduate in 1991. The population of District 4 is about 60 percent Hispanic, 35 percent black, and 5 percent white. The population of CPESS as of late 1987 was 36 percent Hispanic, 49 percent black, 13 percent white, and 2 percent other. Students from CPE I, CPE II, and River East and their siblings are given first preference for acceptance, followed by other students from District 4. Most students from outside District 4 cannot be admitted because of lack of space. Admission procedures pay attention to maintaining a racial and ethnic balance in the school and to equalizing the number of boys and girls.

Students who apply to CPESS spend a day at the school before they are accepted; their parents visit the school and have a conference with the director and assistant director; and an assessment form is filled out by each student's sending teacher. Parents and students are given a CPESS brochure and a letter that explains the philosophy and structure of the school. In addition, one of the CPESS teachers writes an observation of the student during his or her visit to the school, which becomes part of the student's application folder. Certainly, this extraordinary personal attention to each student is radically different from placement procedures in most large urban high schools. This effort is made to communicate the program, structure, philosophy, and expectations of the school to the student and the student's parents. It also serves, through the very process itself, to demonstrate how the school will act in relation to students and their families.

CPESS's approach to curriculum has been derived from the ideas and models proposed by the Coalition and shaped by

CPESS staff to meet the needs of students and the community. It also reflects the experiences of the CPE network. The members of the Coalition share a set of ideas in common, according to Sizer, from which they "create an intellectual atmosphere in which instruction is personalized and students are provoked to take charge of their own learning. The goal is that each student leaves high school with the ability to think, question and reason" (Chion-Kenney, 1987, p. 18). Central Park East Secondary School, according to Chion-Kenney, is further along than other schools in the Coalition in (1) developing an interdisciplinary curriculum built on essential questions, and (2) in creating alternative ways of finding out how much a student has learned. According to the CPE Secondary School Plan, students are expected to engage in writing, reading, and discussion of ideas. Work is both collaborative and individual. Students are expected to make use of the school library and other city library facilities, and to use the various word processors and computers housed throughout the building, which are readily accessible to students and staff.

The school day at CPESS offers a common core curriculum for all students in grades 7–10, organized around two major fields: mathematics/science for half the school day, and humanities (art, history, social studies, and literature) for the other half. The maximum class size is eighteen students. Foreign languages are offered between 8:00 and 9:00 A.M., and sports, computer workshops, woodwork, and arts daily from 3.15 to 5:00 P.M. Every day twelve to fifteen students meet for forty-five minutes in one of sixteen advisory groups, which coordinate students' academic programs and also home/school activities. In addition to their individual advisory groups, students meet in "houses" of seventy-five students grouped by seventh and eighth grades and ninth and tenth grades. Weekly house meetings allow wider student interaction and participation in school decision making. Students spend two hours each week in a service program, which encompasses such activities as working in museums, student teaching, and interacting with senior citizens.

At the end of tenth grade (the first class will begin in 1989) students will enter the Senior Institute, designed for each student by a Graduation Committee made up of the student, the family, and the teacher adviser. The Institute is planned as a personal program of study, with a seminar on books and ideas that have shaped civilization as a unifying core for the Institute. Demonstration of mastery through exhibitions, portfolios, a record of community/school service, and evidence of an appropriate postgraduation plan developed in the Senior Institute are necessary to gain graduation approval. Graduation requirements also include: completion of a CPESS-mandated four-year course of study; an approved Senior Institute Plan and completion of specified items; success in a second-language proficiency exam; passing of five basic minimum competency exams; evidence of ability in paper-and-pencil tests from CPESS, the city, and the state; and, most important, overall evidence of the student's ability to take charge of his or her future. The promise made to students by CPESS states: "We are committed to the idea that a diploma is a meaningful piece of paper, not one that says only that the student has 'stuck it out' through high school. A CPESS diploma tells the student—and the world— that the student has not only mastered specific fields of study but has also mastered the ability to think critically and to evaluate" (Central Park East Secondary School, 1986a, p. 10).

Curriculum and the Role of Teachers.   Fifteen teachers provide the structure, energy, imagination, and strength to create and sustain the program of the Central Park East Secondary School. They are experienced, certified New York City teachers, who opted for and have been chosen by their peers to collaborate in a reform effort in secondary urban education. Their main focus has been on the design and teaching of the four-year common-core curriculum in Humanities/Social Studies and in Science/Mathematics. The content, approach, and structure of the courses are owned by the teachers; they are free to collaboratively design courses and draw on their own strengths and on the resources of content experts to support their plans.

The structural elements and philosophy described above are givens for the school; the curriculum is up to the teachers. Freedom, with responsibility, creates incredible demands on teachers at CPESS, but it also enables them to initiate exciting and innovative ways to teach and learn. An overall governing principle of the Coalition "requires a radical change in the way teachers think of themselves," from that of a giver of information to that of a coach. Teacher-as-coach and student-as-worker demand a basic shift in the way schools operate; as a way of teaching, it is as often discussed in theory as it is ignored in practice. These methods are in operation at CPESS.

The teachers at CPESS are empowered to schedule their classes and to purchase a diverse array of teaching materials and experiences to support their teaching, so that students can proceed with their learning. Their curriculum work is the foundation of the school. Teacher interaction in the design of the curriculum and their freedom to teach in small classes, with sufficient time to examine issues in depth, is the key to teacher autonomy at CPESS.

An example of teacher direction is the decision made collectively by staff that the entire school would do mapping together. The walls of classrooms throughout the school were labeled N, E, S, and W as part of a schoolwide study of geography; every classroom had globes and maps, including subway maps and aerial maps of New York City, on which students identified their homes. In one particular classroom, homework assignments included making an aerial map of the student's bedroom and writing five entries in a journal on directions. Students asked one another where they lived and marked the locations with colored yarn. Students worked in groups, while the teachers helped individual students with problems and brought the groups together at the end of class to read a story. Discipline was clearly exerted through mutual respect for one another and for the teacher. The collective choice to do mapping was also cited by teachers as an example of how the high school teachers are more likely to make joint decisions than the elementary school teachers. The house system creates a collective body of teachers who spend a lot of time together as a team planning and monitoring their teaching. Although the subjects to be taught in the high school grades are semiprescribed by the common-core curriculum, the teachers select the content and, together, design how they will be taught.

Perceptions of Power

"We decide." This statement by a humanities teacher at CPESS is the answer to the question—what do teachers feel they have power over in the school? The strength of the teacher content teams is the motivation to work on curriculum together, to reach consensus agreement on what and how they will teach, and to take responsibility to help others teach. Teachers observe one another, give feedback and suggestions for change, team teach on particular topics, share assignments, and help one another learn how to teach. This activity is teacher-driven and teacher-led. The ultimate power, they feel, is having the power to make decisions. Once an agreement is reached, can it be reexamined? Do teachers have the power to change a decision? At CPESS the answer is a resounding yes. Teachers at CPESS felt that the structure of the school supported their freedom to exercise the power for which they were trained—to teach. Explicitly and implicitly, teachers stated, in response to questions about their desire to control and manage activities at CPESS, "I want to be a teacher."

"I have everything I need to make curriculum work," including a library, support staff, other teachers to share formal and informal staff development activities, flexible schedule, and financial resources, said another teacher. This experienced teacher believes that teachers in other schools might try to exercise the kind of professionalism and autonomy of teachers at CPESS, but they would feel alone and wouldn't have a school structure to support their efforts. "I have the freedom to do so much more, to create so much more." Teacher conversations about autonomy, power, and decision making constantly referred to the teacher's interest in curriculum, teaching, and individual interactions with students. Assistant Director Herb Rosenfeld stated: "Here anyone can have an idea, argue in favor of it, and go for it. There is no hierarchy to block it."

The democratic history of CPE schools encourages the professional role teachers have assumed in policymaking at CPESS. Their responsibility for policymaking is accompanied by their participation in the implementation of policy. Forms were changed four times in one year at the suggestion of teachers; the timing and focus of advisory groups were shifted; staff development activities have been shaped and run by teachers; and teachers are involved in hiring teachers new to the school. To accomplish this shared decision making, teachers meet in their houses, meet as a school for breakfast on Friday mornings, meet in content teams to plan curriculum, and have weekend retreats for the staffs of all four CPE schools. Together, the teachers at CPESS help decide on the curriculum, scheduling, grading, professional development, personnel, discipline, student recruitment and selection, and issues of general administration.

Role of the Teacher: Classroom Versus Administration

It has been suggested that a line needs to be drawn to protect full-time teachers so they can do their job and do it well. A balance must be established between what teachers want and have time to control, and what can be decided by the educational leadership of the school. The teachers at CPESS persistently expressed their preference for autonomy and control over what went on in their classrooms. They were delighted to have as their principal a skillful educator who would assume the onerous tasks of dealing with the bureaucracy of District 4 and the central Board of Education. Teachers wanted power in leadership at the school level. They clearly valued the structure of decision making at CPESS, which enabled them to discuss and plan for the school and to raise questions about any decision. Several teachers expressed the view that they did not want the same kind of information and control over budget and resources that Meier and Rosenfeld had, because they did not want to take the time to deal with the complexities, the politics, and the work. They clearly did want to continue their role in policymaking, but not with the same detailed responsibility for implementation that the principal had.

CPESS operates by making staff decisions with a substantial number of people who are directly involved in the issue at hand. The small size of the school, the supportive political environment provided by both the families of students and the administration, and educational leadership enables this process to work. Teachers did express interest in knowing how funding for the school was allocated, in so far as it affected what they would be able to secure for their classrooms. It is likely, with time, that the staff will become more interested in knowing more about funding when their vantage point expands to cover the school as a whole. At this point, however, the teachers are most appropriately dedicated to working out ways to make a difference for individual students in the school.

Leadership and the Role of the Teachers

A complex balancing act between staff and principal continues to take place on roles and on matters of decision making. The energy and vision of the principal of the CPE network has guided, led, prodded, and pulled these schools into being. It is also clear that the principal is committed to democratic decision making with staff as a way to run the schools. The process of deciding with staff on details of how to run the school is complex and exhausting and, at times, must try everyone's patience. Strong leadership is absolutely necessary to keep the process in motion and to challenge and respond to staff on complex issues as they arise. Such leadership also protects staff and enables them to exert the power and autonomy they have as teachers. Conversely, the school depends on, and is literally defined by, the structures and classes managed by the teachers. The balance between protection and power created by this interaction determines the limits of autonomy for the teachers.

Other Issues

Several issues in regard to teacher autonomy and effectiveness are raised by the program at CPESS: (1) differences between elementary and high school reform, (2) the role of teachers in administration and classrooms, and (3) the part played by central bureaucracy.

1. *Differences between elementary and high school reform.* "The obstacles that block the path of reforming a high school are harder to budge than those that face elementary schools" (Meier, 1987, p. 756). Many of the teachers new to CPESS have not been trained in the techniques of open education; they need support to shift their role from teacher as giver-of-information to teacher as coach. Because of their lack of experience in open education, they have different expectations of what students should be doing in classrooms. Moreover, they were trained to teach a solitary subject rather than an interdisciplinary curriculum. It takes time for professional support and staff development to help teachers make the leap into the new curriculum demanded by the philosophy and promise of CPESS.

In addition, there are more city- and state-mandated requirements at the secondary school level, which need to be negotiated and integrated into the program. Teachers at the high school do not all come from one shared training program as did the teachers in CPE I, II, and River East. It will take time for CPESS teachers to build their own network, based on their experience at CPESS and their participation in the Coalition.

2. *The role of teachers in administration and classrooms.* The changing emphasis on the role of the teachers in both policymaking and in curriculum development will continue until the school has passed through the initial implementation phase. It is obvious that CPESS needs and wants teachers to be involved in both decision making for the school as a whole and in writing a new curriculum. The balance will be determined by the time and skill of the individual teachers as well as by shifting models of decision making for the school. Teachers want to focus on their classrooms as well as participate in school governance. As time passes, teachers will develop a shared history of creating a school, which will give them a firmer base from which to expand the limits of their autonomy.

3. *The part played by central bureaucracy.* In interview after interview, and in her work in CPE, Meier has called for the central bureaucracy to create a system in which Central Park East Secondary School could be the rule, not the exception. The major task for school reform, as she sees it, is the reconceptualiza-

tion of the role of the central office to one of support and technical assistance to schools. The central office should be examined to find out what prevents people of intelligence from working within the system, and then those roadblocks should be removed. If the system could honor entrepreneurs and welcome them in, there would be hope for change. If the central Board of Education bureaucracy would ''open up'' this process, it ''could encourage talented educators to take on the continuing challenge of reform. Whether CPE's success will be often replicated depends on how much the system as a whole becomes amenable to, and even supportive of, attempts at change'' (Bensman, 1987, p. 47).

The educational leadership of Deborah Meier, the continuing protection of the District 4 office, the assistance of the Alternative High School Division, the intellectual and financial support of the Coalition of Essential Schools, the active encouragement of the leadership of the United Federation of Teachers, the support of the MacArthur Foundation, and the wealth of experience and skill that reside in the teaching staff of CPE I, II, and River East all encourage the community of parents and students of Central Park East Secondary School. These elements, and probably more, are needed right now to maintain the momentum and direction of CPESS. How long can this coalition be sustained? What other structures are needed to assure that this experiment can succeed and continue? The answers to these questions are not yet apparent. What is certain is that Central Park East Secondary School is giving teachers greater responsibility for the development of an educational model committed to serving young people well.

15

Restructuring Education:
A New Vision at
Hope Essential High School

by Thomas B. Corcoran

Hope Essential High School (EHS) is a school within a school located within Hope High School, in Providence, Rhode Island. Hope, a distressed inner-city school, is a member of the Coalition of Essential Schools, the national network of schools working with Theodore Sizer and his staff at Brown University to reform the structure and content of secondary education. Through the development of the EHS, the staff of Hope is attempting to translate the Coalition's principles of reform into a program to renew Hope. Working under adverse circumstances, they are literally attempting to restructure an urban high school from the inside out. The program is new and it is still small, but it represents ideas that could have a profound effect on the structure and quality of American public education and on the nature of the teaching profession. What follows is a description of this effort and a discussion of some of the central issues and problems faced by the teaching staff at Hope.

This chapter examines the role teachers are playing in planning and implementing the program at Hope and assesses its implications for changes in the roles and responsibilities of teachers in the larger system in which the EHS operates. However, the question of teacher empowerment cannot be divorced from the program itself. Changing the roles of teachers is not perceived as an end in itself at Hope, rather it is seen as a means to raise the quality of education for students. The new roles being assigned to teachers are influenced by this superordinate goal as well as by practical, fiscal, and legal constraints within which the program functions. Moreover, the continuation and expansion of these new teacher responsibilities are likely to be determined by the success of the program in raising the academic achievement of students. Therefore, the discussion of teacher involvement, or empowerment, must be embedded in an understanding of the program, its objectives, its problems, and its potential.

The chapter is organized into seven sections. The first section is a description of how the EHS staff are attempting to realize the Coalition's principles of reform and its effects on the roles and responsibilities of teachers. The next two sections cover the context of the program and its short history to date. This is a departure from the usual sequence in papers of this type, but it may avoid some redundancy and help the reader understand the complexities of the situation. The fourth section addresses the central question of teacher involvement in decision making in the EHS. The fifth section reports on the initial impact the EHS has had on its students and on the larger school. Issues and problems associated with the EHS are discussed in the sixth section, and the final section contains some speculations of the author about the interaction between the goals of the program and the realities of its implementation and expansion in Providence and how they could shape its future.

Hope Essential High School

The current staff of the EHS consists of a full-time head teacher, four full-time teachers (one for each of the four core subjects), and a secretary. Working from four classrooms and a small office on the third floor of Hope, this team serves 104 ninth and tenth graders who applied for admission to the EHS. Most of these students live within the Hope feeder pattern; the exceptions are students who were admitted to the Arts magnet located at Hope and who also applied to the EHS. According to the current plan, additional teams of four teachers and 104 new ninth graders will be added to the EHS each year for the next three years.

Table 15.1 displays the ethnic composition of the student body enrolled in the EHS and that of Hope High School. The two student populations are roughly comparable in ethnic make-up. The EHS has a significantly larger white population and smaller proportions of Hispanics and Asians. The EHS students also differ slightly in their academic profiles. In his report on the first year of the EHS, the head teacher, Albin Moser, de-scribed the students as below average in reading and math on national scales; most of them were in the 4th and 5th stanines on national tests (Moser, 1987b). This is only slightly higher than the academic performance of Hope's general enrollment. Moser also noted that there were twenty to twenty-five students in the EHS whose academic work was quite good. Clearly the EHS students do not constitute a gifted population in the con-ventional sense, but it seems reasonable to assume that their motivation levels and their attitudes toward school might be more positive than the general student population at Hope, given that they had to apply and that the EHS staff did examine achieve-ment measures during the admissions process. No cutoff scores were used, but staff interviewed indicated that the Hope staff referred better students to the EHS.

Table 15.1. Percentage of Student Enrollment
by Race and Ethnic Group, Spring 1987.

School	Black	Hispanic	White	Asian	Portuguese	Cape Verdean
EHS	43.3	11.5	25.0	2.9	11.5	5.8
Hope	45.6	20.6	14.3	7.9	6.5	5.1

Source: Compiled from data provided by the Providence School Department.

Perhaps the best way to communicate what the EHS staff are doing with these students and how it differs from what goes on in traditional schools is to describe how the nine principles set forth by the Coalition are being implemented at Hope. The

Coalition explicitly rejects the prescription of a specific model for reform and the use of top-down approaches to change, advocating instead that the staffs of each member school adapt the principles to fit their contexts and their strengths.

At one level the goals of the EHS appear to be quite straightforward—design and implement a program based on the nine principles of the Coalition. The team hopes to develop tenacious students who will master the essential skills in the core curriculum and who know how to learn, work harder, and can get help when they need it. In his April 1987 report on the EHS, Albin Moser wrote: "Our goals are consistent with the principles of the Coalition. . . . Succinctly, we wish to develop well-rounded, inquisitive, friendly students who are able to demonstrate their willingness and ability to continue their learning. Within the classroom, this means greater emphasis on discussion, group work, writing, and problem-solving across the four subject areas" (Moser, 1987b, p. 1). The staff of the EHS, working in concert with faculty from Brown, are applying the principles as follows:

1. *An intellectual focus.*   The team has developed new curricula in English, mathematics, science, and social studies that emphasize "strong reading, writing, speaking, and thinking skills as well as essential content development in courses required for college entrance" (Moser and others, 1986, p. 3). The team has been given the discretion and the time to make decisions about course content and materials. Working within the general framework set by the curricular objectives of the PSD, they have attempted to define what is essential in their disciplines. In the classroom there is expected to be a greater emphasis on discussion, group work, writing, and problem solving. Moser (1987b) describes the difference from traditional programs as being "the concentration on coaching as the method, the interdisciplinary teamwork, the high expectations, and the manner of arranging the course work so that students who complete their work either 'on time' or ahead of schedule will have the opportunity to do more with what is usually their fourth year of school" (Moser, 1987b, p. 2). All students are required to take four academically rigorous courses that are taught in double periods every other

day. Leahy (1987) suggests that the use of double periods in the four core areas helps focus attention and permits coverage in depth.

The city course requirements for graduation from high school in mathematics and science also have been extended by one year. And perhaps, most significantly, the team has adopted a form of mastery learning in which course credit is awarded only to those who perform A or B work. In practice, this means achieving a mark of at least 80 percent on all assignments or redoing the work until this standard is reached. Students not meeting the standard are given incompletes at the end of the quarterly marking periods and are expected to make up this work. Failure to do so results in no credit being awarded for the course.

2. *Simple goals.*   The intention is to have students master a limited number of essential skills, not merely cover content as in conventional courses. The EHS team has worked toward this end, but Diane Leahy notes in her paper that this is an area in which theory and practice are difficult to bring together: "Students may not see (and I admit, sometimes the teachers may forget) the inter-relatedness of the various assignments, the goals that we are building toward. There is a tendency among the students, at least in English, and, I would suspect, in other disciplines as well, to see each homework assignment as a discrete unit, perhaps related to class work from that day but certainly divorced from other homework assignments" (Leahy, 1987, p. 7). Yet while the principle may be elusive in practice, the EHS teachers are conscious of it and that in itself is an achievement. It is discussed within the team and with the staff from Brown. The effort to integrate and reinforce skills and knowledge, while intermittent and inadequate, is also unusual and admirable.

3. *Universal goals.*   All students in the EHS are required in theory to demonstrate mastery of the same essential skills and to meet the same standards. In principle they will take the same sequence of courses in the core curriculum. Yet the students have been grouped for these courses according to their math achievement, and it is expected that there will be some differentiation in the curriculum. There is a set of minimum expecta-

tions defined for mathematics, but some students will follow a traditional course sequence and reach different levels of attainment in math than other students. In the other subjects the staff seems to have come closer to setting universal expectations. This principle also is reinforced by the use of the mastery learning approach.

4. *Personalization.*   The double periods, the emphasis on coaching and collaborative work in class, the physical location of the program, and the team planning are intended to intensify the relationships between the teachers and their students. The teachers discuss students in team meetings and attempt to act in concert to deal with individual cases. Their attention, of course, is most often directed toward the needs of problem students. Their decision to have teams continue to work with the same students for at least two years is likely to further strengthen their relationships with students. The teachers are also serving as advisers and meet with students three times weekly in what are referred to as EHS classes. They are becoming involved with their students personally as well as academically.

Ironically, the higher attendance in the EHS means larger daily classes and to some degree undermines the effort to strengthen student-teacher relationships. The EHS staff is responsible for over 100 students rather than the 80 recommended by the Coalition's guiding principle. However, they have had assistance from student teachers in English, social studies, and biology and from the clinical professors in the first two areas.

5. *Student-as-worker.*   Diane Leahy (1987) in her review of the EHS expressed optimism about the progress that had been made toward the realization of this principle. Students are expected to work while in class rather than sit passively while a teacher presents. They are given assignments that challenge their intellects. They are expected to work in teams. They are often asked to present or to demonstrate. In class, teachers move among the students, explaining, demonstrating, motivating, and reviewing work in progress. The traditional classroom with its passive students and the teacher up front presenting has been replaced by a student workroom supervised by an academic coach. The double periods and the ability of the team to alter

the schedule enable teachers to plan activities that make significant demands on the students.

6. *Diploma by exhibition.*   The staff is still working to define
what constitutes an acceptable demonstration or exhibition of
mastery and has devoted considerable time to discussion of that
issue. This remains the most significant unresolved operational
question. The team has explored the use of tests, papers, projects, and presentations as examples of exhibitions but has not
yet settled on an approach to demonstration or agreed on standards of acceptability.

7. *Attitude.*   This principle calls for faculty to set unanx-
ious expectations for students, exhibit trust and decency in their
relationships with students, and collaborate with parents. It is
not possible to assess the degree to which these values are being
acted on at the EHS in a two-day visit, but it is obvious that
there is a positive, can-do attitude among the teaching staff.
Relations among students and between staff and students seem
warm and friendly. There appears to be mutual respect and,
as a consequence, there is a relaxed tone in the classrooms and
in the halls. There have been discipline problems, particularly
with a few chronic troublemakers, but the problems are fewer
and less severe than in the larger school. There has been an
energetic effort to reach out to parents through phone calls,
parent-teacher conferences, and an Open House. The parent
response has been positive and more parents have participated
in these events than expected.

8. *Staff.*   This tenet asks staff to assume the role of gen-
eralist teachers rather than content specialists. Certification requirements and provisions of contract, however, prevent teachers
from teaching out of their field. The spirit of the tenet might
be realized through team teaching, but as yet that has not occurred in the EHS. Teachers, however, have taken on new
responsibilities for curriculum, are serving as advisers, and, as
team members, are engaging in planning and policymaking.
The team members are still functioning as content specialists,
but they are assuming collective responsibility for the EHS.

9. *Budget.*   The EHS team operates on a modest budget,
but it does have significant discretionary resources beyond the

normal school budget. Additional funds have been provided by the Hewlett Foundation, and the district has made special allocations of Chapter II funds, the state Basic Education Program grant, and local funds. These monies have provided for the head teacher, an initial semester of planning time for the entire team, the two weekly team planning periods, the secretary, new texts and instructional materials, consultants, supplies, equipment (including a computer for the EHS office), and travel funds to participate in Coalition meetings and workshops. In addition, a grant from the Champlin foundation of Rhode Island is paying for physical improvements on the third floor, such as painting, renovations to classrooms and the school library, and much needed repairs to student restrooms. In addition, the team has been supported by additional human resources in the form of two clinical professors who work at Hope half time and student teachers.

Teacher Work Load in the Essential School.   The overall work load for teachers in the Essential School is difficult to assess. Each day they teach two double academic classes per day, attend a team planning meeting (twice a week) or monitor an EHS class (three times a week), have an individual prep period, and time for lunch. This schedule is similar in outline to that of the larger faculty who teach five classes. However, EHS staff have been relieved of noninstructional duties such as monitoring the cafeteria, and they may have only one formal class preparation each day rather than the two or three typical of other faculty. Furthermore, they report that their schedule is better because teaching every other day gives them more time to prepare and to grade papers. They also have been assisted by student teachers in three subject areas and, of course, provide support to one another.

On the other hand, the philosophy of the school that stresses student work and the higher average daily attendance in the EHS combine to produce more work to be assessed. And the mastery learning requirement generates more record keeping and paperwork because they have to keep track of incompletes. Three of the teachers interviewed reported spending an average of eight to ten hours per week beyond the normal school day on schoolwork, and even more at the end of quarters. They all indicated this was an increase over their previous work load.

Their new roles as student advisers bring additional work and worry as well. Time is provided for advising, but as one staff member put it: "You get more involved with the kids. You see them all of the time and get to know them better. You serve as their adviser, but they have terrible problems and you don't know how to help. We need help with guidance, with referrals. You feel an increased obligation, but you don't know how to help and you may not have time to help. You feel frustrated." The teachers are not yet comfortable in their roles as advisers, and they may have neither the time nor the resources to do the job, but for the moment they are accepting the responsibility.

The EHS staff also has responsibilities for curriculum that exceed those of typical teachers. They were given a semester to plan the four-year curriculum, but the work is ongoing as they elaborate and revise it. They are supported in these efforts by the two clinical professors from Brown but, ultimately, the success or the failure of the curriculum, and the larger program, rests on their shoulders.

The EHS staff work as a team and this also brings new responsibilities. They can no longer function in splendid isolation, ignoring the problems of students outside of their classroom or the concerns of colleagues. Teamwork demands new skills, new behaviors. They have to present and defend their ideas. They have to listen to conflicting opinions and different ideas. They are expected to collaborate to solve problems with students and to integrate the curriculum. Their relationships with colleagues have been fundamentally altered. Fortunately, the first EHS team is a compatible group. They have a positive attitude and do support one another. Even so, they have their disagreements and the team meetings can be volatile. The author observed one such meeting in which the issue of recruitment of students led to an emotional debate about the program's purposes and who it was intended to serve. The issue was left undecided in order to permit calmer consideration of options. The five members of the EHS team function well as a unit, but they are still learning how to make collective decisions.

In spite of the new responsibilities and additional work outside the classroom, the EHS staff do not believe that they are working significantly harder than before. They do acknowledge that they are working differently. They also indicate that they are deriving more satisfaction from their work. The larger faculty believes that they work harder, but they contend that this is the result of misinformation or lack of understanding about this new program.

The nine principles of the Coalition provide the theoretical framework for the development of the EHS and redefining the work of the teachers. The members of the team have made substantial progress toward putting this theory into action, but they have encountered obstacles and problems. To fully appreciate the extent of their achievement and to comprehend the issues they are now addressing, it is necessary to first understand the context within which they work and the varying expectations that different stakeholders hold for the program.

The Context for Change at Hope

Providence, a small, attractive city, has an ethnically diverse population of approximately 154,000. Historically, its neighborhoods have been divided by ethnicity, and that pattern generally holds true today. New groups have been moving in, most notably Hispanics and Asians, and there has been some gentrification of older neighborhoods, but the overall pattern of ethnic and social residential segregation remains intact. The ethnic and social divisions in the larger community are reflected in the structure of education. Over 19,000 students attend some 30 separate public schools, but about a quarter of the city's children attend private or parochial schools. Slightly less than 40 percent of the public school students are white, about 24 percent are black, 19 percent are Hispanic, 11 percent Asian, and over 6 percent Portuguese or Cape Verdean. While the school system is not highly integrated at any level, magnets have been used with limited success to integrate the secondary schools.

Hope High School is located on the edge of Providence's affluent east side, only blocks from Brown University, and across the street from one of the city's most prestigious private schools, Moses Brown Academy. The beautiful, well-maintained campus of the latter stands in stark contrast to the run-down, dingy appearance of Hope. The school sits on the crest of a hill, overlooking the center of the city below. To the east are elegant, expensive homes on tree-lined streets, many dating from the eighteenth century. These are the homes of the city's power elite. To the immediate west of Hope, there are more modest frame houses, the residences of lower-middle-class white and black families.

Hope is the smallest of the city's four public high schools, with an enrollment of about a thousand, almost three-quarters of whom are from minority students. It has the smallest proportion of white students—only 15 percent. Table 15.2 presents the ethnic makeup of the four high schools. Classical High School, the city's most prestigious public school, has selective admissions and is predominately white. The children from the affluent east side surrounding Hope either go to Classical or to private schools. Central, the vocational school, is racially balanced as a result of the popularity of its business and vocational magnets. Mt. Pleasant serves the white enclaves in the western and northern areas of the city.

Table 15.2. High School Enrollment by Ethnicity, 1986 (in percent).

School/Enrollment	Asian	Black	White	Hispanic	Other
Central HS 1,888	11	26	32	25	6
Classical HS 1,068	7	10	75	5	4
Hope HS 970	8	44	15	21	12
Mt. Pleasant	18	17	52	10	2

Source: Compiled from data provided by the Providence School Department.

In many respects, Hope is the stepchild of the public school system. Once considered an outstanding academic high school (Hope regularly attracted tuition students from the surrounding suburbs in the 1960s), it has suffered from almost two decades of academic decline and physical deterioration. A critical turning point in the school's fortunes came in 1969 when racial tensions among students broke into open conflicts. The school's public image plummeted and white parents began to withdraw their children. There were attempts to improve conditions in the early 1970s through special programs, but the school's condition and reputation continued to decline. Its high concentration of poor, minority students, poor physical plant, and a constant turnover of principals earned it a reputation as a tough place in which to teach or learn.

Many of the students who attend Hope are bussed in from south Providence, the city's poorest area. Enrollment, once over 2,000, has declined and is now stable at about 1,000, even though the facility could easily house 1,200 or more, including the special programs in the building. The vast majority of Hope students enter reading below grade level and need remedial assistance. The ESL/Bilingual program serves several hundred students. Many of Hope's students have experienced failure in primary and middle school and do not expect to succeed in high school. Only a quarter of the entering students are believed to be able to do college preparatory work. The location of the Arts and Communication magnet at Hope has attracted some talented students to the school but not enough to alter the overall climate of failure.

In contrast to the students attending the magnet, many students attend Hope reluctantly; it is not their neighborhood school and it offers neither the academic excellence of Classical nor the career programs of Central. The population is also highly mobile; the annual turnover is about 30 percent. Not surprisingly, attendance is poor—below 80 percent on average. Tardiness and class cutting are endemic problems, and between 40 and 50 pecent of the students drop out of school. In sum, Hope suffers from a malaise similar to that found in other schools serving the urban poor, and it has many of the same symptoms.

The students at Hope are as diverse in style as they are in background. In spite of their colorfulness, their poverty is evident in their dress. They fill the halls with noise and motion between classes, but there is none of the hostility that is often found in urban schools. Nor, however, is there a sense of purposeful activity; instead, the students seem to be apathetic or bored. They seem to be generally well behaved and the school is quite peaceful when classes are in session. Some teachers even teach with their doors open. Relations among the ethnic groups appear comfortable, but there is the usual self-imposed segregation in the halls and the cafeteria.

The building itself is in terrible condition. The outside looks dirty and neglected. Inside, the most visible symbols of the school's fall from grace are the lockers. Painted in garish colors of orange, blue, green, and brown in some earlier, half-hearted effort to alter the climate, they have been wrenched and torn as though a gang of vandals had passed through intent on destruction. Nearly half of them have been rendered useless, and their twisted metal leaves a powerful impression on the visitor.

Although less dramatic, the rest of the facility suffers from similar neglect. The halls are poorly lit, giving the school a dreary appearance even on a sunny day. There is litter on the grounds and in the halls. The restrooms are in a horrible state but repairs (paid for by funds brought in by the EHS) are underway. The cafeteria is a bleak area in the basement. The classrooms obviously were once attractive but now are dirty and in need of renovation. There have been problems with the roof, causing several ceilings to collapse and grievances to be filed. In spite of these miserable conditions, repairs to the building have been repeatedly delayed because the district lacks the resources or the will to do the work.

Working in this bleak and oppressive atmosphere, a largely veteran staff share a gallows humor about the school. Some refer to it as "Hopeless High" (Brown students have added to the disparaging idioms by referring to the Essential School as the Superfluous School). Some of the teachers remember when conditions were different, and they express bitterness about the way conditions have been permitted to deteriorate. The staff face difficult, unmotivated students under poor circumstances and their faces show their fatigue. Yet one hears few raised voices in the halls or from the classrooms, and the teachers still come into the halls between periods to keep order and get students into class. In the faculty lounge, considerable cynicism and frustration are expressed, but it is apparent to even the casual observer that not all of this faculty are resigned to failure. One comes away from the school with a sense of sympathy and respect for people who continue to struggle to teach under such conditions.

The Origins of the Essential School

The most recent effort to renew Hope High School dates back to the appointment of the current principal, Paul Gounaris. Formerly the director of a successful alternative program in the district, Gounaris took the job reluctantly in 1983. In his own words, the school was in serious trouble and someone was needed to restore order and straighten things up. He perceived it to be a short-term assignment and expected to turn the school over to someone else after a few years. Initially, he had to focus on issues of safety and discipline. Rejecting the police state approach, Gounaris chose to become highly visible and personally involved in keeping order in the school. He and his administrative team are constantly in the halls; using radios to communicate, they move quickly to deal with intruders or problems among students.

Gounaris was not satisfied with just restoring order at Hope; he had a vision of how the school ought to operate and his own theories of how to succeed with the population served by Hope. His ideas were rooted in his experience with alternative education. He believed in faculty involvement, bottom-up change, and giving students multiple opportunities to succeed. He wanted to be a facilitator of change rather than just another directive administrator, but the severity of conditions of Hope demanded that he be in charge. Then in the fall of 1984, while attending a conference, he met someone who shared his vision—Ted Sizer of Brown University. Together with former superintendent Robert Ricci, Paula Evans of Brown, and Marsha Reback of the Providence Teachers Union (PTU), Gounaris and Sizer set in motion the process that eventually led to the implementation of the EHS.

The EHS emerged from a confluence of different interests held by the leadership of Hope, the Providence School Department, the Providence Teachers Union, and Brown University. Their common interest was improving the quality of education at Hope, but there also were other agendas that led them to support the new program. Gounaris wanted to get his faculty involved in the renewal of Hope, to light a spark under their initiative. The superintendent wanted to attract white students back to Hope and to attract eastside students back from the private schools. Marsha Reback, long-time president of the PTU, was concerned about the working conditions at Hope, and she wanted to demonstrate the practical value of empowering teachers. She also is a graduate of Hope and, in the words of Gounaris, "gave her support from the heart." Sizer needed an urban site for his nascent coalition and a spot near Brown to train student teachers. In addition, Brown, a large tax-free institution, felt an obligation to do something for the Providence schools.

These leaders went to the Hope faculty and gave them the opportunity to discuss Sizer's ideas. Sizer himself made several presentations at the school. He described the coalition and the philosophy and debate that underlay its nine principles. Four months of discussion and debate ensued. It was Marsha Reback who finally moved things forward by shifting the focus from issues of philosophy to issues of responsibility, work load, seniority, and job rights. She told the faculty that the proposed program would be good for kids but that it could be good for teachers as well. Many were skeptical about the value of such an approach; some did not believe that the faculty would be permitted to make the decision about joining the coalition. Practical issues were raised: What were the implications for teachers' roles and responsibilities? What effects would the new program have on their jobs? Some faculty members were concerned about suggestions that Sizer wanted to conduct a national search for the faculty positions. There were annual layoffs in the district, and faculty were afraid of forced transfers and loss of positions at Hope. The PTU worked with a faculty committee and the administration to develop an amendment to the bargaining agreement that addressed the concerns of the teachers. The issues and their resolution are briefly summed up in Table 15.3.

Table 15.3.   Resolution of Issues Relating to the Adoption of EHS.

Issue	Resolution
Eligibility for the EHS positions and the selection process	The Hope faculty were given preference in filling the new positions. Only if there were no qualified candidates from Hope would they be open districtwide. And only if no candidates appeared in the district could outside applicants be considered. A special committee to interview applicants was defined in the contract.
Teachers working as generalists and teaching outside of their areas of certification	No teaching was to be permitted outside of areas of certification.
Transfers or RIFs at Hope as a result of the EHS	Teachers working at Hope prior to September 1985 were protected from transfers or RIFs that were related to the EHS.
The rights of teachers who accepted positions in the EHS	Teachers hired for the EHS were granted the option of voluntary reassignment after their first year.
Teachers assuming duties of administrators	The head teacher role was defined as nonsupervisory and nonadministrative. Team planning periods and clerical assistance were guaranteed.
The departmental status of EHS staff and the compensation of Hope chairpersons (based on the number of members)	The EHS was not a department; EHS staff would remain members of Hope departments and would not cause a reduction in the chairperson's compensation.

After resolving these issues, the Hope faculty took a vote on the initiation of the new program. They were given ballots that offered them two options: uncertainty but a willingness to let the program proceed, or opposition. Two-thirds of the faculty selected the first option and the EHS was born. Most people seem to be agreed that the faculty would not have voted favorably without the intervention of the PTU and the amendment to the agreement. The PTU president feels that the issue of compensation for department chairs alone could have blocked implementation of the program.

Following the vote, the position of head teacher and four teaching positions were posted and filled. All five were filled with veterans from Hope. Albin Moser, a highly respected social studies teacher with seventeen years experience, was hired as head teacher. The other four, selected from among ten applicants from the Hope faculty, also were mature professionals with experience ranging from ten to seventeen years. The new team was granted a semester without teaching duties to plan the new program and develop the curriculum. This work was supported by a grant from the William and Flora Hewlett foundation obtained with assistance from Paula Evans of Brown University.

The Role of Teachers in the Essential School

Teachers are taking on new roles and responsibilities in the EHS and they are doing it with enthusiasm. They are serving as coaches in the classrooms, advisers to students, curriculum developers, team members, and decision makers. The scope of the changes is ambitious and radical in its implications for the operation and management of schools. There are constraints that may yet limit the application of these ideas at Hope but, for the moment, the EHS team is functioning with a broad mandate to alter the roles of teaching staff.

Clearly, it was the opportunity to play a broader role in decision making that attracted the original group of teachers to the EHS. One team member said, "My motivation for being here was to have some say. That really motivated me. You work for years and have ideas about what works, what should be done, but only occasionally do you have a chance to influence what is done. Everything is determined by policy; downtown makes all of the decisions." In response to a similar question, another replied, "My motivation was the idea of a change. I needed a change badly. Philosophically, the (program) involved getting students to do more work, to take more responsibility for their work. It was an opportunity to do more of what I knew worked with these students, to have a free hand. . . . " One of the teachers recruited for the second team, who will join the EHS in the fall of 1987, commented: "I was disillusioned with what was happening in the classroom. Students came to class and sat there, but when you tested them, it was clear that they didn't understand. They were making no effort, they were apathetic. . . . I used to be able to close the door and teach. That used to work for me but it isn't working anymore. I wanted something different; I couldn't do it on my own anymore. I thought it would be good to be a member of a team. . . . The Essential School staff have each other for support. They can make decisions. They seem to be getting more satisfaction out of their work.''

There is genuine effort on the part of the administration at Hope, the PSD, and the PTU to give the EHS team broad latitude and discretion in making educational decisions. There are constraints, of course, set by law and district policy or created by resource limitations. The nine principles of the Coalition also act as constraints as they define the parameters within which decisions are made. These decisions generally emerge from discussions in the team meetings, but there is also considerable informal discussion among team members at lunch, in the halls, and during prep periods. The simplest way to describe the scope of teacher decision making in the EHS is to review the team's actions area by area.

1. *Curriculum.* The team developed their own curriculum and, while they generally adhered to the objectives of the PSD, there were few constraints placed on their decisions about essential skills and content or materials. They were able to purchase the new books and materials they felt best fit the curriculum. They continue to revise their work and feel that it remains fluid and flexible.

2. *Scheduling.* The team made the decision to use double periods every other day, and they have considerable flexibility in allocating time within the schedule for special events or community meetings. The logistics are worked out by the head teacher. However, the EHS has had to work within the constraints of the larger school's six-period day in order for students to take electives and gym. And a compromise worked out with the Arts magnet to permit students to be dually enrolled has prevented the use of periods 1 and 2 for academic classes. The scheduling of a foreign language for dually enrolled students

is a current problem that threatens the use of double periods. Scheduling constraints are a problem and may worsen as the school expands.

3. *Grading and reporting.* The teachers, as reported above, have developed their own version of mastery learning and are struggling with the problem of incompletes that has accompanied it. They seem to have the freedom to determine standards for promotion in the EHS and to decide how work will be assessed and graded. They also have been issuing their own report cards, but they are required to follow the school's quarterly schedule and to use computerized report cards as well. This has produced excessive paperwork, and the team is now discussing how to adapt to the school's report cards and still report on student progress within the new program. The quarterly system does not meet the needs of a system that is based on mastery.

4. *Professional development.* The team has funds for consultants and has been able to make their own decisions about who to use. They also have access to the workshops and meetings planned by the Coalition but appear to be able to make their own decisions about the utility of attending these events.

3. *Personnel.* They have played a limited role in the selection of the new EHS staff through the representation of the head teacher on the interview committee. They also interviewed the candidates for the clinical professor positions and were consulted in those decisions.

6. *Discipline.* EHS students are subject to the rules of Hope High School, and discipline is administered through the normal procedures by the school administration. The EHS staff has had no discretion about setting school rules for students.

7. *Student recruitment and admissions.* Decisions about student admissions in the first year were made by the team as were decisions about assignment to classes. The team also helped with recruitment by talking to students they knew in the school. This year recruitment and admissions seem to have become the responsibilities of the head teacher. He says that assignments will still be done collectively. Issues of recruitment and admissions have become a source of conflict within the team and will be discussed later in the chapter.

8. *General administration.*   The entire team has been involved in decisions about time and resource allocations, but there seems to be a tendency to rely on the head teacher to define the options and make day-to-day decisions. The head teacher represents the EHS in dealing with the administration.

Clearly, the teachers in the EHS are exercising broad responsibility and are making decisions that are normally within the purview of administration. While precedents can be found for teacher involvement and decision making in each of the areas discussed above, the comprehensive role played by teachers in the EHS is exceptional. One teacher summed up the situation this way: "We have made decisions in many areas: curriculum, scheduling, the grading system, admissions, special activities. The bureaucracy has been eliminated and we have taken its place. We don't feel ignored or manipulated anymore."

The Impact of the Essential School

It may seem premature in 1987 to discuss the impact of the EHS, since it has been operational for less than a year. Yet the early returns are so promising that they cannot be ignored. The effects to date are discussed below under three headings: the EHS students, EHS staff, and Hope staff. (This section was written in June 1987 and reflects the information available at that time.)

The Students.   There is very limited quantitative evidence but considerable anecdotal information suggesting that the EHS is having the desired effects on its students. First, the drop-off rate for students has been small in spite of the increased work demands, high standards, and incompletes that must be made up. One hundred four students were enrolled when school opened in September 1986. Ten were no-shows and their places were quickly filled. Five more dropped out due to changes in residence or fear of delayed graduation because of the standards. These spots were also filled. Only one additional student has left the program since these early withdrawals.

Student daily attendance is much higher than in Hope itself. The daily attendance for the EHS hovers between 88 and

91.5 percnt, while Hope's rate usually is around 75–80 percent and occasionally is lower. On each of the pleasant spring days that the author was at Hope, more than one-third of the enrollment was on the absence list. It may be that the EHS students are more highly motivated and would have had higher attendance wherever they enrolled, but the disparity is impressive.

The EHS staff reported that students had difficulty handling the work at first. Most of the students had not been active workers in the past. Many were accustomed to putting work off and doing it at the last moment or not at all. This is one reason for the large numbers of incompletes in the first two quarters of the year (158 and 194 respectively out of a theoretical possibility of 416 each quarter). More recently, the teachers say, the students have been adjusting to the new demands and are handling the work more successfully. There were fewer incompletes in the third quarter (114) and many incompletes had already been made up. A study of students with incompletes by Joe McDonald, a Brown clinical professor, concluded that the incompletes were more frequently due to procrastination or lack of organization skills than a lack of ability to do the work.

The team has taken steps to reduce the number of incompletes by providing time in class to work on them and by posting records of work completed. In English, work has been broken into smaller units to help students keep up. In biology, students were forced to complete all incompletes before beginning the fourth quarter work. Once students became convinced that the work would not just go away and the team was not backing down on the issue of makeups, the situation began to improve. Contrary to normal patterns, the student work effort has increased as the year has progressed. However, there still will be sizable numbers of students who will have to make up work next year (twenty to thirty in biology alone).

Discipline in the EHS is better than in the larger school. Teachers say there are fewer incidents and they are less severe. This was affirmed by the principal, who indicated that there were fewer problems with the students enrolled in the EHS. The team has resisted pushing out a few chronic disciplinary problems in order to avoid a rift with the rest of the faculty.

Another measure of success in the first year is acceptance of the new program by the students. The low drop-off rate, high attendance, and the steady progress toward reducing the incompletes indicate general acceptance of the program, but the team also surveyed student opinions about the various program elements. Ranking high were working with other students, double period classes, and reading and writing assignments. Negative ratings were given to phone calls home, the student leadership committee, and the grading system. The latter is an important issue. Students would like a system with A-B-C-I grades instead of the current A-B-I (Moser, 1987a). The team is reluctant to abandon its standards, however, and has deferred making any changes in the system until the following year.

As of this writing, the team has not yet received the results of the Metropolitan Achievement Test, which the students took in April 1987. Staff are concerned that the district may expect too much too soon and may place too much emphasis on test scores. There is, however, some other positive evidence of student academic achievement. Analysis of grades revealed that 30 percent of the students had earned A's and B's in all four subjects after three quarters and another 14 percent had A's and B's in three subjects (Moser, 1987b, p. 7). That left 56 percent of the students with two or more incompletes.

EHS Staff. The staff of the EHS say they are highly satisfied with their new jobs and all those interviewed felt they were having more fun. One Hope teacher said the EHS staff ''were the only ones who always came into the faculty lunchroom with smiles on their faces.'' The morale of the team seemed high, and that is unusual at the end of the school year. Informally, several sources said that their attendance was better than the rest of the faculty, and team members themselves indicated that they no longer felt the need to take mental health days. On the contrary, they said they wanted to come to school and felt an obligation to be there. They also reported, as indicated earlier, that their level of effort was up somewhat over former years. In one specific instance, a team member indicated that she had stopped phoning parents a few years ago because it didn't seem to make any difference and she often took abuse. Now she is phoning again and it seems to be working for her. Why? She suggested that parents had made a commitment when they supported their children's application to the EHS.

Impact on Hope High School. The new program is already having an effect on the larger high school. Some of these are quite concrete, such as the renovated restrooms, the displacement of English faculty from the third floor, scheduling conflicts with the Arts magnet, and the involvement of Brown faculty and student teachers with the rest of the staff. Faculty attitudes also are being affected. There is some envy among the Hope faculty of the resources and "privileges" available to the EHS team. Some Hope teachers feel that the team works with better students and under better conditions than they do. Some simply don't believe that such a program can make any significant difference and feel that it is just an aberration that will disappear when the money runs out. A few resent the presence of the Brown staff. A much larger group appear to be taking a "wait-and-see" attitude; they are not hostile and they cooperate with the team but they are not volunteering to join them either. Some are openly enthusiastic about the EHS and the concept of teaming; they see the new program as a model for restructuring the school. The faculty clearly are divided over the EHS.

It is hard to assess the direction of the shifts in faculty attitudes. Most respondents agreed that the faculty were divided but felt that there was movement toward support of the approach and its adoption throughout the school. There is one important negative piece of evidence about faculty attitudes and one equally important positive piece of evidence. The former involves the alarmingly low number of applications for the second EHS team. Only six applicants applied for four positions and, because of the amendment to the agreement, four had to be selected from the limited pool. The EHS head teacher suggested two reasons for this disappointing display of faculty interest. First, staff have to apply for the jobs and compete with their peers, risking loss of face and running counter to the usual norms of conduct. Second, the staff believe that the EHS team works harder and faces greater pressure than other teachers (Moser, 1987a, p. 5).

The positive evidence is the growing momentum behind the effort to extend some of the principles of the EHS to the larger school. There is a genuine effort on the part of the Hope administration to get the faculty involved in the school and to give them a greater voice in determining its future. This began with delegation of the original decision to begin the EHS, and it has continued during several faculty dinners held this year to discuss the development of a five-year plan for the school. Initiated by Paula Evans of Brown and Paul Gounaris, the voluntary dinners were more successful than anyone expected them to be. Over forty teachers out of a staff of seventy-two came to the first one and, although attendance declined somewhat at the next two, momentum is developing behind the idea of inventing a new future for the school. The dialogue begun at the dinners has been sustained by a faculty study committee of fifteen members. This group is meeting weekly after school and intends to work through the summer to produce recommendations for restructuring Hope. There seems to be growing support for some kind of house or team arrangement, using the EHS, the Arts Magnet, the ELS/Bilingual program, and, perhaps, a humanities team or a program for highly mobile students as the focal point for reorganization.

The principal is strongly supportive of this process. He is staying out of the deliberations at present because he feels the faculty are sensitive to administrative involvement. He says that they have to learn that they really can influence events to overcome their cynicism. So he is patiently watching the process from the sidelines. He describes the situation as a case of a public school trying to reform itself from the inside out.

Throughout this process, the EHS team have been active participants. They clearly are advocates for change at Hope but they have been careful to be not too prescriptive, too partisan in their interactions with other staff. They have tried to maintain good relations with other faculty but being isolated on the third floor and being busy, they have little time to socialize. They report little informal contact with others on the staff, except at infrequent faculty meetings. They are aware of the controversy over the EHS but they seem to feel that the momentum in the school is on their side and that the best arguments for change at Hope will be the success of their efforts with students.

Issues Identified by Respondents

The ultimate success of the EHS and the extent of its impact on Hope High School will be shaped to a large degree by the manner in which a number of programmatic and policy issues are resolved in coming months. Many of these issues have been discussed in Albin Moser's progress reports on the program, and almost all of them have been discussed by the team at one time or another. Among them are critical decisions about student assessment, the management of incompletes, student recruitment, and relationship between the EHS and the larger school.

First, the procedures for demonstrating mastery must be clearly defined and some standards set for student exhibitions. Fuzziness, subjectivity, and too much variation in assessment practices will undermine the credibility of the entire program. Fortunately, there is a large literature on competency assessment that can be tapped to solve this problem. Colleges and high schools have been wrestling with such issues since the 1960s and 1970s when experiential learning and competency-based instruction became popular; many of the assessment tools and materials developed for these purposes could be adapted to the EHS. Similarly, the grading and reporting system for the EHS and the computerized system for the larger school must be reconciled into one system to reduce paperwork and confusion. Here too, there are precedents to draw on. These problems are not insurmountable but would be more easily solved if the EHS team were not left to develop their assessment procedures on their own.

The team also must resolve the problem of the incompletes or risk being overwhelmed by the complexity of tracking them. Students also may choose to flee their accumulating deficits unless something is done to contain the problem. This could compound the recruitment problem (discussed below) in future years. If large numbers of incompletes are carried from one year into the next, some form of tracking is likely to emerge to provide for the makeup work. This seems antithetical to the philosophy underlying the program. In addition, the already complex schedule would become further strained by tracking to deal with incompletes. Worse yet from the district's perspective, more staff might be needed and program costs might rise.

To deal with the incompletes, Leahy (1987) recommended dividing class time into separate periods of group work and individual work to permit students to keep up. This might reduce incompletes, but it would also risk introducing elements of control and rigidity into the classes, making them seem more like conventional settings. She also proposed breaking the curriculum up into smaller units or chunks and charting students' progress in some visible manner to keep them aware of their progress. Similar techniques are used successfully in other mastery learning programs and they might help here. Providing a thorough orientation to incoming freshmen that clearly set the work expectations and explicitly taught study skills might also help. Perhaps the first month of the EHS program should be an intensive study skills program combined with some developmental work in writing.

The most pressing problem facing the EHS is the need to attract sufficient numbers of students to continue the planned expansion of the program next year. The problems encountered in recruiting students were discussed earlier. As of May, the program had enrolled only three-quarters of its new freshman class and this after six months of effort by the head teacher. Why are students not applying? Are there problems with the approach to recruitment? Are there elements of the program that deter students from applying? These questions remain unanswered. The discussions of recruitment instead seem to be focusing on questions of who should be eligible to apply and the size of the applicant pool rather than on questions about the efficacy of current recruitment techniques or the attractiveness of the current program to different groups of students. Access to the EHS now is restricted to the Hope feeder area or to students who enroll in the Arts magnet. This excludes large numbers of students across the district. A consensus seems to be developing among the district leadership that this problem could be most easily solved by opening up the program to all students in the district. In effect, the EHS would become another magnet program. This is attractive from both a practical and a political standpoint because it would simplify the recruiting process and it might bring more white students into Hope.

This approach to recruitment has implications for the program's role in the renewal of Hope itself. The leaders who initiated the program agreed that it should serve as a mechanism for the renewal of Hope. Their intention was, and is, to have the EHS expand each year until about half of Hope's students are enrolled. Simultaneously, the other parts of the school might be reorganized into teams or houses along the lines of the EHS. Paul Gounaris, the principal at Hope, describes it as a Pac-man design that will eventually eat up the entire school. It is partly for this reason that the EHS was originally restricted to serving the Hope feed area and is not just another magnet program. It is not at all clear that converting the EHS to a magnet school in order to integrate Hope will prove to be compatible with this effort at renewal. If the EHS becomes just another magnet, will the Hope faculty accept its approach as a model for serving the rest of the students? If open access brings higher-achieving students into the EHS, will the curriculum development effort be directed away from the needs of lower-achieving students? Will the EHS be forced to set higher and more specific academic admissions standards to justify its admissions decisions to students and parents? Will quotas become necessary to preserve places for minority students? If the program attempts to serve a wide range of ability levels, will tracking reemerge in some form? These are critical issues that are coming to the surface as the debate over recruitment and access to the EHS emerges.

The former superintendent wanted to renew Hope but believed that attracting white students back to the school was an essential element in such an effort. He also hoped that the EHS would eventually attract students back from the private schools. The desire to desegregate Hope is shared by several members of the EHS team who want to solve the problems of recruiting and to attract more and better students to the EHS. Apparently the new superintendent shares their desire to open up access to the EHS and will propose such a change to the school committee.

Marsha Reback of the PTU also believes that the goals of renewal and open access are compatible in the long run. She rhetorically asked, "Wouldn't the problem of too many applicants be a wonderful problem to have?," and suggests that the problem could be solved by speeding up the expansion of the program. But this suggestion assumes that the program could drop its selective character and without altering its special character and, perhaps, diminishing its overall effectiveness. Reback believes that the program will eventually become a model for general education in Providence. It may eventually reach this point of acceptability, but it has to establish itself first. At the moment this appears to require a delicate balancing act, remaining special and unique but not being perceived by other faculty members as privileged or elitist.

Some members of the Hope faculty had simpler, more immediate needs in mind when they voted affirmatively for the EHS. They felt that the presence of Brown faculty in the school would generate powerful pressure for the PSD to speed up improvements in the physical conditions in the building and to provide additional resources to the staff. This was probably not the role that Brown expected to play nor was it the stated intention of the school committee. Nevertheless, faculty felt the adoption of the EHS would be an action-forcing event. To some degree their hopes are being realized; work has begun on the restrooms and improvements will eventually be made to the library. But visible changes have been slow to appear and there continue to be delays. Faculty acceptance of the EHS may in part depend upon improvement in the overall working conditions at Hope.

One indirect measure of the attitudes of the current faculty toward the EHS is the number of applicants for the new teaching positions created in the program. This year there were only six applicants in total, and for two positions on the new team there was only a single applicant. This virtually denies the intent of conducting a search, and it suggests that the Hope faculty are not yet persuaded that the EHS offers better working conditions for teachers. Moser (1987a) has proposed that the positions be open to the entire district if there is only a single applicant from Hope. He also has proposed that the applicants' classrooms be visited as part of the process. These proposals are in conflict with the amendment to the agreement and might alienate some faculty at Hope. However, some new approach must be taken if Hope faculty do not compete for the positions.

These and related issues will dominate the discussions of the EHS team over the next year and will challenge their commitment and creativity. They may, as issues often do, fade with time—students could make up their incompletes or more applicants might appear without altering the policy on access. But it seems more likely that the team and its allies at Brown will have to make some difficult decisions to solve these problems. The nine principles of the Coalition provide some guidance for their decisions, but those concerned about the EHS will also have to face some difficult political choices. It seems safe to predict that the EHS may become more controversial at Hope and in Providence before its enormous potential is realized.

Some Final Observations

It is not reasonable to make an assessment of a complex effort to restructure a school in its first year, and it certainly should not be done on the basis of a brief two-day visit. Conclusions cannot be drawn as yet about the strengths or weaknesses of the program or about the validity of the educational theory that underlies it. The initial evidence about the program's impact on students and teachers appears to be positive. But its impact on academic attainment or retention in school or on the ability of teachers to sustain their levels of effort and involvement over time remains to be determined. The only appropriate summative statement that can be made at this point is that what is being undertaken at Hope is important and ambitious and the individuals involved deserve the whole-hearted admiration and full support of those concerned about the education of the poor and minority youth.

It does seem appropriate, however, to speculate a bit about the program and its future. Such speculation by an outsider might contribute to the dialogue among the participants and their own ongoing formative evaluation of the EHS. There are some questions that the site visit raised for the author that may not yet be part of the participants' dialogue about the EHS. The first of these concerns resources. Are there sufficient human and material resources in the EHS and at Hope to create the opportunity for long-run success? In his normal progress report, Moser raises a number of resource questions: the student–teacher ratio is too high, the lockers need to be replaced, the EHS needs a guidance counselor, the expansion will require more head teachers to lead teams, and so forth. He might have added that two team planning periods a week are inadequate (most schools with team teaching provide one per day) and that as the EHS expands it will require more clerical help. Students who are asked to write frequently should also have access to a computer lab. The point is that even with the external funds that have been provided, there remains an enormous resource gap. Conditions are even worse in the larger school, where cutbacks have created shortages of custodians and clerks, textbooks are often old and inadequate, and teachers are asked to perform noninstructional tasks that could be carried out by aides. How is Hope going to renew itself without additional resources? Is dedication alone sufficient? I don't believe that it is. Even if a small pilot program works because of enormous dedication, is it reasonable to expect that kind of commitment from everyone? It seems to me that the development of the full potential of the EHS and the renewal of Hope depend upon the willingness of the Providence school committee to come up with the funds to make a major investment in education.

Another nagging concern is the role of the head teacher. He is supposed to be the chair of a committee that makes decisions and acts as a collective. He is not an administrator, or so the contract stipulates. Yet he represents the program to the outside world, handles recruitment, communicates with the administration and the school committee, makes day-to-day decisions about the schedule, and otherwise acts like an administrator. In the team discussion of the recruitment issue, a teacher questioned his right to reach an important agreement with the superintendent on open access without consulting the entire team. He replied that he thought he had that right and other team members supported him, saying it was his job to handle recruitment. It is not that the current head teacher is seeking to become an administrator. He is simply trying to solve practical problems and make things work. The teachers are swamped with the classroom work and the head teacher is the only one free to handle routine "administrative" matters. It is easier to leave matters to him. As the program expands and he is dealing with several teams, his responsibility and his informal authority are likely to increase. Is a new administrative role being defined? If so, what does that mean for the empowerment of the teaching staff? If not, what steps should be taken to formalize the responsibilities of the team and the head teacher in order to avoid the natural drift of responsibility and authority to the one person who has both the time and communication networks to handle them.

A third concern is even more fundamental, it concerns the appropriateness of the essential skills curriculum for high school-age students who are not collegebound and who lack vocational skills. If they complete the program, will they be more employable? By whom? With what prospects? The answers to these questions seem to have been assumed. Perhaps it would be better to be developing such a curriculum for grades 6 through 8 or 9 so that it would prepare them to take full advantage of good technical education. The so-called Minnesota Plan proposes something along these lines, a common-core curriculum in the intermediate grades, followed by program options that prepare students for college or work. Are we deluding ourselves that a better form of general education is the universal answer?

And, finally, there is the issue of uniqueness or rather the absence of it. There is nothing about the EHS, its curriculum, the coaching, the team planning, the teacher advising, the assessment, or the selective admissions that is new. All of these strategies are being used elsewhere and, in some cases, are well established. Teaming, for example, is common to middle schools and is used in many high schools. The coaching model of instruction is used in the various cooperative learning programs. And so on. A significant reform need not be based on new ideas or approaches, of course, but its advocates ought to be aware of its roots and make an effort to learn from the previous applications. Why reinvent the wheel? Why not draw more upon the literature and materials produced by the educational R&D community? Perhaps these connections have been made at Hope through the work of the Coalition staff but, if so, it was not obvious. This was disturbing at first. Then the reason became clear. This effort was bottom-up not only in the character of its teacher participation but in its commitment to permit teachers to take initiative, to invent and, if necessary, to reinvent.

The experiment at Hope may not prove to be the general model for renewal of urban schools that everyone keeps looking for; it may not even succeed in turning Hope High School around. Yet it is an admirable effort by dedicated people who deserve to be taken seriously. And there is already one lesson to be drawn: letting people start from scratch or at least with an incomplete road map such as the nine principles may be what it takes to produce the energy and commitment that is needed to renew urban schools. This is an important lesson for state agencies and for educational improvement organizations that prefer to have their "bottom-up" approaches follow predetermined paths, in which teachers make use of the approved strategies. The EHS and other similar efforts are a welcome departure from these canned programs and, if we are serious about empowering teachers, we will have to learn to live with the messiness and apparent inefficiencies that come with it.

16

Nurturing Creativity and Critical Thought: The Interdisciplinary Curriculum of the Humanitas Academy, Los Angeles

by Charles Taylor Kerchner and Charles Donaldson

High school teachers in Los Angeles are simultaneously reshaping their work lives and the content of schooling through an interdisciplinary humanities program that gets spectacular results from ordinary people. "Our kids are not honor students," notes one teacher in the Humanitas Academy program. "But we teach our students to think, and they start acting like honors material."

And the teachers are not all spellbinders and showmen. Some are relatively young or have recently become teachers after experience in industry or elsewhere, but most are classroom veterans whose enthusiasm and idealism have been rekindled by this opportunity to design and run their own educational enterprise. By so doing, these teachers are demonstrating the organizational promise of the autonomous work group in education.

The measure of the Humanitas Academy program, co-sponsored by the Los Angeles Unified School District and the Los Angeles Educational Partnership (LAEP), can be seen in the kinds of questions students answer. In one school, its tenth graders are asked, "How would Machiavelli rate Hamlet and Claudius as leaders?" While at another school, students at the same grade level are considering this question: If "all the world's a stage," what mask is worn by Jack in *Lord of the Flies*, Richard Wright, and Prufrock?

275

Meanwhile, a biology teacher is preparing raw fish and fat—Eskimo sushi, he calls it—to be used as an unknown in the laboratory. The examination question will ask the students to identify the unknown and then tell what they know about a people who would eat such a diet. For the answer to this question, students must draw on information from their anthropology class where they are studying native cultures and their environments.

And, at another school, while students in a social studies class are learning how Calvin's theology helps explain how the Puritans acted at the Salem witch trials, students in an art history class are analyzing portraits of Puritans, explaining how they reflect Puritan values.

"We have to teach the whole world to kids, not just what is in the little boxes," John Brierley, a Westchester High School teacher, says. "There is a vision among the people who do this program that there is so much kids can learn this way, that there is a neat world to be in."

These programs are not designed as "honors" programs for advanced students, and they do not carry the college equivalent credit that advanced placement classes do. The most common requirement for admission is regular attendance at school. One will take any student who can read on a fifth-grade level.

"We are designated for the middle-of-the-road kid," says Bonnie Just, a teacher in Narbonne High's Humanitas program, while Boyd Cook of Gardena High says that at his school the ideal Humanitas student is one who "is making lousy grades, but is not really dumb."

How Humanitas Works

The Humanitas Academy Program is the product of public and private cooperation. The Los Angeles Educational Partnership is a private—corporate- and foundation-supported—organization designed to serve as a laboratory function for Los Angeles area schools. Peggy Funkhouser, the organization's president and executive director, describes the Partnership as a "hothouse" for new ideas and a "tugboat" for school reform. The Partnership raises funds and accounts for them to donors, but it is also an operating organization that institutes programs in schools.

The relationship between the Partnership and the school district is best described in terms of Humanitas itself. The Humanitas Academy is modeled after the successful interdisciplinary humanities program of the Cleveland High School Magnet School in Reseda, a suburban community in Los Angeles' San Fernando Valley. The central idea was to take Humanitas out of the magnet school context, where critics claimed they simply skimmed off the best inner-city youth, and make the idea work within the context of schools citywide. Using Cleveland's expertise and experience, Humanitas Academy programs have been established in thirteen schools, many of them in areas of high minority population.

The Humanitas Academy forms a small school-within-a-school. Humanitas students take a core of classes together, and both the curriculum and interpersonal relationships carry over from one class to the next. Assignments, lessons, and projects are linked across classes. For example, at Lincoln High School, history, English, art, and philosophy are combined. During one six-week period students focus on the historical period 1865–1914, just as they might in a conventional history course. But Academy students integrate around the theme: "What Price Progress?" They study writings of Charles Darwin, Upton Sinclair, and Eugene Debs, the political cartoons of Thomas Nast, and the Ashcan School painting of John French Sloan. They'll make sense out of a world that contained both romantic landscapes and the Pullman Strike, reformers and machine politicians, immigration, and the rise of labor.

The participating faculty at Lincoln High School became a Humanitas Academy by applying to the Partnership. The teachers, all volunteers, designed their program and wrote a detailed application to the Partnership. The programs were not required to look the same, and, thus, the curriculum varies between schools: at some, art production is brought into the mix, and at others, science is included. As did all the other site administrators, the principal at Lincoln had to endorse the application and support it with a statement of how the interdisciplinary program would fit into the work of the school. Fewer than half the applicants were selected.

The Los Angeles Educational Partnership provides external funding and direct operating leadership for the program. Neil Anstead, who founded the Cleveland Magnet Program, is the educational director. He remains a school district employee, but he is on released duty this year to oversee the program. His district salary is supplemented by a monthly consulting fee and summer stipend from the Partnership. Administrative responsibility for the program is carried by Judy Johnson and Patrick Scott, Partnership staff members. The teachers remain school district employees subject to the work rules of the school district and the authority of the school principal. Teachers also receive a stipend from the Partnership for their planning time and attendance at Academy events. The Partnership has raised funds from the Rockefeller Foundation, which supports nine large Humanities Programs in school systems nationwide, and the Ahmanson, Stuart, Times-Mirror, and Mellon foundations, as well as the Neutrogena Corporation. The California State Department of Education contributed a small amount, and the Los Angeles Unified School District has supported the program through its own budget with additional planning time pay, field trips, and substitute teacher funds.

The relationship between the Partnership and the school district is characterized by both a high degree of informality and a network of interpersonal relationships and influence that allows Partnership programs to work in the schools without being a part of the school district bureaucracy. The Partnership has no contractual relationship with the school district, and it must work through district personnel to implement its programs. However, the Partnership is not without influence. Its board of directors includes the former school superintendent plus a cast of influentials from the city's industrial and financial communities. Besides Humanitas, the Partnership sponsors a number of other projects, including a small grants program for teachers to engage in curriculum improvement projects, a dropout prevention program designed to link schools and other social service institutions, two math/science programs, and a community relations program for principals called "Going Public."

The Partnership's independence from school district control allows it freedom of movement, but it also subjects it to continuing scrutiny by school administrators. Part of the organization's success is attributable to its judicious avoidance of projects that are at the center of district political conflict. For instance, the Partnership has avoided programs in bilingual education, and it approaches the politically sensitive issue of year-round schools only obliquely.

While the Partnership does not operate on the basis of trust alone, the interpersonal relationships are crucial. In the case of Humanitas, it has been able to cultivate the support of top administrators. "My first reaction was very positive," said Daniel Isaacs, assistant superintendent in charge of senior high schools. "It was a refreshing concept." Isaacs noted that he calls attention to the program at each monthly meeting of high school principals. In the world of large public bureaucracies, such attention sends clear signals to principals that this is a program which the central office wants to succeed and through which a principal's leadership can be noticed.

Although many of the Humanitas Academy teachers are active union members, and some are the building representatives in their schools, there has been no direct relationship between the program and the United Teachers of Los Angeles, a merged AFT-NEA local. All the teachers involved in the program are volunteers, and there is no apparent conflict with the contract. From the labor relations standpoint, the program operates with a kind of tacit approval.

Inside Humanitas Classrooms

Visits to Humanitas classrooms and the classrooms at the Cleveland Magnet School bear out what the teachers say. Streetwise and articulate black students, Hispanics, second-language Asian students, blond cheerleaders, and sizable football linemen proudly wearing numbered jerseys are the mix of students, and they have one common denominator—they are involved in the business of their classes.

At Jefferson High School, in a room outfitted with wet sinks, gas jets, ring stands, the normal insignia of a chemistry lab, Roland Ganges, a compact man in a leather vest and cowboy boots, engages his 30 eleventh graders in a discussion that links the method of science to the stuff of the social system.

Ganges paces a path between two sets of movable student desks, writing on chalkboards on each side of the room. His style is precise and formal. The class is composed of "ladies and gentlemen," not Bobby and Maria. "What does it mean," he asks, "when we say that a culture has socially transmitted behavior patterns? . . . If that is the case, what's a dominant culture? What's a subculture?"

Some giggle when he asks for examples of deviant cultures, but straight answers follow when Ganges shows he is serious.

Students take detailed notes following the general outline they were given when the period began. They include lots of tough words—pathogenesis, odyssey, dynamics—and words whose meaning has been transferred from physical science to philosophy—static, macro, micro.

The lecture-discussion moves on to questions of values in American society. "Can anyone think of an example of the society operating at odds with the state belief that 'all men are created equal'?" Animated discussion follows about the differences between science, which finds systematic differences between people, and a politics of equality. Even the controversy over genetics finds its way into the discussion.

As the class closes, Ganges ties it up: " . . . and we shall see how science along with economics, politics, and religion shapes these values we call culture."

At the same time in another Jefferson classroom a less formal teacher, Mike Pace, has his math class of 29 tenth graders writing the definitions of different words they have learned—postulate, theorem, thesis—on chalkboards. "One reason you write so much in here," he declares as they work, "is to learn to write exactly what you mean." Skill at written language cuts across the whole Humanitas program.

Pace, a one-time master's candidate in philosophy who turned to math teaching when money for school ran out, obviously enjoys the ensuing discussion that involves Aristotle, Locke, and Kant, and, while drawing an illustration on the board, laughingly notes, "This will show you the reason to have some art in your curriculum." His lecture ends with a call for a half-page essay due the next morning.

Across town at Lincoln High School, Richard Stewart was engaging his students' interest in a philosophy class with a totally different style. Soft-spoken, almost terse, Stewart's speaking style virtually forced his students to come to grips with the subject.

This session is to integrate material about Puritanism, and groups of four or five students set to work on such questions as "How were the Calvinists' beliefs of the Puritans related to their conduct during the Salem witch trials?" A different culture for a class of roughly equal parts of Hispanic and Asian.

The assignment is difficult; not everyone knows what to do, but leadership emerges in each group. Soon students find they don't have enough information to answer the question, and they begin, with Stewart's guidance, to make a list of what they need to learn from teachers in *other* classes.

At the same time, in Chris Biron's classroom, eleventh-grade art history students, using guide sheets, each complete peer assessments of two other classmates' homework essays on how Colonial American painting reflected Puritan values. Only two of the twenty-four students did not turn in the work. During the process, Biron urges the students to write about good things they notice in the essays, saying, "We want to encourage each other as much as possible." The students work with a hum of chatter that equals the room's air conditioner, punctuating the steady murmur with an occasional, "Uh oh, man," and sharp whispers, "I should've included that!"

The peer assessments completed and the papers with their rating forms returned to the front of the classroom, Biron quickly picks out the top efforts and calls the authors one by one to the front to read. A Hispanic student, Alex, leads off. He wears a football jersey, and Biron comments that he had better be as prepared for that afternoon's game as he hands him his paper. The writing contains a few grammatical glitches, but the organization and content would gladden the heart of many a college freshmen English composition teacher. A black student reads, next, followed by Edgar, another football lineman, who proudly lumbers to the front to read. After an Asian student reads the fourth paper, the class discussion turns to vocabulary, and the students demonstrate they have a clear understanding of the term *stereotyping* (''All Mexicans eat beans''; ''All Chinese eat rice''; ''All Americans eat hamburgers'').

After class, Biron observes, ''This tends to be a passive, apathetic school. The kids are passive. They don't have behavior problems, but we have a high dropout rate and generally 50 percent of the kids won't do homework. To get a discussion going in a regular class is like pulling teeth. Humanitas students feel unity and support, which is often missing for other students. They take three classes together. They feel special,'' he says, ''and, as a result they are special.'' One reflection of the cohesiveness is the absenteeism rate, which appears to be less than half that of regular classes in the same schools.

A Teacher-Run Program

Humanitas proceeds with remarkably little bureaucracy and virtually complete teacher control, a remarkable fact in the nation's second largest school system. In each school, Humanitas teachers design and implement their own programs. The whole program must fulfill the district and state curriculum requirements for that grade level, but none of the teachers we talked to found there were problems or reported difficulties in fulfilling district guidelines.

Humanitas teachers are members of regular high school departments—English, art, social sciences—and they each teach traditional classes in addition to those in the interdisciplinary program. There is no such thing as a humanities department, only the tight interpersonal linkage among the teachers who are involved.

The program thrives because of four vital inputs: a large measure of ownership and dedication on the part of teachers and students, time and flexibility in the school schedule, an unobtrusive administrative environment, and relatively small amounts of money.

Ownership. "This is a teacher-run program," says Harry Handler, the recently retired district superintendent under whose administration the Humanitas Academy was started. The teachers agree, and they display extraordinary care and dedication in their proprietorship. Michael Desrochers, who is the lead teacher in the Humanitas Program at Wilson High, explains, "We are creating a new curriculum. We have to decide what to teach."

In many cases, deciding what to teach also implies creating teaching material. Teachers find themselves paraphrasing materials usually presented to college audiences and writing their own essays to convey scholarly ideas to students with limited vocabulary skills. "Our kids can't handle things translated for use at a scholarly level. We have to use the easiest translations we can find. I duplicate a phenomenal amount of material," notes Cathy Nadler at Jefferson High. Photocopy machines have become an essential component of the program.

And, in preparing materials, teachers themselves often have to be learners. ("You have to write your own textbook as you go along. You have to stretch," says Biron. "I've never taught American art history before. I've really had to hit the books.")

All this requires hard work. "We are all working a lot harder, sometimes for reasons we don't understand. But we are doing what we want to do," observes Cook at Gardena High. The joy and also the challenge is that there is no ready-made curriculum. "It is totally our baby," says Biron at Lincoln. "This is the first time I've been treated like a teacher, like I count."

The ownership also extends to students. Humanitas students are not only assigned homework, they complete it. They participate actively in class, even in schools where the norm is often apathy. There is a sense of student expectation for performance coupled with a sense of self-worth that comes from being "special." The teachers have seized on the positive reinforcement their students receive within the student subculture: new-wave Humanitas T-shirts are coming off the silk screen press.

The rewards flow primarily from the work itself, the reactions of the students to making the connections within the social and physical worlds. "I think we taught them to think last year," says Nadler. "You hear them in the [school] yard discussing ideas in college vocabulary words."

Time to Teach and Plan.   Someone has to provide the time so that Humanitas can work. Because each Humanitas Academy exists *within* a conventional high school, the school's pupil scheduling system needs to accommodate the block scheduling that is necessary for all program students to take the same classes. And the program must also allow those same students to schedule other courses required for graduation or college admission. Without this accommodation, the program cannot exist.

The extent to which the school schedule encourages students to enroll in Humanitas varies from school to school. In one high school, the principal has assigned all Humanitas students to a single counselor, "the best one," who keeps track of required courses and runs interference with the scheduling system to see that students get what they need. However, this level of support is not universal, and some teachers reported that Humanitas students had difficulties dovetailing the programs without taking summer school classes.

Teachers also need time. Humanitas programs are tightly linked across class and across teachers. As the classroom vignettes showed, each subject area is integrated across disciplines. Teachers cooperate in preparing an interdisciplinary essay assignment at the end of each major unit of study, and at least two teachers read each student's essay. These teachers require much more personal interaction time than would be the case in a conventional compartmentalized high school program.

Some schools accommodate the need for teacher meetings by providing a period in the day when Humanitas teachers can meet, but the more usual case is for teachers to cram a meeting into lunch hour or to meet after school. Even more than most teaching jobs, the program seems to be a central feature in teachers' lives. "It's the kind of job you take home and think about all night," says Cook of Gardena High. "We are the only ones responsible for what we are doing. I'm starting to feel like a grandmother, I worry so much about the other teachers.''

James Dunlap of Van Nuys High's Humanitas program agrees, saying, ''You are always thinking about what other people are doing and coordinating with them.'' Nadler adds, ''You have to make sure other people have covered what you hope they've covered so that you can make connections with what you do.''

The program also provides important summer planning time, up to three weeks in a university setting for teachers to interact across schools and for school teams to plan the year's work. This process has been central to initiating new teachers into the Humanitas process and providing resources before the school year begins. The last two days of ''summer camp'' were held at an oceanside retreat for corporate managers that had been loaned to the Partnership, a definite psychological plus for teachers more accustomed to the ambience of the school cafeteria.

Unobtrusive Administration.   Although he's far from being a low-key person, Jefferson High School principal Francis Nakano relies on an unobtrusive management style in regard to Humanitas: ''I have confidence in the people who run this program, and I leave them alone.'' Nonetheless, school administration plays a powerful but subtle role in stimulating the program at their schools. Neil Anstead, the citywide coordinator of the program and a teacher at Cleveland High says, ''It boils down to the principal saying, 'I want this at my school.' '' But teachers are also quick to discern the apparent motives of principals in initiating the program, differentiating between those who support the program because they believe in it and those who support it because there is a district emphasis on it.

Subtle but tangible administrative support begins with encouraging students to enter the program. Scheduling and counseling, as mentioned above, either facilitate or choke off the flow of students. The lack of counseling support is a sore point for some teachers.

Second, administrative support means managing the paperwork demands. Like most large bureaucracies, the Los

Angeles schools have generated volumes of arcane regulations and reporting requirements. New and novel programs are particularly vulnerable to paperwork overhead because everything involving them violates conventional reporting routes. Supportive and savvy principals have found ways to allow teachers to order supplies, purchase needed services, and run their programs without adding to the bureaucratic madness.

Third, administrative oversight needs to be aimed at the program as a whole: Over the course of the year, how are students doing? Do they seem to be engaged in learning? How are their attendance records? Do they show gain in scores compared to other students? Do they show achievements in other more subtle ways, such as the way they talk, the subjects they talk about, or the ambitions they have for their lives? Administrative inspection at the micro-teaching level or questions such as "show me your precise learning objectives for next Tuesday" would drive out the needed experimentation and situational responsiveness.

Humanitas is a tightly structured program in some ways and very fluid in others. The strong teacher-to-teacher coordination provides an internal feedback loop about program progress. If necessary material has not been covered in one class, it quickly becomes evident from students' performance in another class. Teachers and students are thus highly dependent on one another, and deviations from the program structure in a single classroom endanger the cohesiveness of the whole program. Conversely, the Humanitas program is inherently a continuing experiment. Reaching an understanding of society is fundamentally unlike rote memorization or skill acquisition. There is no "correct" teaching style or lesson content. This is particularly true because of the newness of the program, but it is not likely that Humanitas will settle down into a lockstep curriculum. Part of the energy that drives the Humanitas program and its teachers is the need to create and to experiment with new and vital teaching materials. Sometimes things flop, students don't engage, they miss the point—as is true with any teaching.

Fourth, administrative support means quietly running interference. There is a certain amount of jealousy aimed at the program from teachers on the outside. Teachers involved in the program have gained the attention of outsiders while regular classrooms go unvisited. Sometimes fellow teachers fear Humanitas programs will draw away the best students, leaving them to teach a class of generally disinterested youngsters. Sometimes Humanitas teachers feel pressure as "rate busters" who work harder than their colleagues. Other teachers are irked because Humanitas teachers spend a great deal of time together, creating the illusion of a clique. These situations are partly interpersonal and exist in any organization. However, because of the departmental structure of high schools, special programs such as Humanitas have to gain access to departmental resources—classroom space, materials and supplies, categorical funds—which are in the main controlled by teachers not involved in the program.

Financial Support.   Although Humanitas rests on the skill and dedication of teachers, it is also strongly supported financially. District and LAEP funds total approximately $464,000 this year, or about $309 per student involved in the program.

Program teachers receive a $1,000 stipend, which includes payment for summer planning time and in-service sessions during the school year. Teachers receive mileage and expense allowances for the summer conferences and for other meetings associated with the program. They also receive a $200 grant, which is usually spent on supplies and photocopying. At each school site, a coordinator receives a salary differential of $1,100, and each school receives small additional funds for departmental grants and community outreach to parents.

There is one citywide academic director, and the Los Angeles Educational Partnership has 1.5 employees involved in the logistics of the program and its oversight. Approximately 75 percent of the program funds flow directly to teachers and classrooms.

The funds involved are not a trifle, but relative to other programs, Humanitas is not expensive. Dividing the annual budget into the 69 teachers involved in the program yields an allocation per classroom of just over $6,724—about $309 for each of the 1,500 students involved. This means that the average

Humanitas classroom is about 7 percent more expensive than the state's "normal" classroom, for which the rule-of-thumb cost is about $100,000 per year. In terms of long-term operations, these costs are probably overstated. Support services and planning time needs are higher than would be the case for an ongoing program, and the numbers of students involved do not yet reach capacity at all schools. In comparison, compensatory education programs such as Chapter I cost an average of $412 per student, bilingual education programs an average of $343 per student, and programs for gifted and talented students approximately $125 per student. In terms of its long-term economic viability, it is important to understand that the structure of Humanitas Academy programs does not require smaller-than-usual class sizes or classroom aides and other auxiliary personnel as do many other special or enriched programs. The major ongoing fiscal implication is tied to the need for teachers to plan and coordinate and the need for supplies and production of teacher-created classroom materials.

Sustaining and Institutionalizing Humanitas

By its own assessment, Humanitas works in Los Angeles. The program is sufficiently new that quantitative data on student achievement are not available, but the anecdotal and impressionistic reports are highly positive. Teachers see better writing, hear improved vocabulary, and feel the student engagement. Principals echo the teacher assessment. Still, institutionalizing innovation, energy, and creativity is a classic organizational problem, one which is not yet solved.

Scale.   Humanitas faces a size problem; too much growth could weaken and kill it. Because the program exists within conventional high schools, at some point it poses a threat to central structures of how those schools work. One principal put the outer limits as something over 500 students in a school of 2,600. Much beyond that, he suggested, master scheduling would have difficulty accommodating the special program students and providing them access to the classes they need in the regular schedule.

Also more political and sociological problems are attached to scale, particularly among the established disciplines and departments. At some point Humanitas moves from being something to be accommodated by the existing structure to something that is a threat to the existing system. One can only guess at where this point may be, but it may be informative to note that the Humanities magnet program at Cleveland High, which operates as a separate school-within-a-school, has just over 600 students in a school of 3,000.

Clearly, there is a point at which the growth of Humanitas at any single high school must either be capped or an organizational structure created for it.

Finding a Permanent Structure.   Eventually, one needs to consider organizational structures to permanently support Humanitas programs. The Humanitas Academy might well become a separate department within a comprehensive high school. Such a structure would legitimate and protect the program's status and assure it resources and a standard internal structure. However, problems of program integration with the rest of the high school would remain. Students would still need access to courses taught outside the Academy, and maintaining the Humanitas class structure would continue to require special schedule accommodation.

Alternatively, Humanitas Academies might be structured as self-contained schools-within-schools in which each program formed a small high school with a complete curriculum. A number of these programs might coexist within an existing school building. Such a structure would offer substantial independence to Humanitas programs, but it would require that they reach some minimum size, perhaps 300–500 students, before it became possible to staff a whole high school program.

Finally, Humanitas might be continued by institutionalizing the existing autonomous work group structure. These structures would appear to offer the most flexible, dynamic form for a changing curriculum. Programs could start and stop easily, because each teacher would have a home department or division. Programs could expand and contract in response to student needs and demands, and teachers could join or leave them without great disruption. Programs could experiment with new combinations of courses and pull back from those which do not work without involving staff in situations where program changes evoked questions of job rights and seniority.

One possibility would be to create a citywide Academy by recognizing the existence of the confederation of teachers created through the District/LAEP program. The Academy could have a budget, staff positions, supplies, and citywide leadership and support services, much as the program now does. Teachers could continue to be members of individual high school staffs as they are now, and schools could continue to opt in or out of the program on an annual or biannual decision. In this way, the program could maintain the cohesiveness and common curriculum of a magnet school and yet be distributed throughout a large-city system.

Resources.   Los Angeles faces the problem of institutionalizing resources for Humanitas. Foundation grants instrumental in founding the program are relatively short-lived, and as a matter of course, foundations expect public agencies to pick up the bill for new programs. Administrators in the Los Angeles district informally assure us of the school board's willingness to continue funding for Humanitas. Still, the political history of relatively small arts and humanities programs is not encouraging. They are easy budget targets when things get tight, which they do frequently. Humanities programs are also vulnerable because, unlike athletic or vocational education, they do not generate powerful external constituencies. Interdisciplinary programs are even more vulnerable because they exist outside the usual department structures.

Sustaining the Effort.   In a very real way, the outside limits of this program are set by the willingness and ability of teachers to sustain it. In Nakano's words, the top is met when "you run out of qualified teachers who will volunteer. You can't force participation in a program like this; it won't work if you do." We know that the program takes extraordinary teacher energy—both physical and emotional. On the day we met, one teacher had spent three hours dancing with his students as a way for them to sample dance as an art form.

Burnout is a common problem in teaching and the other helping professions, and its symptoms need to be watched for in Humanitas. It is entirely possible that the levels of dedication cannot be sustained, and that teachers may need to cycle in and out of the program. However, the early indications in this regard are encouraging. Few teachers have dropped out, and other initially skeptical teachers in the pilot schools have been attracted to the program once they saw it in operation. At the Cleveland magnet school, the program has been sustained for nearly a decade.

Institutionalization. Over the next year, the school district must decide how to institutionalize Humanitas. As is usually the case, private foundations see their role as starting new ventures, and their support will not continue indefinitely. Decisions have not yet been made or even all the options thought through. Consideration is being given to creating interdisciplinary Humanities Departments, thus putting the program on an equal footing with all other subunits within a conventional senior high school. Alternatively, thought is being given to creating a large number of Humanities Magnet Schools or to creating schools within schools so that financing and administrative oversight could flow through that established school district program. But the search for alternatives has just begun and a concrete proposal to the school board is still months away.

Are Teacher Work Groups Models for Organization?

The lessons of Humanitas may well go beyond the program itself. Just as we have rediscovered cooperative learning for children, we may be reawakened to the power of cooperative working for teachers. The work group—a primary, personal contact, social aggregation—may well be the organizational structure with the ability to make a strong difference in teaching lives.

The semiautonomous work group is much praised as a progressive, sometimes utopian invention in modern industry: the stuff of Volvo assembly and innovative labor agreements at General Motors. Although teaching work is nothing like industrial assembly, teaching, too, may have found the limits to minute divisions of labor and strongly rationalized instruction systems. The reform literature in education is a prayer for curriculum that is both rigorous and compelling and teacher-student interaction that is both substantive and human. Attempts to remotely control teaching—the curricular magic pill—have largely been a failure because teaching depends more on the *engagement* of student and teacher than on any specific body of technique. Attempts to transform teaching into an occupation that is simultaneously compassionate and tough-minded have foundered because of the tremendous isolation in teaching work. As Anstead says, "Teaching has become much too private. You close a door and teach, and your colleague next door doesn't know what is going on in your classroom. No one knows whether your teaching is traditional or innovative."

By approaching teaching in groups, the Humanitas project alters the design of teaching as work in fundamental ways but in ways which are curiously consistent with reform in existing public school bureaucracies. For example, over the past five years reform panels by the scores have sought to find ways of making teaching a more attractive occupation, one infused with autonomy and yet responsible and accountable for itself. In a workable way, the Humanitas work groups do just that. From all accounts, we can safely infer that groups of Humanitas teachers enjoy relatively high levels of self-determination and autonomy. Yet they do not suffer the isolation of the teacher with the closed classroom door. The Humanitas group offers a level of feedback about student performance that is not found in even the most rigidly externally examined teach/test/teach/test program. In addition to standardized testing, Humanitas students' work is examined by more than one teacher within the group, and frequently work is examined by fellow students. The feedback loop both allows teachers to monitor progress and to make midcourse corrections in situations that are not working well. The groups thus take on a self-guiding characteristic that is much prized and difficult to achieve in most workplaces.

Perhaps most fundamentally, Humanitas work groups structure teaching work in a way consistent with the professional and artistic requirements of the situation. The work group structure produced a very small but manageable organizational form that appears to be a great challenge and that also produces good results: Students appear to learn and to be engaged in real inquiry. The group structure produces a pedagogy that is responsive to the situation, rather than trying to craft a method of teaching for its own sake. In this respect it avoids some of the classic problems of the team teaching experiments, where "teaming" became an end in itself. However, the responsiveness that appears to be a hallmark of Humanitas is the real hallmark, producing an organization that recognizes the artistic qualities implied in teaching work.

Humanitas exists with a bare minimum of overhead. It does not require class sizes smaller than usual or extensive support personnel, and the program runs with a single coordinator for the thirteen sites.

Finally, these work groups are able to exist within the conventional school structures of departments, bell schedules, administrative hierarchies, civil service rules, teacher unions, and a highly politicized school environment. The work group does not require a special building, a brand new cadre of teachers, or a whole new organizational structure. The implications of this are startling: programs like Humanitas, which rest on a new division of labor, can continue to exist within an organizational structure that was constructed to support quite a different division of labor. This means that work groups are a relatively tractable form of innovation and one with great promise.

17

Strengthening the Humanities in the Classroom: Writing Across the Curriculum in Philadelphia Schools

by J. Lynne White

In the School District of Philadelphia, a project designed to teach writing "in every classroom, at all grade levels" has been extremely successful at achieving that goal. In the process, the project has generated a more important side effect—an awakening awareness of the benefits of administration and teacher collaboration and of the ability and desire for teachers to collaborate among themselves.

Under the guidance of the Philadelphia Alliance for Teaching Humanities in the Schools (PATHS), a private organization, the Writing Across the Curriculum (WAC) project has trained teachers in that city to increase the frequency and quality of their students' writing, to improve the variety and effectiveness of writing assignments, and to use writing as a method for learning all subjects.

Classroom teachers have worked collaboratively with supervisors, curriculum specialists, principals, and district superintendents to develop strategies for achieving these goals. Through PATHS, training, consultants, and financial support have been provided to seven district teams—one in each of Philadelphia's seven subdistricts—implementing WAC in elementary, middle, junior high, and senior high schools. WAC has stressed a "training of trainers" model to introduce and develop teacher skills in writing instruction. The result has been a dramatic change of attitude toward writing among both teachers and students in the School District of Philadelphia.

"Full-Fledged Partners from the Start"

The Philadelphia Alliance for Teaching Humanities in the Schools (PATHS) is a private organization dedicated to strengthening the humanities curriculum in the Philadelphia public schools. PATHS is not part of the school system, although it developed through an initiative of the system's superintendent. With both public and private funding, PATHS was conceived as a partnership organization to serve the school system—specifically to enhance the ability of administrators and teachers to teach humanities-related subjects.

In 1983–84, the new superintendent of the Philadelphia schools, Constance Clayton, was seeking ways to increase private participation in education. She formed a committee of community business leaders and asked them to explore ways to improve the public schools. This ad hoc committee eventually developed into a formal advisory group named the Committee to Support Philadelphia Schools. The work of the advisory group led to the formation of an operations group—PATHS.

The superintendent's firm belief was that improvement in the humanities should focus in part on writing in the classroom. Superintendent Clayton charged PATHS with developing a plan that would address the entire curriculum—systemwide—at all grade levels and that would engage teachers as "full-fledged partners from the start."

PATHS organized a planning group that studied the structure and implementation of other programs in the country that successfully focused the curriculum on student writing, such as the Bay Area Writing Project and its offshoot, the National Writing Project. Looking at a large number of other programs at local colleges and universities, a consensus developed that a successful writing project was collaborative, involving the public schools, universities, libraries, and community organizations. They envisioned a project that would bring together district administrators, school principals, classroom teachers, college-based consultants, and librarians to significantly transform the way writing was taught and used in the public schools.

This broad perspective resulted in Writing Across the Curriculum (WAC), a project which was initiated in the 1984–85 school year in sixty-four pilot schools. It has since grown to become the largest school-based writing project in the country and will eventually involve the participation of every public school in Philadelphia. Program costs for WAC are provided entirely by the school district, which supported a project budget of more than $500,000 in 1987–88. In many ways, the program was initiated from the "top down," but, more important, it has been implemented from the "bottom up." Nothing in the project was put into place without planners seeking vital input from all parties involved.

In fact, Writing Across the Curriculum is notable for the consensus of support achieved among teachers, principals, and administrators, at all levels. Along with other PATHS programs and the programs of PRISM, PATHS' sister organization for mathematics and science education, it is one of only a few projects of its kind to achieve the enthusiastic support of Philadelphia's strong teachers' union. Union support has been important to the success of the program.

"No Real Change until the Practitioners Have a Voice"

The teachers' union in Philadelphia, the Philadelphia Federation of Teachers, is one of the strongest in the nation. Union membership encompasses 95 percent of 20,000 school system employees. Two issues of consistent concern to the union and the school district have been to achieve increased teacher participation in policy decisions that affect the classroom and more staff development time and opportunities.

The union supports strong educational reforms, but its position is that "there will be no real change in education until the practitioners have a voice."

From the start, PATHS respected teacher contracts in terms of structuring the WAC project, understanding that union support was essential and that it would be difficult to attain. The union has historically stayed away from various system-wide "reform" projects that were seen as "top-down."

The structure and goals for the WAC project—that teachers be the decision makers; that the project be structured to meet teachers' identified needs; and that teachers train one another—matched very well with union and individual teacher concerns and needs. And, in the end, the union decided to throw its weight behind WAC as a workable model of peer assistance and support it as a way to increase district staff development opportunities.

"Active School-Level Ownership"

The Writing Across the Curriculum project was implemented in the 1984–85 school year in all seven districts of the Philadelphia school system, beginning with a small number of schools in each district. In 1986, 158 schools (109 elementary, 49 secondary) participated, and in 1987 the number of Philadelphia schools involved climbed to 210 out of a total of more than 250 system schools.

For the pilot year, each district selected schools for participation based on interest; if the principal and staff seemed enthusiastic about trying the program, they were selected. After the pilot year, schools began to initiate the process—that is, teachers or principals contacted the district about getting involved.

Beginning in 1986–87, schools must now submit a written proposal indicating school goals and objectives, and a program of planned activities to reach these goals. The proposal is submitted to the District Executive Committee, which reviews its content and direction.

This change in procedure does not reflect a tightening of district control, but rather a loosening. At first, it was necessary to disseminate the concept and structure of the project from the district level to the schools, but now the flow has been reversed. The district uses school proposals to set an agenda for the district

program—to suggest workable ideas to the other schools. But
the individual school develops a plan to meet its own set of needs.
Hence individual school programs differ across the districts.

The proposal process is an indication or symbol of active
school-level ownership and involvement, and the Writing Across
the Curriculum project has become increasingly "decentralized"
since its inception. Individual schools depend on the district for
resources to implement its activities and for in-services to provide training for the teachers, but ultimately, the project as it
manifests itself at the school level is designed by administrators
and teachers in the individual school.

Much of this movement toward decentralization has been
a direct result of having the project directed by PATHS, an outside organization. According to participants, this has enabled
planners to honor the teachers' contract and bypass many of
the more confrontational union-management issues concerning
teacher input and involvement. For example, the initial planning committee was convened by a full range of concerned parties, from the superintendent down to the classroom teacher.
Participants in planning sessions felt that they were not bound
by titles and bureaucracy, or by the pro forma compositions
of many district committees "designed to change things." They
did not feel bound to follow precedent or the narrow guidelines
traditionally found in their large urban school system. This is
important in explaining why there is an unparalleled level of
teacher input into the WAC project (as confirmed by the union).

Because WAC was organized and directed by PATHS,
planners were able to create new structures to share decision-
making power. PATHS created the basic framework, starting
with district programs, and then moved to emphasize school-
generated projects. The decision to move heavily toward the
school level is supported by district administrators.

"Structures of Collaboration"

The PATHS office serves as the overall administrative center
for the systemwide WAC project. The Central Steering Committee of PATHS provides the core leadership group. It is re-

sponsible for formulating and approving writing project guidelines for districts and schools, evaluating outcomes on a periodic basis, and recommending adjustments to existing guidelines as needed. Members of the Central Steering Committee include

- district superintendents
- directors of reading/English language arts
- curriculum specialists from other divisions
- teachers and principals from each district's executive committee
- teacher consultants

The PATHS office conducts special workshops or activities for school principals, with particular emphasis on principals of schools new to the writing project. Specialists work with leadership in various subject areas to create writing-related programs to serve the purposes of staff in those divisions, and provide assistance to the Writing Assessment.

"Seven Districts, Seven Programs"

The School District of Philadelphia is divided into seven districts by geographical division. To implement and operate the Writing Across the Curriculum project, each district has an Executive Committee, a District Team, and a Teacher Consultant program. The leader of the district program is typically the district Supervisor of Reading/English Language Arts (R/ELA).

The Executive Committee is the core leadership group for district-level projects, responsible for communicating district-based guidelines, expectations, and opportunities to participating schools.

In addition to teachers, the membership of the Executive Committee usually includes the district superintendent, the Reading/English Language Arts supervisor, a supervisor from a different subject area, and elementary, junior high, and secondary school representatives (principals, teachers, librarians, and a School Writing Leader). The Executive Committee, which meets four or five times a year, coordinates the individual schools.

Especially important is the committee's role in monitoring the school-based projects, and providing advice and assistance to School Writing Teams.

Where appropriate, the committee is charged with facilitating "decentralization" for schools that have been involved in the project for two or more years and would now thrive on a program that is more fully school-based and locally generated. As part of this process, committee members work to identify outstanding leaders from among the district's participating teachers and administrators. Efforts focus on the special needs of schools that are new to the project, as well as the newly developing needs and interests of "old" schools.

The District Team has been the primary project vehicle for initiating teacher training in each district. The District Team offers workshops to prepare teachers and administrators to conduct "turnaround training" for their colleagues in their own schools. Teachers and principals from all participating schools who attend District Team training sessions serve as the leadership group for the writing projects in their respective schools.

The third district level component is the Teacher Consultant Program, which provides an array of opportunities for teacher-to-teacher collaboration. Teacher Consultants are recruited from among teachers, who participate in the Summer Writing Institutes at the University of Pennsylvania. Graduates from the Writing Institutes become Fellows of the Philadelphia Writing Project and are designated Teacher Consultants. Teacher Consultants attend voluntary meetings at the University of Pennsylvania throughout the school year to discuss various aspects of the program and to pursue a collective inquiry into the writing that takes place in their own classrooms.

Teacher Consultants then provide direct "outreach" to individual teachers and schools. They organize and present to their peers specialized, intensive workshops, focused on specific issues and techniques. They work one-on-one with other teachers through an exchange of visits within and between schools, called "cross-visitations."

The strategy of the Teacher Consultant program is not to have consultants work with large numbers of colleagues at any one time, but rather to work over an extended period of time with a few teachers on an intensive basis.

School Writing Teams interested in having a Teacher Consultant work in their schools request it through the R/ELA supervisor. Upon request the Teacher Consultant will meet with the School Writing Leader, the principal, a language skills teacher or other interested teachers; he or she may make a short presentation at a faculty meeting or meet with the School Writing Team. From initial discussions, a more long-range plan is worked out for ongoing collaborative work.

School systems are often supportive of peer assistance and observation programs ''on paper,'' but these programs never get off the ground because teachers are ''tied to their class-rooms.'' Therefore, the school system's commitment to pro-viding long-term substitute teachers to cover the classrooms of Teacher Consultants and teachers participating in cross-visita-tions is a crucial project component. Substitute teachers are hired specifically to make cross-visitations possible, and one such teacher is provided by the school system to each of the seven district writing projects. Without these long-term substitutes, known as ''writing support teachers,'' this aspect of the project would probably also have remained on paper.

The role of the Teacher Consultant might best be summed up in one teacher's own words:

> I became a TC because I felt a need to improve how I taught writing. First, I talked to the Language Skills teacher who told me about the pro-gram. The district had made it clear that writing was a priority for every classroom. I was selected with another because of my expressed interest to attend initial trainings. In order to participate in the training, I had to agree to do turnaround training back at school. When I went back into the school, we created a writing team with other teachers on a volun-tary basis.
>
> My role as Teacher Consultant is based on collaboration. I talk to teachers about what they are doing in writing and what the problems are and areas they want help with. Then they are invited to watch me teach. It is important to have peer observations. Once one teacher hears about the program, then lots of other teachers want the opportunity to observe; there is a snowball effect. It is one of few opportunities to actually discuss teaching ideas with others except at lunch or after school. What distin-guishes this program from others is that they see demonstrations done

by their colleagues; other programs have someone suggesting and talking from the "top."

The staff really sets the tone for the project in the school, but the principal has to endorse it and lend support to the program or there is no point trying to have it. In most cases, this is not a problem. The principal sees the Teacher Consultant as a needed resource for his staff. This is the only project where teachers stay in the classroom and provide help to other teachers instead of leaving the classroom. This gives the Teacher Consultant more credibility and is a selling point to other teachers.

"Demonstrating Active Support"

At the school level, the Writing Across the Curriculum project is implemented through a School Writing Team and a School Writing Leader, with the input and cooperation of the school principal and individual classroom teachers.

The School Writing Team is the core leadership group at the school level. It is composed of teachers and administrators, responsible for planning, supporting, implementing, and monitoring the school's writing project. The School Writing Team, as designed, is meant to represent the full range of grade levels and subject areas within the school.

Active members of the School Writing Team usually include the principal, the language skills teacher or English department chair, teachers from at least three other subject areas, and the school librarian.

The most important role of the School Writing Team is to develop a proposal for how the writing project will be implemented in the team's school. The proposal sets goals for faculty participation in training, for scheduling cross-visitations with Teacher Consultants, and for collecting evidence of changed classroom practices in writing-related instruction. School Writing Team members work to maximize faculty participation beyond the team's membership and to spread the writing project to all subject areas within the school.

The School Writing Leader is a teacher or department chair who serves on the School Writing Team and volunteers as the school's project resource person and activities coordinator. In addition, the School Writing Leader acts as the key liaison between the school and central PATHS office. In collaboration with the principal and other team members, the leader helps to keep the school program focused on stated objectives.

Each district's cadre of School Writing Leaders is an instrumental group for initiating and sustaining school-to-school networks, and for communicating district-level information and objectives to individual school writing teams.

In collaboration with the School Writing Leader, the principal is expected to demonstrate active support for the writing project, to provide faculty meeting time, and other contributed time and resources. A large measure of this support is to provide regularly scheduled time for teacher collaboration. In secondary schools, the principal may provide common consulting periods for teachers who are teaching in teams across disciplines.

Ultimately, the project depends on individual classroom teachers, who must make a commitment to try out new writing activities and teaching strategies, to share their successes and failure with other teachers, and to attend school and district training sessions. Teachers are encouraged to participate by the offer of a stipend for participating in after-school writing workshops or writing project meetings. Project money has also been allocated to pay for publishing student writing, which stimulates classroom writing activities and rewards both students and effective teachers.

Some understanding of the extent of program diversity among the districts can be gleaned from the examples of two different Philadelphia districts—District Two and District Five.

"Helping Teachers Do Something They Are Already Doing"

District Two developed a writing project with the following components: District Team meetings; staff development workshops; participation in the Teacher Consultant program; and Networking. At District Team meetings, staff development workshops are held for Teacher Consultants and School Writing Leaders with topics determined by reviewing participating schools' proposals. For example, recent staff development workshops focused on Writing to Learn, Looking at Text Structure, Creative Problem

Solving, and Metaphor in Fiction and Nonfiction.

In addition, Carol Adams, the district Reading/English Language Arts (R/ELA) Supervisor, who manages the District Program, meets every month with language arts teachers from participating schools to plan staff development activities. Participants in staff development workshops are expected to share their experiences with their own School Writing Teams and then do turnaround training, either through presentations at faculty meetings or by working with individual teachers.

The district R/ELA Supervisor describes the District Two program as being "teacher directed," and, in terms of true teacher participation, thinks that WAC surpasses any of the other programs. It is important that participation is totally voluntary; the teacher makes the choice to get involved. As one participant said of the project, "They are not giving the teacher something else to do but helping teachers do something that they are already doing."

The Teacher-Consultant Program is considered a valuable resource for the individual district schools. The Teacher Consultant works with other teachers on a voluntary basis and makes his or her own connections, which may be within a school or across schools. The Teacher Consultant keeps a log of these visits to schools, individual contacts made, and subjects discussed. Principals and Writing Team Leaders can request Teacher Consultant assistance through the District Team. According to participants in the school, the Teacher Consultant component works because teachers are involved in one-to-one peer relationships. Because providers of in-service programs are the teachers themselves, a forum for interaction is created, one that arises from teacher interaction and is totally supportive of teachers.

The networking component is District Two's own innovation. It was conceived as a way for teachers from different schools to meet to discuss the practicalities of implementing the writing project. Networking is initially encouraged at the District Team meetings held four times during the school year. Then teachers set up times to get together. District money is made available for teachers from participating schools to compensate them for meeting with others after school five to eight times during the school year. Once again, district money is used as an incentive to make the project work at the ground floor.

The key to the program's success in this district is the collaborative spirit that has been generated. Program participants stress repeatedly that because the program was initiated by PATHS, participants were "free to be interactive, not conflict ridden, and free from questions of power." For the teachers involved, the project seems to embody teacher empowerment; the structure of the project dictates that classroom teachers have a voice.

An added benefit is that the project has created and is continually creating new leadership roles among teachers and building new capacities. For example, some principals treat the Writing Team Leader as an instructional leader in the school, which confirms for teachers that they "have a real say" in defining their improvement goals in writing and a measure of control over the means to attain them. The District Two writing program is constantly evolving as participants try to identify emerging strategies and models.

"The Golden Opportunity"

The model adopted by District Five is what they call a "mini-conference" model. The model was developed after intensive feedback from district teachers. The district's Executive Committee designed and makes available a variety of in-service sessions—miniconferences—each focusing on a topic or technique of interest to a sizable number of participants. Teachers and principals from participating schools attend the sessions that interest them and decline others, but agree to send representatives to a set number of these organizational and information exchange meetings throughout the school year.

Differing degrees of school involvement in the project have been established, from a more centralized, district-controlled option to a mostly school-centered approach. A school selects the option that best suits its needs. Schools that are new to the District Writing Project typically select the maximum amount of supervision and funding, while schools that have already participated for several years can elect greater autonomy.

District Five's innovation has been to establish a writing resource center, under the direction of district Teacher Consultants. Center resources include videotapes, professional books and literature on writing, samples of in-school publications, and classroom writing lessons and activities—all materials which can be checked out for use in planning school in-services. The resource center has proved invaluable for disseminating new teaching practices throughout the district.

George DiPilato, the District Five Superintendent, described the success of their approach: "Our goal was to get students to write districtwide, and this project provided needed awareness towards that goal. It is such a highly visible program that teachers *want* to belong, and when they learn that they can be compensated for professional development, which is unheard of in Philadelphia, they view it as a golden opportunity."

"Writing Has Become a Priority in This School"

In response to questions on how the WAC project has changed attitudes toward writing in his high school, Davis B. Martin, the principal, said: At the top of my daily bulletin, is a quote on writing, and this is just one of the many ways that writing has become a priority in this school. Numerous bulletin boards in the halls display students' writing. We have moved from sports trophies, as the only student recognition, to book awards. I give every English student a journal for writing in." And the principal's enthusiasm seems to have spread. There is an emphasis on writing in almost every classroom; teachers are constantly talking about writing. They have even gotten the principal to write a sample piece, which they photocopied, and sent to other teachers for grading. This was done "to get discussion going about grading ideas versus grading spelling."

In this high school, the principal selected as Writing Team Leader Rayna Goldfarb, a teacher who was respected by and had influence with other teachers. The appointment was made in accordance with contract procedures. The School Writing Leader is released one period a day to assist other teachers and hold Writing Team meetings, which have evolved into a writing support group for teachers in all departments. Not many Writing Leaders in the system have this release time, and it is said that the principal "really stuck his neck out to have it happen."

The principal said, "Some principals feel very threatened about sharing power with teachers instead of seeing it as a joint means to improvement. I know that I can't do everything myself, so I encourage the team approach."

In attendance at this high school's Writing Team meeting were business teachers, a science teacher, the new special ed teacher, the English department chairperson, and a social studies teacher. The business teacher said that she taught shorthand and typing and, until she began to incorporate writing assignments into her class, she never knew anything about the students. She only saw their typed copy work and really had to stand up and teach. She was terrified at first but got support and encouragement and writing ideas from the other teachers. The Teacher Consultant helped her find ideas in her curriculum for writing assignments.

The science teacher's experience was similar. For him, the writing group represented support—a place where he could come to discuss his problems with getting students to write. His problems were often the same problems other teachers had faced and learned to overcome.

One teacher said of the Writing Team and WAC project: "It is teacher owned and principal endorsed. For the very first time, teachers are given both time and money to come together in an unthreatened way to share similar problems in teaching, something that doesn't happen in departmental or faculty meetings. The bottom line is that this is an opportunity for a bunch of very frustrated teachers who want to be doing more with their students, and now we can exchange ideas and interact with our colleagues. This has broken down feelings of isolation for some of us."

Another teacher has changed her teaching approach from skill-oriented writing to more experiential writing, which she says has been a great boost for her students. Her topics for writing now tend to be more provocative and personalized. "I really needed this group to support and reinforce me," she said.

"I am now able to take more risks in the classrooms in trying new writing ideas." She often brings students' papers to the group meetings to discuss and share the results.

For the new special education teacher, the Writing Team was a way to be in the building and meet other teachers and build collegiality. She hopes to use writing techniques to build literacy among her own students.

Teachers agreed that they tend to reject programs that come from outside or are mandated by the district, when teachers have had no part in the design. The Writing Project has brought into the school the concept of peer assistance. In this high school the principal has endorsed the program verbally, then backed up his words with time, money, and special scheduling arrangements.

"It Doesn't Have to Look Like Any Other School's Program"

Michael Clayton, the principal in a District Four k–6 neighborhood school with 770 students and 45 staff members, was concerned about the level of writing ability in his school. Generally, teachers were teaching writing as part of language arts, but before the WAC project there was no impetus for moving writing into other curriculum areas.

When the district initiated the WAC project, one teacher in this school trained to become a Teacher Consultant, and then formed a School Writing Team with two other teachers, the language skills teachers specialist, and the principal. As a Teacher Consultant, the teacher observes in other classrooms and conducts demonstration lessons. Then they trade roles. The teachers observe the Teacher Consultant's own classroom practices, and then volunteer to work with the Teacher Consultant, an important aspect of the program.

"We don't force it on anybody," said the Teacher Consultant. "We don't make anything mandatory. The Writing Team meets monthly for the purpose of discussing problems teachers are having with writing and to pinpoint useful topics for future workshops. The principal said of the program: "We cannot overemphasize the need for students to write clearly and well. Tests have shown that our students do not write well enough. This program is very attractive because teachers are not just given a guide and abstract things to do, but learn by doing. It has been incredible to have a Teacher Consultant in the building, and the program has centered around her work with individual teachers. Another desirable aspect of the program is that we can get to work on our particular needs in writing. We decide what kind of program we need, and it doesn't have to look like any other school's program."

One teacher noted the results in her own classroom. She has doubled the number of writing assignments, from the twelve expected by the district to twenty-four. She does different types of writing and gets students to do revisions. The students' work is then displayed in the classroom and in the hallways.

Another teacher also echoed the impact on her own teaching style and the effect on her students: "I used to teach strictly from the book, but now we work on a different writing idea every day. Last year I wrote every morning with my students and in every subject area. It was helpful for other teachers to come in and see that. My class ended up writing a school newspaper, which we are all very proud of. The writing skills of my students have improved immensely, plus they have gotten into the habit of writing. We have tripled the amount of writing from previous years."

This school's Teacher Consultant, Peggie Johnson, has also worked with three teachers in another school who requested her assistance. One of these was a new teacher, and the other two were veterans. She observed their classrooms, and then they were given the opportunity to visit her classroom three times during the school year. Other teachers from the school then began to request help, until she had more requests than she could handle.

"The project has empowered teachers and generated a lot of excitement about writing among the kids and teachers," she said. "Because it is a teacher-directed project, it doesn't seem to be mandated, even if it is."

"Writing Has Assumed a New Status"

PATHS and the school district conducted a careful survey evaluation in 1986–87 as part of a new citywide writing assignment to discover where the project stands in Philadelphia and how successfully it has met its goals. The purpose of the survey was to gather information on classroom writing practices within the system, such as the kinds of instructional strategies used by teachers, the type and length of writing assignments, and methods of evaluating student writing. Also elicited were answers on teacher collaboration and project involvement.

The survey was administered to a self-selected sample of third-, fifth-, seventh-, and eleventh-grade teachers. By looking at those responses given by teachers who reported involvement in WAC, it was possible to obtain information about the effects of WAC on classroom teaching, on students' writing, and on the schools.

Teachers who identified themselves as WAC participants were overwhelmingly female (83 percent) and had many years of teaching experience (90 percent reported having taught for at least eleven years). WAC participants did not differ, however, from other survey respondents in respect to years of teaching experience or other demographic factors.

The qualitative results read like a testimonial for the project, which, above all, measures a significant shift in teacher and student attitudes toward writing in the School District of Philadelphia.

Most respondents (92.5 percent) reported that a school's involvement in WAC had an observable schoolwide effect: teachers wrote more with their students; new writing strategies were being used; more student writing was displayed in school; student writing had improved; and there was more schoolwide sharing of writing practices. The large majority of WAC participants (133 or 70 percent) stated that their students' writing skills or attitudes toward writing had improved. Of the 91 WAC participants who elaborated on student effects, almost three-quarters reported an improvement in students' attitudes toward writing.

A third grade teacher stated that participation in WAC made her aware of the importance of a positive attitude toward writing as a first step to improve student writing. "My first concern was attitude," she said, "which I felt was negative. By stressing expressions and ideas, I think their attitude has improved, and they are more willing to write and do so extensively."

A high school English teacher reported that his students now "expect to do more, consistent writing. The increase in volume and regularity has facilitated their organizational skills, and the quality of the finished product."

A fifth grade teacher said, "My students have become more actively involved in writing their stories and poems. . . . I submitted writings of some of my students in two contests. We had a number of winners, and that has sparked lots of writing interest."

When asked to comment on the effects of WAC participation on her classroom teaching, one fifth grade teacher wrote: "It was the first time I became aware of the writing process. Since these programs, my classes and I are doing much more writing. I have always been cognizant of the importance of writing as a communication and thinking method. Now I have the ability to transmit that knowledge to my students." And a junior high teacher commented: "Writing has assumed a new status—it's no longer only an English subject, but a subject that surfaces in every content area."

In addition, teachers were asked if they had been involved in the training of other teachers. This question was of interest since WAC stressed the training of teachers by their peers as a desirable model for staff development. It was found that there was a significant relationship between program type and training of others. That is, WAC participants were more likely to be involved in training other teachers than their counterparts in other programs. Since other programs do not generally stress the "turnaround" training of teachers, this difference was not unexpected.

A junior high school English teacher described the effects of teacher collaboration as "our faculty and student body have become more aware and conscious of the need for better writing.

Our School Improvement Plan will include joint subject involvement in across the curriculum writing activities.''

Another teacher said, ''I have gained confidence in my ability to share constructive writing ideas with other professionals, and they have shown me that I had good, useful information to share. I have developed my teaching skills in the writing area.''

One high school teacher said: ''It is a good program because of the level of teacher input, which is genuine. Teachers can decide what the program looks like at their school. However, the biggest problem is getting involvement of teachers outside of English. Teachers in other subject areas pay it a lot of lip service, but the fact is that they don't want to grade extra papers. That is the biggest hurdle the program in our school has to overcome.''

In a paper written as much to exercise his new writing ability as to extol the virtues of collaboration with his colleagues, Robert Fecho, a teacher, wrote of the effect of WAC on his attitude toward teaching: ''I had never seriously considered the effect of spending six hours a day teaching in a solitary classroom. It was expected of me. It was what I knew. I even prided myself on how I kept my little corner of the world neat and tidy. I was the long-distance teacher. I knew the loneliness and accepted it, as did a majority of my colleagues. But the teaching profession, like all things worthwhile, is in constant flux. To education's credit, there is a movement afoot that dares suggest that teachers might have something to say to each other, that educators, given time to discuss professional matters, will actually discuss professional matters, that a staff in one school can learn from the staff of a second school.''

''There Is Nothing to Prevent Staff and Principal from Getting Together Now''

Each district has its own version of the WAC project for participating schools, and each school designs a specific application of that design, which is developed by a school-based team. Originally, the district program dictated project structure, but, under PATHS' direction, schools began to develop their own capacities. The nature of district programs has changed. The "basic engine" driving WAC is no longer at the district level. Project directors at the school level now find themselves in the role (which is probably unique) of deliberately responding to their school's needs. Schools now set the district agenda in terms of objectives, staff development, and other project activities.

Writing Across the Curriculum is a teacher-directed project, and it is not mandatory—which are two very key points. In recent history, there has been much mandating of change from the top down, which is to say that designers of programs to improve education have not taken classroom teachers' needs and limitations into consideration. Teachers suggest that they very quickly lose faith in a program if it is mandatory; they are distrustful of programs coming out of the central office.

In this context, the role of PATHS as an "outside" mediator between administration requirements and teacher needs is extremely significant. PATHS has been able to implement an effective change in both teacher and student attitudes toward an essential learning skill—writing in the classroom. This has occurred because PATHS was able to sidestep traditional areas of administration-union confrontation, by insisting on the need for school-level control of the WAC project and by providing an effective channel through which this can operate.

The Teacher Consultant role, as it has developed in the WAC project, is also very significant. It represents the only opportunity for teachers to go into other classrooms outside the context of supervision or evaluation. Teacher Consultants set their own agenda with other teachers. Therefore, the program has become a rallying point for the teachers' own enthusiasm for change in the classroom.

Currently, teachers view the WAC project as a real opportunity to gain training in an area that produces notable results. The concern among teachers is to maintain ownership of the project.

Also important is that workshops offered continue to be run either by teachers or by outside experts selected by teachers. The belief is that within schools, the project *has* to have had an impact—especially in those schools where teachers are actively involved both in design and implementation. For the future, in making a decision to support the project, teachers will look at several factors: Does it meet contractual obligations? Do teachers feel they need it? Will it really be in the hands of teachers?

As one teacher remarked, "There is nothing to prevent the staff and the principal from getting together now." And this should be taken to heart. The WAC project has demonstrated the beneficial results of a collaborative effort. When the administration and teachers can work voluntarily together, when teachers can collaborate among themselves, then a true change in learning attitudes can take place in the classroom.

18

Teacher Renewal
and Revitalization:
Pittsburgh's Schenley High School
Teacher Center

by Janet L. Bourdon

A different set of 3 "R's" in education—reform, renewal, and revitalization—are occurring in the Pittsburgh Public School District in Pennsylvania. These three action words describe the nationally recognized Teacher Center Program at the Schenley High School Teacher Center (SHSTC) in Pittsburgh, a unique experiment in the in-service training of secondary school teachers.

The center is not only a comprehensive high school, offering students a wide range of academic, elective, athletic, extracurricular, and social opportunities, but also an intensive school-based staff development program—the first such program for high school teachers in the United States. The program brings approximately fifty secondary school teachers into the Schenley High School Teacher Center each quarter for eight-week "minisabbaticals," during which they can learn new techniques of teaching adolescents in a collegial environment and also upgrade their knowledge of course content.

This working high school is staffed with master teachers, many of whom have a reduced work load so that they can teach seminars of other teachers, orient teachers coming to the center, monitor the research activities of the visiting teachers, and also serve as models of excellent teaching. The classrooms are "laboratories," in which visiting teachers observe and put into practice new methods of teaching under the supervision of resident teachers. According to the Superintendent of Schools Richard C. Wallace, Jr., the administration of Schenley High School Teacher Center is a responsibility shared by the principal and the director of the Teacher Center program. ''The principal is responsible for all programs affecting the students and staff within the framework of the high school. The Teacher Center director is responsible for designing and implementing the program for visiting teachers'' (Wallace, 1986, p. 15).

At the center, visiting teachers may

- participate in seminars with peers and center staff, as well as university, business, and industrial personnel;
- become involved in a clinical experience, for example, observing an effective teacher, watching a planning session, actually teaching, and meeting in conferences;
- fulfill their individual teacher plans, which may include working with university, community, and/or business resources; and
- train in appropriate new technologies, for example, instruction media and computers [Wallace, 1986, p. 14].

After visiting teachers return to their classrooms, they continue to receive reinforcement of their new teaching techniques through follow-through activities, such as seminars, discussions, and observation.

The Schenley High School Teacher Center is located in the historic Schenley Farms neighborhood of Pittsburgh, on Bigelow Boulevard, a major crosstown artery. It is within walking distance of the campus and hospitals of the University of Pittsburgh and the Carnegie Library and Museum and is geographically accessible to every other Pittsburgh neighborhood by virtue of its central location. Every student living more than two miles away from the school and every part-time Schenley student whose high school is over a mile and a half from Schenley receives free transportation. The school has an exceptional faculty, teachers who are masters of effective teaching and who are dedicated to improving student achievement. Student enrollment in September 1986 was 1,070 in grades nine through twelve. Average and low-achieving students benefit equally from small class size and a favorable teacher-student ratio of fourteen to one.

The school offers magnet programs with a sharp focus and intensified curriculum in three different career areas: high technology, international studies, and health careers. These programs and the presence of the Teacher Center program have, in effect, desegregated the school, once 87 percent black, by attracting more white students.

"Reform, Renewal, Revitalization"

One must remember where Schenley High School was in the late 1970s. The Pittsburgh Public School District was like many other urban school districts that were struggling at that time with very serious problems. Court-ordered desegregation, declining enrollments, declining student academic performance, and teacher burnout were ailments at the top of the list. The city itself was suffering from unemployment problems, industrial closings, and generally poor economic growth.

Schenley High School, in particular, was identified as a prime example of a depressed inner city school, viewed by many as one of the worst schools in the city. The school was under a desegregation order, the physical plant was deteriorating, the student academic performance was generally poor, reading and math scores were well below the national norm, the drop-out rate was soaring (34 percent among ninth and tenth grade students), and the teachers were feeling a real need for a renewal of their professionalism in education. The school district was considering closing three high schools due to declining enrollment and focused on keeping Schenley High School open, as it was located so close to the University community. School improvements were not only necessary in Pittsburgh but critical to the survival of Schenley High School.

Where did reform, renewal, and revitalization all begin? In 1980 a crucial, workable desegregation plan was finally put in effect in Pittsburgh, mixing voluntary and mandatory shifts in student assignments. The implementation of this plan allowed the energy of school administrators to focus on other critical issues at hand.

Richard C. Wallace, Jr., took charge of the school district's administration as superintendent in late 1980. Superintendent Wallace, known as a strong instructional leader, placed a firm emphasis on improved instruction within the district. He worked closely with William Cooley and staff, experts from the University of Pittsburgh's Learning Research and Development Center (LRDC) to develop a districtwide needs assessment. The needs assessment surveyed concerns of parents, children, teachers, administrators, and others in the community. When the findings were compiled, Superintendent Wallace took the report to the school board to discuss the list of problems identified. There were five priorities to be addressed on the list, three of which are listed as follows:

1. Improve student achievement.
2. Improve staff and personnel evaluations.
3. Deal with declining enrollments.

The board agreed to address the five priorities identified by the needs assessment in the next six years. Wallace stated that the board's unanimous approval of these and other priorities was "the most significant thing that's happened in the district." The board also united behind the programs designed to meet those priorities, which included: Monitoring Achievement in Pittsburgh (MAP), Pittsburgh's Research-based Instructional Supervisory Model (PRISM), and Teacher Center Projects. An Instructional Leadership Task Force was asked to define instructional leadership in the district. This task force consisted of fifteen to twenty volunteer educators, who used Madeline Hunter's model on effective teaching principles to check the elements of instruction in the district classrooms.

Wallace envisioned an all-district staff development program and decided on a plan of action. One of the first staff development programs began with the training of principals and vice-principals in PRISM (Pittsburgh's Research-based Instructional Supervisory Model), based on research into the instructional strategies that should be used to provide every student with the opportunity to learn. Teamwork was an important element of the program. With cooperation and shared responsibilities came an improvement of attitudes and, in time, the establishment of a principals' network.

The tenets of good teaching in the PRISM model included teaching to an objective, monitoring learners, and consistent observation of teachers. The principals and vice-principals were asked to go into the classrooms and conduct twelve observations per month. The principals were also asked to teach teachers this model. John R. Young, principal at Schenley High School Teacher Center, was one of the four people who developed the PRISM plan. He recognized the need for department head and teacher involvement in a staff development plan so instructional methods would not be dominated by administrative staff. Young states, "I feel it is important to be able to delegate responsibilities to the staff, to share information, and to build trust among colleagues. We have had the opportunity for teacher retreats where I listen to the ideas that my teachers have about curriculum issues, building environment, student problems, etc. My door is always open and I feel that my teachers and department heads can come to me at any time concerning any issues in the building."

Developing a Teacher Center

Wallace presented an outline to form the Teacher Center, where teachers would teach teachers. He felt that the center should develop staff training by focusing on teachers training teachers, rather than on administrators training teachers. Several committees of teachers and technical support personnel were formed for the purpose of developing a detailed program of recommendations for the following areas: needs assessment, orientation/follow-up, subject matter, externships, replacement teachers, staff selection, in-service, preservice, and public relations. The reports of these committees were submitted in the spring of 1983 and became important resources for the core planning group. Judy Johnston, now director of the Teacher Center, served on the Teacher Center Training Committee. She has extensive experience as trainer of teacher trainers, as head of an English Department, as dean of instruction, and as coordinator of instruction at Brashear High School. She has brought all of her experience and expertise to her role as director of the Teacher Center, working closely with Dr. Young, to develop the Teacher Center programs.

The teacher center evolved from a desire not only to improve instruction and student achievement but to save Schenley High. By choosing to add magnet programs, Schenley High reduced the black population from 87 to 63 percent. In the first year of development (1982–83) time was spent in defining roles, selecting staff, planning program content, scheduling, evaluation, and consultation with the union. Planning and development took eighteen months, with the target date for opening the center set for September 1983.

The most important concern for the appropriateness of the center was to address the needs of the teachers and to be responsive to those needs. The committees surveyed 805 secondary teachers in the district to determine the needs for professional development. They then analyzed the data for the district as a whole and by subject area of respondents. It was then possible to categorize the needs identified generally across all subjects as well as those unique to certain content areas (Table 18.1).

This needs assessment completed by teachers became the foundation for all subsequent development efforts. It was a landmark approach to recognizing teachers as professionals in their field.

A full year of program development involved 180 teachers, who voluntarily served on 15 committees. The entire process for the development of the Teacher Center was a districtwide effort. It has been a cooperative venture involving key decision-making organizations. One of the most important organizations represented was the local teachers union. Many elements have been involved in making Schenley High School Teacher Center work, one of which is a dynamic group of union officials: Al Fondy, PFT president; John Tarka, West representative; Paul Francis, vice-president; Rufus Jordan, vice-president. These union officials were open to an experiential program that would enhance the professionalism of teachers and allow them the professional staff development they deserve. Districtwide collective bargaining was crucial. Union officials felt that (1) there was a strong need for teachers to be recognized as "professional" in the school setting, (2) that teachers should be responsible for their own staff development, (3) that staff development should occur in the school during school hours, and (4) that the depart-

Table 18.1.   Secondary Teachers' Perceptions
of Needs Relevant to Professional Development.

Area	Topic*
Instructional skills	Recent developments in research on teaching and learning Teaching study skills Instructing students with special needs (in mainstream classes) Technological update (educational hardware and software, etc.) Motivational theory and technique
Content area	Knowledge of subject area Recent curricular developments in subject area Innovations in field of study Applications of subject area to world of work Review of appropriate supplemental and enrichment materials
Classroom/student management	Classroom discipline and control Options for enforcement of rules and regulations for students Approaches to dealing with difficult students Dealing with absenteeism Preventing students from dropping out
Human relations	Teacher burnout and stress management Recent findings on adolescent psychological development Cooperative problem solving between teachers and administrators Sharing the responsibility for the educational enterprise
Technical/routine management	Facilitating recordkeeping for students Judicial decisions and legislation affecting educational practices School district management (administrative viewpoint) Efficient handling of routine management duties

*Topics are based on a survey of 805 secondary teachers. Included here are those common to all subject areas; separate analyses were carried out by content areas as well.

Source: LeMahieu, 1984, pp. 11–12.

ment head should have more instructional responsibilities and be a "trainer" in a particular discipline.

"The experimentation and innovation that was about to take place at SHSTC was not something that could be cemented at the bargaining table," states Albert Fondy, PFT president. The existing status of Schenley High School had to be changed. This type of change had contract implications, and the entire family of Schenley High School was going to be affected. There needed to be an agreement about closing Schenley temporarily, transferring teachers to other schools, and then posting openings so that teachers could apply for the Teacher Center positions. The district wanted to attract the best secondary teachers from throughout the district. To have that type of opportunity meant that the district would need a negotiated agreement regarding faculty changes: some faculty would transfer to other schools, some would remain for continuity with students, and those teachers applying for transfer to Schenley would have their positions held open for them at their home schools throughout the four years of the project. A progressive union agreement made it possible to attract outstanding teachers in the district because they were not asked to give up their rights at their former schools. This provision has opened the door for success at the SHSTC.

The other major concern for union officials was that the center provide a positive experience for teachers, giving them the opportunity to broaden their teaching abilities and experiences, provide professional training; and allow the exchange of ideas in a professional instructional setting, colleague to colleague, without the fear of constant administrative interference. The main thrust in the design of the center is that teachers are recognized as professionals, able to identify their needs and address those needs with a sound staff development program. Thus, the Pittsburgh Federation of Teachers, an affiliate of the American Federation of Teachers, has been willing to work closely with the district to "professionalize" classroom work.

Reform, renewal, and revitalization were moving ahead throughout the district, but all of the committee work, organization involvement, and planning and development activities would not really work without money. Financial support was a necessary element of success. In the summer of 1982, a $119,000 grant from the Ford Foundation was approved to pay for the planning and development stage of the Teacher Center. When the center opened in the fall of 1983 the school board allocated $1 million to operate the center; it planned to maintain the funding for the first four years of the center's operation until other funding sources could be found. Superintendent Wallace says the board is looking to local foundations and the community to provide additional financial assistance.

In addition to funding from the Ford Foundation, the Teacher Center received grants from the Pittsburgh Foundation, the Heinz Endowment, the Pittsburgh National Foundation, the ALCOA Foundation, the Mellon Bank Foundation, the Buhl Foundation, the Benedum Foundation, the Henry C. Frick Educational Commission, and the Pittsburgh National Trust.

Operating the Schenley High School Teacher Center

In the fall of 1983 SHSTC opened its doors, and the center was ready to receive the first cycle of fifty visiting teachers. This means the visiting teachers check out of their home schools and spend eight weeks with pay at the SHSTC revitalizing themselves and their teaching techniques. While these visiting teachers are at the center, a corps of replacement teachers covers the regular teaching duties. These fifty replacement teachers were crucial to the success of the staff development plan. Without agreement between the district and union on the retention and use of these fifty teaching positions, the center would not have been able to function.

The objectives of the staff development center addressed the needs that were identified by teachers in their needs assessment in 1982. The objectives also address the school district initiatives as established by the school board and administration. The experience at the center incorporates six basic objectives:

- To apprise teachers of districtwide initiatives;
- To make teachers more sensitive to adolescents;
- To update teachers' knowledge in their specific content areas;

- To refine and expand teachers' instructional skills;
- To provide teachers with the opportunity for personal and professional enrichment; and
- To enable teachers to follow through on individual and interactive plans for continued professional growth [Johnston, 1984, n.p.].

In a 1984 brochure describing the Schenley High School Teacher Center, Johnston outlines the center activities as follows:

Program.   Each visiting teacher goes through a three-phase process:

- Orientation and self-assessment;
- Direct involvement; and
- Follow-through

The first phase, orientation and self-assessment, occurs at the visiting teacher's home school. A center staff member visits the incoming teacher and acquaints him or her with experiences available at the center. The teacher, with principal and other staff, preselects those activities regarded as beneficial.

This self-assessment, coupled with the district's more global objectives, forms the basis for an individual teacher's "diagnostic summary." The teacher uses this summary to develop an eight-week plan.

The direct involvement phase occurs at the center over an eight-week period and incorporates five types of activities:

- *Refinement of instructional skills.*   A research based model of instruction has been adapted by the district to the teacher center program. The visiting teacher practices the instructional strategies in the classes of the clinical resident teacher and receives feedback from the clinical resident teacher.
- *Training seminars in school district initiatives.*   These are conducted by school district staff involved in developing new programs to meet these initiatives.
- *Seminars on adolescent development.*   These may be conducted by resident teachers or guest lecturers and include related readings.
- *Content area update.*   This activity places a teacher in a close working relationship with his or her content area supervisor. Together they plan appropriate activities designed to update the visiting teacher in the content area knowledge base.
- *Personal enrichment.*   Teachers are encouraged to select seminars and speakers for their own personal and professional enrichment. They may visit a corporation or pursue a professional goal.

At the end of the eight-week experience, teachers review their goals and prepare for the third phase, follow-through. They design objectives and look to the principal, the content area supervisor, and most importantly, their peers for support when they return to school.

Process. Three groups of teachers are central to the program—the resident staff, visiting teachers, and replacement teachers.

The resident staff is comprised of teachers chosen from applicants and recruits across the city. Their work load combines regular teaching duties with activities involving visiting teachers. Resident staff members may develop and teach seminars on a wide range of topics, serve as role models, and direct the clinical program for visiting teachers. To fulfill these roles, resident teachers receive special training. A third of the resident staff are clinical resident teachers (CRTs) who serve as "peer coaches" for the visiting teachers. This corps receives intensive training in all aspects of the program, including all new initiatives instituted by the district.

Visiting teachers (VTs) are participants in the eight-week Teacher Center Program. Each session the clinical resident teacher works with two visiting teachers. Visiting teachers learn and practice new skills and techniques and receive feedback from the clinical resident teacher. Practice usually occurs in the classroom of the resident teacher, but only after joint planning to insure continuity in the instruction of students.

This collegial relationship between the clinical resident teacher and the visiting teacher is at the core of the program and forms a model to be replicated in other high schools in the district.

While the visiting teachers are at the center, replacement teachers (RTs) take their place in the home schools. Replacement teachers, who were the first to take part in the Teacher Center Program, also continue to receive intensive training.

Impact. The Teacher Center is having an important impact on participating high school teachers. Data collected from each group of teachers that completes the training at Schenley indicate a wide range of significant results. In their own words, many teachers are finding the experience "rewarding," a time of "self" and "professional" renewal.

Increased effectiveness in instructional skills, understanding of the adolescent, and knowledge of the district's expectations for instruction are three of the most frequently mentioned results.

Perhaps the most common observation made by teachers who complete the program concerns the value of teachers' stepping back from the rigors of daily classroom instruction and reflecting on their professional experiences in a collegial atmosphere. The professional sharing of ideas and solutions to problems may well be a start toward reducing teacher isolation and, with it, the much publicized "teacher burnout" syndrome.

Nationally, the center has the potential of becoming a model for staff development programs. "Teachers teaching teachers" has proven to be an effective, powerful resource for the improvement of secondary instruction.

Further, the commitment of the district to a serious, sustained staff development effort illustrates both the importance of the goals and the level of effort required to make an impact. The Schenley High School Teacher Center offers the promise of significant, positive change for secondary education (Johnston, 1984, n.p.).

Janet Primus, a teacher at Oliver High School, said, "The CRT/VT experience reinforced my teaching strengths and gave me an opportunity to observe effective teaching behaviors in others. The board's decision to invest in the teacher center concept was quite audacious, but it certainly proved to be very beneficial."

Gerald Halpern, a teacher at Langley High School, said, "It gave me a chance to reflect—to settle down professionally— and redefine the goals I've set after fifteen years of teaching."

Mary Finley, a teacher at Carrick High School, stated, "You tend to become very insular, staying in your own school building, barely meeting the teachers that teach with you. Coming to the teacher center was like walking through a mirror and finding that there is a different world out there."

George Riley, a replacement teacher at Schenley High School Teacher Center, said, "The program is there if you want it. It's funny how back in the schools you get interpretations of the program. Some people call it boring, others call it exciting. Personally, I didn't know exactly what to expect. As a result of the program, I found out a lot about myself. On a scale of 1-10, I would give the program a 9—my opinion is extremely high."

The testimonials stated above are taken from a brochure describing the Schenley High School Teacher Center (Johnston, 1984, n.p.), but others that have been spoken to reflect the same messages in their own terms.

As John Young, principal, says, "There is a very positive professional attitude that prevails among the teachers at SHSTC. They are constantly modeling for other teachers and the attitude is that they are part of a team. They help make decisions in the building, and they own the program as operated in the school. When I go to the teachers throughout the building, they have an attitude of "how can we do this" instead of complaining about additional tasks that need to be done."

Jackie Perhach, a parent representative and magnet program recruiter, says, "I found the High Technology Magnet excellent and the teachers competent and professional. I had my sons apply for the program. I discuss the magnet program with many students and parents and offer to take them on tour. The programs at SHSTC are the selling point."

There is concern that parents in the community do not understand the function of the Teacher Center well enough. Perhach indicated that she speaks with parents daily about the programs at Schenley. Many think that the Teacher Center is a magnet program for students to learn how to become teachers. She said, "Parents are not aware enough of the CRTs, the "cream of the crop" teachers in the district. Now that Brookline is opening, it is helping parents to realize that SHSTC is not a magnet program, but is providing their youngsters with the top teaching professionals in the community."

Ann Haley, chairperson, English department, has noticed a change at Schenley due to the staff development programs. She said, "I feel relaxed now in discussing departmental issues and problems. I think there is more discussion and an element of trust that has developed in the building in order to have this program work."

Teacher Charlie Granigan, states, "Being here really raises your sensitivity to group dynamics; when we go out and observe other faculties, we see how the group works, who sets the tone, what the tone is, and whether there are negative patterns that need to be broken up At Schenley they have had the opportunity to observe a different approach and a different, more positive, relationship with their colleagues."

According to Haley, "There has been a positive impact on students. The use of the PRISM model raises expectations for students to perform better and they do perform better. There is a closeness here and a great deal of sharing. For example, as a CRT you are with other teachers much of the day. You share classrooms and you share a workroom. As department heads we are expected to be 'instructional leaders.'"

All staff at SHSTC, including counselors, staff assistants, and vice-principals, indicated that staff attitudes were now more positive, sharing, and instructional. All staff concerned expressed the conviction that the main goal was to provide better instruction for students and to raise student performance. Teachers at first were skeptical of a staff development process occurring during instruction time when students were present in the classrooms; however, they found that the staff development was extremely rewarding and beneficial and that students did not mind that they were participating in teacher training sessions.

Evaluating the Schenley
High School Teacher Center

One of the most important aspects of the Schenley High School Teacher Center development and implementation has been the data-based evaluation that was begun at the inception of the center program. The commitment that the evaluation would be objective, reflective, responsive, and flexible, and that it would provide systematic feedback during the entire process was important to the success of the program. Key researchers were involved from the beginning. William Bickel, Learning Research and Development Center, University of Pittsburgh, and Paul LeMahieu, testing division, Pittsburgh Board of Education, were two people who are totally involved in the evaluation of the program. They have developed the data in report form for the Ford Foundation.

Schenley High School completed its fourth year of operation in June 1987. Certain effects could be identified as a direct or indirect result of the center activities. The program of research focused on three broad areas: the behaviors and attitudes of teachers who visited Schenley; the performance and attitudes of students at Schenley and in classrooms of teachers who went to Schenley; and the structure and organization of secondary education in the district, including traditional professional roles and their functions.

In general, the surveys suggest that there is positive teacher perception of the benefits of the eight-week experience. The availability for positive peer interaction, sharing information with colleagues, and the CRT/VT interactions were consistently among the most strongly endorsed sections of the questionnaire, thereby corroborating other sets of inquiry that have highlighted the importance of peer interactions.

Many teachers reported an enhanced sense of professionalism, a greater sense of competence in interacting with adolescents, and a more accurate awareness of future trends in the teacher's areas of instruction.

Many teachers displayed marked increases in the amount of time spent in direct instructional interactions and the overall amount of time on task.

The center has had a positive impact on student achievement. Achievement levels were generally among the lowest in the Pittsburgh Public Schools. Since the opening of the center, the long-observed trends of depressed student performance have been reversed. It can be noted that in nine of ten subjects, student performance was higher in the most recent testing (1985) than it was before the opening of the center. Example: Scores in total language, as measured by CAT in 1983, were 27 percent and rose to 61 percent in 1985. Total reading, as measured by CAT in 1983, was 28 percent and rose to 45 percent in 1985. The most dramatic increases are observed in physical science, where an additional 50 percent of the student body moved above grade level from 1983 to 1985. The gratifying trend in the achievement data is found in an analysis of academic achievement by race. Nationally, such analyses typically reveal an achievement gap between blacks and whites. Differences of 30 to 35 percentage points are not at all uncommon. These differences have been reduced to 9 percentage points; in no subject area was it higher than 18 percentage points.

School climate surveys indicated that teachers were demonstrating more concern about student learning, reflected in the teachers' willingness to provide extra help and in their seriousness about their jobs. Students also reported that their teachers expected them to do well, attend school, get to class on time, and spend the majority of time focused on academic activities.

Schenley High School Teacher Center continues to receive considerable local, national, and international attention. It clearly is demonstrating the importance of the involvement of teachers as professionals with the educational process. It is a program that has a broad base of community support, including school administration, school board members, teachers, parents, students, community members, business, local teacher union officials, and so on.

Much more is happening in the Pittsburgh School District. The Teacher Center is moving to Phase II—institutionalization of the concept citywide; an additional program has been implemented called, "Critical Thinking Project"; and Brookline Elementary Teacher Center is forming, where teaching professionals are fulfilling major leadership roles in the innovation process.

All of the district's secondary school teachers completed the Teacher Center Program by the end of the 1986–87 school year, according to Superintendent Wallace. "In the future the center will undoubtedly serve as the site for orientation of new teachers," he notes (Wallace, 1986, p. 15).

What is occurring and has occurred at Schenley High School Teacher Center truly demonstrates the importance of "the teacher as ally in educational reform."

Appendix

How Eleven Schools/School Districts Achieved Reform

School Districts	Types of Reforms Initiated	Mechanisms for Change
1. ABC Unified School District, Cerritos, California	A streamlined management organization and partially decentralized budget process, which has increased funds for schools and school-level control of funds	Management associations of school administrators, which meet regularly with the district superintendent
	District-wide curriculum development and evaluation by teachers	A Curriculum Master Plan Council and subject-area committees made up of teachers from each school and management facilitators
	Mentor Teachers	Selected by teacher committees
	Instructional Resource Teachers	Appointed by administration
	Teacher involvement in staff development and in-service training, selection of principals, determination of disciplinary procedures, and development of new instructional techniques	School site councils, departmental forums, off-site retreats, and staff development workshops
2. Cincinnati (Ohio) Public Schools	A peer appraisal plan, new teacher allocation methods to relieve overcrowded classrooms, new grading and promotion standards, improved professional teaching and learning conditions, and career ladders for new teachers	Joint union-administration committees
	Improvement of certain low-performing neighborhood schools through implementation of all-day kindergarten programs and several other reforms	A joint planning committee for identifying eligible pilot schools and conducting a selection process; teacher involvement in specific improvement plans

School Districts	Types of Reforms Initiated	Mechanisms for Change
3. Dade County (Florida) Public Schools	School-Based Management/ Shared-Decision Making program which has included a wide variety of school reforms, such as a new bilingual and basic skills curriculum, nontraditional staffing techniques, and new scheduling procedures	A joint union-administration task force to oversee the school-based improvement program; various school-site structures to carry out reforms, such as quality circles, faculty councils, and departmental committees
	Satellite learning centers established at business sites	A joint union-administration program implemented in conjunction with the business community
	Saturday morning tutorial programs established at inner-city schools	Regular teachers, who are paid for their extra tutorial work
	Dade Academy of the Teaching Arts, a nine-week professional development program for teachers based at a functioning high school	Mentor teachers who work with other teachers; overall project is collabo-ratively run by the administration and union with participation of consultants from local universities
	Partners in Education, a school improvement program focused on inner-city schools	A joint program of the administration, union, as well as other local organi-zations; teacher-administration school committees
	Teacher Recruitment Internship Program	A collaborative project between the University of Miami, the school district, and the American Federation of Teachers
4. Duluth (Minnesota) School System	Participative Management/ Quality of Work Life process, which has focused on improvements in instruction, teacher evaluation, staff development, and budgeting to increase school-level control over financial resources	A district-wide Quality of Work Life Steering Committee, composed of school board and central administration representatives, school principals, and union members; joint school-level quality circles and problem-solving groups

(continued)

School Districts	Types of Reforms Initiated	Mechanisms for Change
5. Hammond (Indiana) School District	A School Improvement Process, which has included improvements in such areas as curriculum development, instructional strategies, professional development, peer evaluation, disciplinary procedures, staffing needs and hiring, and scheduling	Joint school improvement teams, which may set aside elements of the master contract in order to carry out improvement plans
6. Jefferson County Public Schools, Louisville, Kentucky	A district-wide restructuring effort including the following components: Professional Development Schools, participation in the Coalition of Essential Schools, a school district/ University of Louisville project to redefine the induction process for the teaching profession, Learning Choice Schools, and a Middle Grades Assessment Program	At district level, led by the Gheens Professional Development Academy, a human resource development center for teachers and principals; at school level, a variety of teams and other participative structures

Schools

7. Central Park East Secondary School, New York City	A totally restructured school, in which teachers have designed a common core curriculum in humanities/social studies and in science/mathematics. Teacher involvement in staff development activities, grading scheduling of classes, hiring new faculty, student recruitment, discipline, teaching strategies, selection of teaching materials, and some issues of general administration	"Houses," groups of 80 students, each led by a team of four faculty members; content teams to plan curriculum; weekly faculty breakfast meetings, and weekend retreats
8. Hope Essential High School Providence, Rhode Island	A "school-within-a-school," in which teachers have developed new curricula in English, mathematics, sciences, and social studies; teacher involvement in selection of teaching materials, scheduling, grading and reporting, professional development, and some issues of general administration	Team planning sessions held twice a week

Special Programs	Types of Reforms Initiated	Mechanisms for Change
9. Humanitas Academy, Los Angeles Unified School District and Los Angeles Educational Partnership	An interdisciplinary humanities curriculum completely designed and implemented by teachers	Semi-autonomous teams of teachers organized at the school level
10. Writing Across the Curriculum, School District of Philadelphia and Philadelphia Alliance for Teaching Humanities	A teacher-directed program to improve teachers' skills in writing instruction and student writing skills, and to increase the use of writing as a means of learning all subjects	At district level, Executive Committees including distrtict superintendent, curriculum specialists, principals, teachers, and librarians; District Teams, which conduct training sessions for teachers and principals; and Teacher Consultants, specially trained teachers who work one-on-one with other teachers; at school level, a School Writing Team, composed of teachers and administrators; School Writing Leader, a teacher or department chair who serves as the school's project resource person and activities coordinator
11. Schenley High School Teacher Center, Pittsburgh, Pennsylvania	A teacher development and renewal program based at a functioning high school, designed jointly by the district and union, and focused on teachers training teachers	*Visiting teachers*, who spend eight weeks in the program; a core of *replacement teachers*, who cover the regular teaching duties of the visiting teachers; *resident teachers*, chosen from applicants and recruits across the district, who combine regular teaching with training activities involving visiting teachers; and *clinical resident teachers*, who serve as "peer coaches" for the visiting teachers

References

Bensman, D. *Quality Education in the Inner City: The Story of the Central Park East Schools.* New York: Central Park East School, 1987.

Berger, E. "Pat Tornillo's Transformation: Confrontation Is Out, Cooperation Is In: Tornillo Pushes Revolutionary Reforms as He Works with the School Board." *Miami News,* February 20, 1988, p. 1.

Bluestone, I. "Joint Action and Collective Bargaining—and Vice Versa." In J. M. Rosow (ed.), *Teamwork: Joint Labor-Management Programs in America.* Pergamon Press/Work in America Institute Series. New York: Pergamon Press, 1986.

Boyer, E. L. *High School: A Report on Secondary Education in America.* New York: Harper & Row, 1983.

Carnegie Forum on Education and the Economy's Task Force on Teaching as a Profession. *A Nation Prepared: Teachers for the 21st Century.* New York: Carnegie Forum on Education and the Economy, May 1986.

The Carnegie Foundation for the Advancement of Teaching. *An Imperiled Generation: Saving Urban Schools.* Princeton, N.J.: The Carnegie Foundation for the Advancement of Teaching, 1988.

Central Park East Secondary School. *Central Park East Secondary School: Program Description.* New York: Central Park East Secondary School, 1986a.

_____. *Central Park East Secondary School: Six Year Plan.* New York
Central Park East Secondary School, 1986b.

_____. *Newsletter.* Fall 1987 (entire issue).

Chavez, L. "Two Bronx Schools: A Study in Inequality." *New
York Times,* July 2, 1987, Section 1, p. 1.

Chion-Kenney, L. "The Coalition of Essential Schools: A
Report from the Field." *American Educator,* winter 1987, pp.
18–27, 47–48.

Coalition of Essential Schools. *Prospectus.* Providence, R.I.:
Brown University, 1985.

Corcoran, T. B. *An Assessment of Common Models of Teacher Participation in Public School Decision Making.* Coalition of Essential Schools, Brown University. Unpublished paper commissioned by Work in America Institute, 1986.

Dade County Public Schools. *Statistical Highlights, 1987–88.*
Miami, Fla.: Dade County Public Schools, 1987.

Denton, S., and LeMahieu, P. G. "Evaluation Research as an
Integral Part of Pittsburgh's In-Service Staff Development
Center." *Evaluation News,* Aug. 1985, pp. 45–50.

Duke, D. L., Showers, B. K., and Imber, M. *Teachers as School
Decision Makers.* Palo Alto, Calif.: Institute for Research on
Educational Finance and Governance, Stanford University,
May 1980.

"Education Quiz." *Cincinnati Post,* Dec. 22, 1984.

Fernandez, L. "Pine Villa to Offer Saturday Classes." *Miami
Herald,* Nov. 19, 1987.

Fisher, R., and Ury, W. *Getting to Yes: Negotiating Agreement
Without Giving In.* Boston: Houghton Mifflin, 1981.

Fiske, E. B. "Miami Schools: Laboratory for Major Changes."
New York Times, Jan. 10, 1988, p. 1.

Golen, L. L. *Participative Management: A Labor-Management Process That Works for Kids.* Duluth, Minn.: Independent School
District No. 709, 1987. (Pamphlet.)

Goodlad, J. I. *A Place Called School.* New York: McGraw Hill,
1984.

Governor's Commission on Equity and Excellence in Education (Connecticut). *Teachers for Today and Tomorrow.* Hartford,
Conn.: Governor's Commission on Equity and Excellence
in Education, June 1985.

_____ . *Teachers for Today and Tomorrow: One Year Later.* Hartford, Conn.: Governor's Commission on Equity and Excellence in Education, June 1986.

Guthrie, J. W. "School-Based Management: The Next Needed Educational Reform." *Phi Delta Kappan,* Dec. 1986, pp. 305–309.

"Harlem School Stresses the Basics." *New York Times,* May 24, 1987, Section 1, p. 42.

Harrington, D. *Beyond the Four Walls: Teacher Professionalism in Action.* New York: United Federation of Teachers and the Edwin Gould Foundation for Children, Apr. 1987.

Hope High School. *The Hope High School Student Handbook.* Providence, R.I.: Hope High School, 1986.

Hovey, S. "Teachers at the Center." *American Educator,* fall 1986, pp. 26–29.

Jessup, D. *Teacher Unions and Change.* New York: Praeger, 1985.

Johnson, S. M. *Teacher Unions in Schools.* Philadelphia: Temple University Press, 1984.

_____ . "Teachers as Policymakers: The Role of Collective Bargaining in School Reform." Unpublished paper commissioned by Work in America Institute, 1987.

Johnston, J. *The Schenley High School Teacher Center.* Pittsburgh, Pa.: Pittsburgh Public Schools, 1984.

Kerchner, C., and Mitchell, D. *The Dynamics of Public School Collective Bargaining and Its Impact on Governance, Administration, and Teaching.* Washington, D.C.: National Institute of Education, 1981.

_____ . "Teaching Reform and Union Reform." *The Elementary School Journal,* March 1986, pp. 449–470.

Kochan, T. A. *Worker Participation and American Unions: Threat or Opportunity?* Kalamazoo, Mich.: W. E. Upjohn Institute for Employment Research, 1984.

Leahy, D. E. "Hope Essential High School: Portrait of a School in Transition." Paper prepared for Ed. 208, Brown University, Providence, R.I., May 11, 1987.

LeMahieu, P. G. "An Assessment of the Needs of Secondary Teachers Relevant to Professional Development." Paper presented at the annual meeting of the Educational Research Association, New Orleans, La., 1984.

Levin, H. M. "Finance and Governance Implications of School-Based Decisions." Unpublished paper commissioned by Work in America Institute, 1987.

McCormick, K. "Richard C. Wallace." *Executive Educator,* Nov. 1986, pp. 13–14, 30.

McDonnell, L. M., and Pascal, A. *Organized Teachers in American Schools.* Santa Monica, Calif.: Rand Corporation, 1979.

_____. *Teacher Unions and Educational Reform.* Santa Monica, Calif.: Rand, 1988.

Malafronte, A. *History of the Dade County Classroom Teachers' Association.* Unpublished doctoral dissertation, School of Education, University of Miami, Miami, Fla., 1974.

Meier, D. "Central Park East: An Alternative Story." *Phi Delta Kappan,* June 1987, pp. 753–757.

_____. "Why a Kindergarten–12th Grade School?" New York: Central Park East Secondary School, 1987. (Mimeographed.)

Moeser, E., and Golen, L. L. *Participative Management: A Labor-Management Process That Works for Kids* (unpublished paper). Duluth, Minn.: Independent School District No. 709, 1987.

Mooney, T. "Don't Blame the Teachers." *Cincinnati Enquirer,* Dec. 12, 1983.

Moser, A. *Head Teacher's Summary of Hope Essential Questionnaire.* Providence, R.I.: Hope Essential High School, 1987a.

_____. *Hope Essential High School: Year One.* Providence, R.I.: Hope Essential High School, 1987b.

Moser, A., and others. *Hope Essential High School Interim Report.* Providence, R.I.: Hope Essential High School, 1986.

The National Commission on Excellence in Education. *A Nation at Risk: The Imperative for Educational Reform.* Washington, D.C.: U.S. Department of Education, Apr. 1983.

Office of the Deputy Superintendent, Dade County Public Schools. *Report on School-Based Management (Learning-Centered Schools).* Miami, Fla.: Dade County Public Schools, 1986.

_____. *Professionalization of Education: Executive Summary.* Miami, Fla.: Dade County Public Schools, 1987.

Office of School-Based Management, Dade County Public Schools. *School-Based Management/Shared-Decision Making.* Miami, Fla.: Dade County Public Schools, 1987.

O'Hara, P. S. "Dade Breaks School Tradition." *Florida Trend,* Mar. 1988, p. 48.

Olson, L. "Less Is More: Coalition Rethinking the Basic Design of Schools." *Education Week,* Feb. 18, 1987a, pp. 1, 22–24.

———. "The Sky's the Limit: Dade Ventures Self-Governance." *Education Week,* Dec. 2, 1987b, pp. 1, 18–19.

———. "Study Groups Giving Committed Teachers the Chance to Reflect, Share, Learn." *Education Week,* June 3, 1987c, pp. 1, 23–26.

Providence Teachers Union and Providence School Board. *1985–1988 Agreement.* Providence, R.I.: Providence Teachers Union and Providence School Board, 1985.

Rallis, S., and Highsmith, M. C. "The Myth of the 'Great Principal': Questions of School Management and Instructional Leadership." *Phi Delta Kappan,* Dec. 1986, pp. 300–304.

"'Restructured' Schools: Frequently Invoked, Rarely Defined." *Update* (Newsletter of the Association for Supervision and Curriculum Development, Alexandria, Va.), Jan. 1988, pp. 1, 6–7.

Rosow, J. M., ed. *Teamwork: Joint Labor-Management Programs in America.* New York: Pergamon Press/Work in America Institute Series, 1986.

Schlecty, P. *The JCPS/Gheens Professional Development Academy: Present Status and Future Prospects.* Louisville, Ky.: Gheens Professional Development Academy, 1987.

"Schools to Give Home Rule a Try." *Miami Herald,* May 5, 1987.

Siegel, I. H., and E. Weinberg. *Labor-Management Cooperation: The American Experience.* Kalamazoo, Mich.: W. E. Upjohn Institute for Employment Research, 1982.

Sizer, T. *Horace's Compromise: The Dilemma of the American High School.* Boston: Houghton Mifflin, 1984.

"Spelling It Out." *Cincinnati Post,* Dec. 10, 1984.

Teacher Development Committee. *The Duluth Plan: Report of the Committee.* Duluth, Minn.: Independent School District No. 709, 1987.

"Teachers: Reaction to Passage of School Levies Shows Their Priorities Are in Order." *The Cincinnati Enquirer,* Nov. 19, 1984.

"Union Chief Remains in a Class by Himself." *Miami Herald,* Dec. 21, 1986.

Wallace, R. C., Jr. "The Teacher Education Dialogue: Priming Participants for Reform." *Educational Record,* fall 1986, pp. 13–17.

Wanner, F. "President's Message." *Duluth Federation of Teachers Newsletter,* Nov. 6, 1987.

Warren, A. S. "Quality of Work Life at General Motors." In J. M. Rosow (ed.), *Teamwork: Joint Labor-Management Programs in America.* Pergamon Press/Work in America Institute Series. New York: Pergamon Press, 1986.

Wiggins, G. *Away from Trivial Pursuit, Toward a More Thought-Provoking Curriculum.* Providence, R.I.: Coalition of Essential Schools, Brown University, 1987.

————. *Horace.* (Newsletter of the Coalition of Essential Schools.) Providence, R.I.: Coalition of Essential Schools, Brown University.

"Year of Honor in East Harlem Schools." *New York Times,* June 27, 1987, p. 29.

Zager, R., and M. P. Rosow, eds. *The Innovative Organization: Productivity Programs in Action.* New York: Pergamon Press/Work in America Institute Series, 1982a.

————. *Productivity Through Work Innovations.* New York: Pergamon Press/Work in America Institute Series, 1982b.

Index